Praise for
Feature Filmmaking at Used-Car Prices
By Rick Schmidt, "one of the world's top independent
film gurus" (*MovieMaker*)

"Rick Schmidt, whose *Feature Filmmaking at Used-Car Prices* is the undisputed champ of low-budget bibles, was the guru of choice for many of today's top indie moviemakers long before this new trend [of DV moviemaking] began."
—Glen Berry, *MovieMaker*

"Intelligent, personable, and carnivalesque . . . An intriguing book that takes on Hollywood with a healthy, 'do-it-yourself' attitude. . . . I can think of a lot of studio heads who should read this one and meditate!"
—*Cineaste*

"It's as much an inspirational book as a step-by-step guide to the process of making 'no-budget movies.'"
—John Hartl, film critic, *The Seattle Times*

"I wish I could have read this book thirty-five years ago, before I made my first low-budget features."
—Vilmos Zsigmond, cinematographer, *Deliverance, The Deer Hunter, Close Encounters of the Third Kind, The Crossing Guard*

"Rick Schmidt is the only person on Earth who could shoot an entire feature film *inside* a used car . . . and then sell the film (and car) for a profit." —Nicholas Kazan, screenwriter, *At Close Range, Reversal of Fortune, Patty Hearst, Dream Lover* (also directed), *Fallen*

"An indie's A to Z . . . If you want to jump on in, Rick'll get you rolling."
—Jon Jost, feature filmmaker, *Speaking Directly, Last Chants for a Slow Dance, Frame Up, Sure Fire, All the Vermeers in New York*

PENGUIN BOOKS

EXTREME DV AT USED-CAR PRICES

Since the early 1970s, Rick Schmidt has written, directed, shot, edited, and produced more than twenty indie features, which have been presented at over fifty film festivals, including the Sundance Film Festival's Dramatic Competition, New Directors/New Films, San Francisco International, Berlin International (Panorama), London Film Festival, and Channel Four (England) (see *www.lightvideo.com/films.aspx*). His first no-budget feature, *A Man, a Woman, and a Killer*, directed with then roommate Wayne Wang (*Joy Luck Club, Smoke, Maid in Manhattan*), won Director's Choice at the Ann Arbor Film Festival. When his fourth feature, *Morgan's Cake*, premiered at New Directors/New Films in New York, Janet Maslin of *The New York Times* called it "[A] deadpan, unpretentious delight . . . one of the most promising of the festival." His fifth feature, *American Orpheus* (Seattle International, Rotterdam International), was awarded the Gold as "The Best Low-Budget Feature of the Year" at the Houston International Film Festival.

Recently Schmidt has had the distinction of cowriting, codirecting, coproducing, and executive-producing *Chetzemoka's Curse* (Dogme No. 10) on DV, only the second American feature to receive this official certification from Denmark. *Curse* was coproduced with his son, cinematographer Morgan Schmidt-Feng, in a seven-way writing and directing collaboration at Schmidt's ongoing Feature Workshops.

Besides producing cutting-edge, award-winning movies, Schmidt has influenced a generation of moviemakers with his classic how-to,

Feature Filmmaking at Used-Car Prices (Penguin Books), which *MovieMaker* magazine calls "[T]he undisputed champ of low budget bibles. Schmidt was the guru of choice for many of today's top indie moviemakers long before this new trend began." His list of distinguished readers includes filmmakers Kevin Smith (*Clerks, Chasing Amy, Dogma, Jay and Silent Bob Strike Back*) and Eduardo Sanchez (*The Blair Witch Project*), as well as action star Vin Diesel (*The Fast and the Furious, Pitch Black, XXX*), whose mother bought him Rick's book to help encourage a filmmaking career.

Schmidt has proven himself an able spokesman for the new DV revolution. Interviewed at *www.wired.com* (February 2002) he had this to say: "Digital video gives the little guy the illusion of big budgets, and that helps people make *Dogme* movies. The timing is so well aligned with the digital-video explosion. There may be 25 official *Dogme* films, but there are probably 20,000 working on their movies. A 12-year-old kid can be making a movie. The timing is extraordinary to make a new wave of art-house hits."

EXTREME DV

AT USED-CAR PRICES

HOW TO WRITE, DIRECT, SHOOT, EDIT, AND PRODUCE
A DIGITAL VIDEO FEATURE FOR ⌈**LESS THAN $3,000**⌉

RICK SCHMIDT

With a Foreword, "The Path of the Artist,"
by Ray Carney

PENGUIN BOOKS

PENGUIN BOOKS

Published by the Penguin Group

Penguin Group (USA) Inc., 375 Hudson Street, New York, New York 10014, U.S.A.

Penguin Group (Canada), 90 Eglinton Avenue East, Suite 700, Toronto,
   Ontario, Canada M4P 2Y3 (a division of Pearson Penguin Canada Inc.)

Penguin Books Ltd, 80 Strand, London WC2R 0RL, England

Penguin Ireland, 25 St Stephen's Green, Dublin 2, Ireland (a division of Penguin Books Ltd)

Penguin Group (Australia), 250 Camberwell Road, Camberwell,
   Victoria 3124, Australia (a division of Pearson Australia Group Pty Ltd)

Penguin Books India Pvt Ltd, 11 Community Centre, Panchsheel Park, New Delhi – 110 017, India

Penguin Group (NZ), cnr Airborne and Rosedale Roads,
   Albany, Auckland 1310, New Zealand (a division of Pearson New Zealand Ltd)

Penguin Books (South Africa) (Pty) Ltd, 24 Sturdee Avenue,
   Rosebank, Johannesburg 2196, South Africa

Penguin Books Ltd, Registered Offices: 80 Strand, London WC2R 0RL, England

First published in Penguin Books 2004

10   9   8   7   6   5   4   3

Grateful acknowledgment is made for permission to reprint the following copyrighted works:
Selections from "The Path of the Artist" by Ray Carney. Reprinted by permission of the author.
"Laws and Admonitions of Madcap RV Nomad" by James Crotty. Reprinted by permission
of the author.
"Dogme 95—Vow of Chastity" manifesto by Lars von Trier and Thomas Vinterberg.
Reprinted by permission of the authors.

LIBRARY OF CONGRESS CATALOGING-IN-PUBLICATION DATA

Schmidt, Rick.
   Extreme DV at used-car prices : (how to write, direct, shoot, edit, and produce a digital
video feature for less than $3000) / by Rick Schmidt.
      p. cm.
   ISBN 0-14-200435-9
   1. Motion pictures—Production and direction. 2. Low budget motion pictures. 3. Digital video. I. Title.

PN1995.9.P7S33 2004
792'.023—dc22   2003070746

Printed in the United States of America
Set in Adobe Garamond with Corporate
Designed by Daniel Lagin

For Julie

Always stay in your own movie.

—Ken Kesey

A PREAMBLE

Hello, new moviemaker, and welcome to the world of extreme digital video (DV). This book will show how you and your friends can make a DV movie even if you lack funds or past experience. The low $3,000 price tag for writing, directing, shooting, editing, and producing a DV feature, as sited on the cover, refers to the purchase of an affordable Mini-DV camera, a computer and monitor, and nonlinear editing (NLE) software (a DV moviemaking workstation). But if you have access to DV equipment through school or friends, the production costs can drop to almost nothing. As opposed to producing a feature-length movie in film, where just the film stock and lab processing costs can easily exceed $10,000, DV moviemaking may be accomplished with just a few inexpensive DV cassettes. Anyone can go out and purchase an hour-long Mini-DV cassette for less than $10!

In fact, this book could have been titled "How to Make a DV Feature for $10" if more videographers reused their tape, as Arkansas-based moviemaker Beau Anderson does. While I was visiting the Ozarks Foothills Film Festival in Batesville, Arkansas, I got to chat with Beau in front of the historic Melba Theater there and learned how he'd rerecorded over a certain Mini-DV tape *thirty* times and that only around the thirtieth time had there been some fuzzy dropout on one section of the tape. That means that only after he'd shot 29 hours of DV was there a breakdown in the overall quality of the Mini-DV tape. For several of my films, including *A Man, a Woman, and a Killer, 1988—The Remake,* and *American Orpheus,* shooting 8–10 hours per production provided enough footage to cut those feature-length works. Beau's $10 recycling process would supply that total amount of raw material.

For his movie, Beau would *capture* (called "log and capture" in the terminology of most nonlinear editing software systems) each hour of Mini-DV images into his computer before reshooting on the tape again, sort of like using the Mini-DV cassette as a water bucket that he could refill and empty again and again. Of course, there was the risk of not being able to retrieve the images from a computer's hard drive if something bad were to happen (the dreaded computer crash!). But if he had a stable editing software program and a dependable brand-name external hard drive for storage (and backup) of image and sound files, he could then edit each hour-long cassette down to the crucial shots, achieving a fine-cut, then export the short sequence back to another master DV tape, filling up that cassette with the accumulating movie before clogging the computer's memory with the next hour's worth of raw footage. Off-loading rough cuts in full resolution to DVD-R disks, using the Mac G4/G5 Super Drive DVD burner, is another option. But regardless of the editing process Beau used, his frugal money-saving attitude for shooting is to be commended. Perhaps this method of rerecording will help some fledging moviemakers with literally no budget get started making their DV features, by making use of what's available at home and at school—perhaps a parent-owned consumer DV camera and an iMac with built-in iMovie editing software. The point is that, in this day and age, there are plenty of opportunities to acquire the equipment you need to make movies if you're determined enough.

A postscript: Beau was off using his $10 worth of Mini-DV tape to make his feature while helping his friends Alder and Jessica shoot a 35mm epic feature, *Barbarian Poet.* The location was a 200-acre spread near Fayetteville, Arkansas, where the group also launched something called "Progressive Cinema Convergence." This event is to be attended by such indie luminaries as John Sayles, Mary Steenbergen, and others, to help signal the beginning of a new progressive cinema movement in rural America dedicated to making affordable DV features and getting them distributed without going mainstream. (Check out their interesting approach at: *http://stonesoupstudios.com.*)

For others with a good used car to sell, $3,000 for making DV features seems like a reasonable cost commitment to get started. By purchasing a DV camera with a FireWire connection, buying a personal home computer and adding a powerful editing software program, moviemakers can create their own production studios to kick the dream into gear. Subsequent features will cost only the price of videotape, after the initial expense for this first feature is incurred. And over time, the daily handling of one's own DV camera will not only increase proficiency with that tool, but may well lead to the invention of new shooting techniques. Working with NLE software on a computer at home can't help but encourage originality, as each person discovers his or her new editing skills. So that relatively small amount of money (the cost of most good used cars you'd consider buying for simple transportation to and from work) is enough to get started on a professional-track DV moviemaking career.

Within these pages, I'll explain how to deliver the professional-level DV images and sound recordings necessary for a broadcast-quality DV movie. I'll also give precise, detailed instructions on how to cut the footage using the leading NLE software systems available, helping you produce a movie you can be proud of—a work that can compete at important film festivals (Sundance, even Cannes), screen on TV, sell on DVD, and stream on the Internet.

So even if your wallet is empty, stick with me through the book and I'll do my best to fill your pockets with the latest information, ideas, and anecdotes, to move you toward your feature-length DV moviemaking goals. Hey, we're wasting time, so let's get started!

Good luck,

Rick Schmidt
lightvideo@aol.com

CONTENTS

CONTENTS

FOREWORD

"THE PATH OF THE ARTIST"
BY RAY CARNEY (*www.Cassavetes.com*)

AUTHOR'S NOTE: Just as with the 1995 and 2000 Penguin paperback editions of my previous how-to, *Feature Filmmaking at Used-Car Prices*, I have asked Boston University professor, critic-at-large, and author Ray Carney to share some of his invaluable insights about the artistic process. For this new installment he has contributed an incredible array of notes and observations molded into concise paragraphs, duly noted as his copyrighted material. (Thanks must extend to Tim Rhys for first publishing these aphorisms as a three-part series in *MovieMaker* magazine.)

Whether these gems make you immediately yell "Right on!" or infuriate you when your favorite Hollywood movie is summarily dismissed, there is much to learn from Ray's succinct phrases. In fact, the essence of your life's work as a moviemaker dwells somewhere within this critical information. Ray's Foreword asks the question, "To what moviemaking god will your creative life be devoted?" Will your movies be just another surface retelling of tired, rehashed Hollywood-style plots, or will your DV work leap off the screen (Web or other media) with a refreshing vitality, to show us new ways of living, new truths, offering new views into the human condition? That's really what's at stake. Perhaps the result of Ray's brilliant offerings will be that they help save some promising artists from being lured down the money path, where ideals are tampered with, ideas turned to mush. Perhaps this provocative material will empower you to more strongly stand alone (if that's what it takes) in your quest to become a new, great, and true moviemaker.

If these aphorisms strike a chord, you can benefit yourself further by delving into Ray Carney's extensive Web site (*www.Cassavetes.com*), checking out his definitive books about John Cassavetes, works on Carl Dryer, Mike Leigh, and others, enjoying his posted letters, discussions, and numerous articles attacking the status quo. Again, I feel honored to include Ray's insightful words in my book. (Thanks again, Ray!) I hope it spurs some deep and meaningful conversations between you and your fellow DV moviemakers. Enjoy!

■ ■ ■

I teach film at Boston University. My students have access to dozens of books that tell them how to budget, shoot, or edit their movies. But there are precious few that grapple with what I feel are the really important questions: What makes one movie better than another? What can movies do that a sitcom can't? Why make films at all? Those are the questions we end up talking about most of the time—in classes, in my office, and over coffee. I've kept notes from many of our conversations, and, at various students' requests, I recently gathered some of them together into a packet, which I distributed in my American Independent Film class.

My roommate in my freshman year had a weird habit. Every time he came across a thought-provoking idea in a novel, poem, or essay, he would print it in big block letters on an index card and stick it up somewhere in the room. Putting a slice of bread in the toaster, I would be faced with William Blake's "Energy is eternal delight" taped on the side. Shaving in the bathroom mirror, I'd have to scoot down a little to see myself underneath Clement Greenberg's "All profoundly original art looks ugly at first." Climbing into bed, I'd see Marshall McLuhan's "When first proposed, new systems of knowledge don't look like revolutions or breakthroughs—but like chaos" posted with a stick pin on the opposite wall. The nuttiness only lasted a couple of months. As the semester wore on, he got busier and busier, and ultimately discontinued the practice sometime around Thanksgiving break. The funny thing was that though I had begun by hating them, when he stopped doing it, I missed those index cards with their mysterious, inspirational ideas.

That was a long time ago in a galaxy far away, and to tell the truth I forgot all about it until recently. But something from those days must have stayed with me, since I've now become an inveterate keeper of my own lists of aperçus, insights, and quotes—though I don't write mine on note cards, but scribble them on dog-eared tablets thrown in the back of drawers. A lot of them are on ratty scraps of paper stuck in the folders behind my lecture notes, because they are prompted by something the students in my Boston University film classes say. At least once a week, in the middle of a discussion, someone says something so thought-provoking that I stop the class for a minute to write it down before I forget it. Those comments (and the counter-observations they frequently provoked in me) were the source of many of the following aphorisms. All of the others came from puzzling over films I've seen.

These notes represent a series of random and not-so-random thoughts about the meaning of art and life. They are not really intended to be read at one sitting from start to finish, but rather to be dipped into at odd moments—for inspiration, for encouragement, or for something to argue with and rail against. But before I present these aphorisms, I want to mention that none of the observations that follow come out of books I have read or classes I took as a student. Without exception, they come from artists' letters and diaries or from the works they created. Everything I know about art and much of what I know about life, I owe to the artists. They are the real teachers—much more than the professors and critics I have known. I dedicate this piece to them and to my students—to the artists of the past, present, and future.

—Ray Carney
(*rcarney@bu.edu*)

Never forget that to be an artist is, above everything else, to be a truth-teller, one of the few left in a culture seized in a death grip by media-induced fictions and journalistic clichés. You speak secrets no one else dares to whisper. You exist to share your most private feelings and personal observations with others. They are where truth lies. Don't be afraid of being too personal, too private. Your most secret fears, your private doubts and uncertainties are everyone's.

It's hard to see the truth because emotional clichés are everywhere, waiting to trap us. Most movie emotions are as unreal as the ones in pop songs. But fake emotions are not confined to the movies. They fill up the radio, television, magazines, and newspapers: All the things we pretend to care about but really don't. All the things our culture tells us matter but really don't. Make a movie about what you really feel, not what you think you are supposed to feel.

■   ■   ■

Leave the plastic feelings to the after-school specials. Leave the recycling to Hollywood. Our films have so many imitation emotions that if a real one ever intruded, it would shock us or make us laugh. Mike Leigh tells the story of the time a table collapsed on stage and, as the actors scurried to keep the dishes from tumbling, the sudden honesty of their performance revealed the falsity of the entire preceding play.

■   ■   ■

Recipes, formulas, avoidances of reality are everywhere. Any hack can create loneliness with a long shot and a little music. Danger with a hand-held, point-of-view shot. Fear with key lighting. Surprise with an editorial jump. Leave the tricks to magicians. They are not life. If you are about to use a snappy, jazzy, exciting way to get something on film, it means you're not really in touch with what is going on in a scene. You're falling back on a routine, a formula, a shortcut for understanding.

■   ■   ■

My teachers told me that filmmaking was about telling gripping stories. It took me years to realize that that's not an ambitious enough goal. You can do much more than that. You can give viewers new eyes and ears. You can change their states of awareness so that they see, hear, care, and feel differently. Your work exists to express things too delicate, too fluttering, too multivalent to be said in any other way. You're doing something much more radical than telling a story. You're rewiring people's nervous systems. You're doing brain surgery. Art gives us more than new facts and ideas; it gives us new powers of perception.

The problem with a storytelling conception of what you are doing is that it makes you pay attention to comic book trivia: plot, event, psychology, characterization, motivation. Things that don't exist or matter in real life.

■　■　■

You speak the most subtle language ever created—the language of art—a form of expression more nuanced than verbal language, more complex than a theorem in physics, truer than anything in the newspaper. Storytelling does not get anywhere near the complexity of art-speech.

■　■　■

A work of art is not a mirror but a house of mirrors. It is not a tape recording but an echo chamber of connected, compared, contrasted feelings and points of view.

■　■　■

Context creates content. Structure is meaning. Scenes and events shift in significance because of what precedes and follows them. Emotions in one scene mix with the emotions in the next to make a whole new emotion. Objects and events mean nothing in themselves. You *make* them mean. A telephone is just a telephone, but when Cassavetes has it ring in different scenes in *A Woman under the Influence*, it accumulates enormous emotional power. In his *Minnie and Moskowitz*, a pair of sunglasses means something different every time the title character puts them on.

■　■　■

We put too much emphasis on the words in the script. Watch a children's puppet show or a ballet to see how unimportant dialogue is. In film, facial expressions, body language, gestures, pauses, and tones of voice are far more important than the actual words the characters' say or actions they perform.

Just as sculptors make the space around the figure as important as the space of the figure, your characters' silences should be at least as expressive as their words and actions. The silences in Bresson are more eloquent than the chatter in Woody Allen.

The plate tectonics of a work should allow characters to stress each other's faults even without a word being spoken. Look at Mike Leigh's *Short and Curlies* for a crash course in how characters' *ways of being* can collide even when they are doing nothing but engaging in small talk.

Our intentions don't ultimately matter. They are not the deepest part of us. We know this about other people, but forget it about ourselves. Our conscious thoughts, our plans and purposes, are probably the least important aspect of what we are. Capture the emotional and intellectual structures that make us what we are, even if we don't know it. What we really are is almost always the opposite of what we *think* we are or what we *intend* to be.

Most movie characters have goals and follow a set of steps to achieve them. Life is not like that. It's not logical. People outside the movies don't have purposes and goals. We are not rational beings. Our moods swing wildly and unpredictably. Our lives are not logical. We don't follow game plans, certainly not consciously. We keep changing our minds. We almost never know what we are doing or where we are going from one moment to the next. The only times we do know are unimportant moments, like driving to the dentist. All of the rest of the time, we just get by—one step after another. Make a film that shows how irrelevant our plans are, how they are a way of avoiding living. As John Lennon said, life is what happens when we're making other plans.

■ ■ ■

Film teachers love films like *The Godfather, 2001, Blade Runner,* or *Pulp Fiction* because they can be explained to a freshman film class with ten catch phrases in fifty minutes. They require no understanding of people, no cultural awareness or historical knowledge. Make a film that you have to know something about life—about the difference between men and women, about what it is to be a parent or a child, about our states of emotional confusion—to appreciate. Make a film that *you* couldn't have understood when you were in high school or college. Make a film a professor can't reduce to metaphors and symbols.

■ ■ ■

Life is mysterious, but its mysteries are entirely different from the mystifications in *L.A. Confidential, Blood Simple, Blue Velvet,* or *Psycho.* Their mysteries are shallow. They can be cleared up with a few words of explanation. Their puzzlements are trivial—matters of fact and event, of who

Getting an early start, young Jacob Ricks shows off his Lego DV camera, complete with radio mike antennas. What kind of DV camera will he be able to buy in ten years?

did what to whom. Make a film about real mysteries, mysteries that don't involve facts but feelings—like the mystery of who we are, the mystery of why we do hurtful things to ourselves and others, the mystery of why the effects of our actions can be so different from our intentions, the mystery of why we can never see ourselves as others see us.

■   ■   ■

Why should characters have characters? No one in the audience is limited to a character. Only at our worst are we predictable (which is why we hate it when someone says they know what we will say or do in a particular situation). Only when we are afraid or discouraged do we freeze into a pattern of response. At our best, we shift and flow and adapt. At our best, what we are is not a fixture but a power of movement. If your characters are predictable (as Hollywood characters are), that should be a problem.

■   ■   ■

Why should the people in your movie be less interesting than the people watching it? Allow your actors to be at least as surprising, ironic, playful, self-critical, and changeable as people in life. Make your characters at least as subtle, intelligent, and sensitive as you are. If they have problems, let them admit them and work on them. If they are good, let them doubt themselves. If they do bad, let them convince themselves they are doing the right thing. Let them also be as confused and self-deluded as you are.

■   ■   ■

Most characters are as unreal as the ones in the human interest stories in the newspapers. Film what people really are. John O'Brien, a filmmaker friend, tells the story of how when he had real farmers play farmers in his movies, critics savaged him for the "bad acting." They preferred Hollywood's version of what a farmer looked and sounded like. To the extent that there is any reality in your work, be prepared to be accused of unreality.

■   ■   ■

Why are there no sex scenes where a woman is embarrassed about her body? Why none where a man is uncertain about his ability to satisfy her? Why none where strangers feel a sense of emptiness, shame, or regret after making love?

American movies are as abstract as allegories, as generalized as cartoons. There are no individuals, only types; no flesh and blood, only ideas. Characters are fabricated from a screenwriter's ideas, define themselves in terms of their own ideas, and appeal to a viewer as a set of ideas. That's why the acting can be so generic, so pantomimic. Watch the characters in Elaine May's *Mikey and Nicky* ebb and flow, freeze and melt, to see what self-hood freed from abstractions looks like.

Most films (like most articles in the newspaper) define people in terms of racial, sexual, and social categories and types: There's the rebel, the intellectual, the member of a minority group, the feminist, the businessman. But no one is really a type. Everyone is an individual. Make a film about individuals and interactions that are unique, unclassifiable, specific.

America admires brassy certainty. The main characters in most films are as cool, controlled, knowing, and cynical as the host of an MTV talk show. The toughness, swagger, and smart-ass witticisms of the characters in most movies represent emotional problems to be explored, not qualities to be celebrated. Allow your characters to have doubts and uncertainties, to be shy or embarrassed, to reflect on their lives. In this triumph of cockiness, the shyness and pudency of soul are snuffed out.

Why deny your own experience of life with a happy face ending? Go against the insipid optimism—the bows, ribbons, and rewards—of the

American mythos. Why this insane need for happy-ever-afters? Life is disappointing in many ways. It is frustrating. It is sad. It is not fair. It ends with death. Why do we deny that? What are we afraid of? Make a film about failure, frustration, and loss—about what we *can't* do or be. Read *Othello*. Look at Ozu's *Tokyo Story,* Dreyer's *Day of Wrath*, or Gillian Armstrong's *My Brilliant Career.* How much shallower they would be with happy endings. Dreyer and Ozu show us that only when we give up the world can we gain our souls.

■　■　■

The pitch session is designed to create the worst possible films. If your movie can be told in terms of "high concepts" and programmed resolutions distributed across a "three-act structure," you might as well not make it.

■　■　■

Events and actions are a trivial way to create drama. Plot points are simply too coarse a means of documenting the internal events that make up the most interesting parts of life. Furthermore, plot locates characters' problems outside themselves. It's comforting to believe this, to believe that our problems are "out there," but, of course, it's a lie. We create all of our most important problems, and we are the only ones who can solve them.

■　■　■

Why have actions and events in your film at all? Are our problems caused by *actions*? Does anyone actually believe we can save ourselves by *doing* something? What your characters *are* is much more important than anything they *do*. Make behavior the narrative; personality the plot. That's more than enough to build a film around.

–from Ray Carney's "The Path of the Artist,"
www.Cassavetes.com

PREFACE

I once received an e-mail from a college-aged individual saying that he had no money, knew no other moviemakers, and didn't have a clue as to how to go from reading my *Used-Car* filmmaking book to making his own movies. I wrote back a quick note saying that he should go directly to his local college newspaper and submit an ad that read something like this:

> WANTED: Collaborators (actors, camera
> & sound people), who want to make a DV movie.
> Let's get together and talk!

I never heard back, so I don't know if that young person took my advice or whether it helped him.

But there *are* ways to begin making a movie by just wishing it into existence. In the old days of shooting expensive 16mm film stock (a couple hundred dollars for each roll of 11 minutes), getting started seemed impossible. You needed *a lot* of money, and everything you did was a one-shot deal. If your exposures were incorrect or something went wrong with the lab processing, your priceless scenes were ruined. What trepidation! But thankfully, things have changed in this electronic age of digital video (DV) moviemaking. With DV you don't have to wonder if you got an image or recorded clean sound. You just march up to your computer with the tape cassette you just shot and start editing, taking for granted the CD-quality sound and high-resolution broadcast-quality color images.

The one thing you don't get with DV is a week-long forced vacation like those I used to give myself, while I waited for the lab to process and workprint my 16mm footage. When the footage was out of my hands, I'd either grab a bus or hop in my car (a 1939 Dodge half-ton pickup at the time) and travel to some affordable destination near the Bay Area, perhaps Calistoga (hot springs at the motel) or the Mendocino coast (hotel room overlooking ocean). [Back then (in the last century), an off-season hotel room in Mendocino was $38.] There I would try to recover. I could sleep off all the stresses of moviemaking, wander around the cliffs and pastures to celebrate the fact that I had again survived a shoot. I finally got to enjoy being exhausted, instead of worrying about failing my filmmaking job.

For a week or so I'd be in limbo, pretty much just sleeping and eating, reading books, while the many cans of film stock I'd shot made their way through the lab's processing labyrinth. For me, sixteen 400-foot rolls or so would have been the bare minimum for a feature. At any rate, I'd try not to worry, but, given all that free time, I couldn't help running scenarios like: What if there was a power outage right in the middle of my favorite shot going through the chemical bath, ruining it? What if I missed detecting a light leak in one of the film magazines while we were shooting, rendering ALL the rolls unusable? Could there have been an undetected hair in the gate? One tiny strand of hair could destroy all my work (with no money to reshoot the entire movie, as Woody Allen is able to do under the same circumstances). What if the lab darkroom door accidentally opened while the cans of original footage were being unloaded and prepared for processing, exposing everything to the light? Maybe the lab misloaded my precious footage into the workprinting machine and it got scratched by a faulty pulley or printing gate. Knowing that the lowest-paid novice lab employee was the person directed to handle incoming original footage didn't add to my comfort. Knowing that these lab trainees were given the job of rewinding film originals at high speed with a foot pedal control made it easy to imagine a disastrous mistake. With one slip of the toe, the entire 800 feet of ganged-up two-rolls of

16mm footage could suddenly fly off the reel, filling the entire room in seconds (800 feet is almost three football fields in length). Such was the *extreme* paranoia that went along with shooting film.

Yes, it was an *extreme* lifestyle. *But* the moment of seeing the footage, learning that it had come out OK—even beautifully—was such a high that it made the process of shooting film almost an addictive activity. Extreme pain, followed by extreme pleasure.

Flash forward to today. With DV there is no lab lag time, like I once had for rest and recovery. When you shoot DV (any video) you get to see the results instantaneously. So it's totally up to you, as the writer/director/producer of a DV feature, to build in that "vacation" window. You'll need a little time to reward yourself, take a breath, and reflect on the work done before you jump into the long and involved job of editing.

With the new technology, you watch the shots unfold on the eyepiece or LED screen of your DV camera. That's it—the whole ballgame. If you view your shots on a portable TV monitor, the kind most

Rick Schmidt shoots Canon XL-1 open-eyed, to anticipate the next move by actors while framing. (Photo by Galen Garwood © 2000)

professional cinematographers use on the set, then that video feed supplies accurate color balance and exposures, along with precise frame line cutoff. That special monitor shows you exactly the picture quality you're going to end up with when the movie is fully edited and completed. If you aren't completely satisfied with the images, you can and should reshoot. That's the gift of video/DV moviemaking. You've been given the ability to analyze your cinematography and sync sound quality (using professional earphones for monitoring signal during playback) right there on location. With DV you can shoot more unconventionally, take *much* greater risks, since the digital video format (Mini-DV, DVCAM, DVD) is relatively cheap, costing only about $10 per hour of Mini-DV cassette. Without much added expense, you can shoot your DV scenes twice, thrice, even fifty times (have your actors passed out yet?), until you get it right.

Another emotional extreme that's missing from a DV shoot is "screening the rushes." In the old 16mm days, the filmmaker would get the footage back, sync it up to the mag soundtrack, and screen it. A blaze of light from the projector lit up a wall or screen, filling a space with an image larger than any TV, flat or otherwise. The little audience of cast and crew would get to see the clapboards clacked together, like in the releases of cute outtake bloopers shown in Pixar's *Toy Story, A Bug's Life*, and *Monsters, Inc.* It would be intense, but fun to see something on the silver screen, images in sync with on-location recorded sound. When the price of DV projectors comes down, more of us will get to enjoy this big-screen experience. It may be hard to imagine how differently your DV movie will impact an audience when the work is finally edited and shown at a film festival or the IFP Market in New York (more about this in Chapter 8, "Guerilla Promotion"). With DV, you have to edit away on a computer for some time, perhaps several months, to earn that first big, emotional, public moment of "rushes." In the language of extremes, your first high occurs sometime during the editing, where it must all come together in a cohesive cut as seen on your monitor. You will then work toward that moment when you can at last screen your movie (on VHS or DVD) to a small audience gathered in your home or edit suite. That's what you're fighting for now.

Just as I was finalizing this preface, I got a call from San Francisco writer and director Jerry Barrish (*Dan's Motel, Shuttlecock*, etc.), who reminded me that I should explain how we filmmakers actually *bene-fited* from the fact that the film process was so costly. He pointed out that, with so little room for error while shooting film—no money for repeating shots beyond two or three takes—we were forced to *plan, plan*, and *plan* some more. To keep expenses as low as possible, we be-came very focused. For every scene, we'd plot out each cut point or at least take responsibility for designing those cuts as part of the im-provisation on the set. We took such extra care because shooting film footage that didn't cut together had profound economic conse-quences. We racked our brains to make sure we (1) understood the concept of our movie, (2) knew basically where each scene on the shot list fit into the overall filmmatic structure, and (3) had a handle on what overall graphic style we'd use (b&w, grainy or fine-grain, various color tones) to convey our story's emotional intent. The ac-tual planning list was longer than this, but what I'm trying to convey is that the true indie moviemaker who is responsible for a film (i.e., footing the lab bill, etc.) had to pay the utmost attention to each and every aspect of the craft. To roll off footage by the tens of takes in hopes that *something* would cut together was simply out of the question.

So my recommendation for the new millennium moviemaker is to *treat DV as a precious commodity.* Try to maintain a low ratio between footage shot and final length, even though video invites overshooting. Of course, shoot a second or third take if something goes wrong. But if you get it right on the first try (very important when working with non-actors and/or improvisation), then just move on to the next setup. You'll be surprised how this one decision frees up your entire moviemaking process, from facilitating a faster pace on the set to saving hundreds of hours sorting through excessive footage while editing. You'll shoot fast and loose with DV, but it's up to you to shoot looser *in a precise sort of way.* Your new DV style will develop along these lines.

If you understand this kind of methodical approach necessary in film-making—even while you revel in the newfound freedoms of DV—you can expect to turn out better, more accomplished work. In time, once the steps for making a feature are entrenched in your mind, you will be able to launch a project without much of a script or even a full set of actors (see Chapter 1). Your writing will be different, perhaps much more spontaneous; scenes may be created right there on the set. Shots and cuts will be unusual. The feel of the images will be refreshingly original, as will the experience of seeing the finished work on DLP screens or on the Web. Try to maintain that vigilance of *extreme* focus, as you shoot DV.

If you get stuck or discouraged along the way, please feel free to get in touch. Send a (short) question to me by e-mail (*lightvideo@aol.com*) so I can hear about your moviemaking adventures. I'll try to answer all incoming mail, but don't get discouraged if you don't hear back immediately. If I'm lucky, I will be out on a DV shoot myself or sequestered with my nonlinear editing (NLE) software. At any rate, may the production miracles be with us!

ACKNOWLEDGMENTS

Thanks for this new DV edition of my used-car moviemaking books must first go to my wife, Julie Schachter, who helped me firm up the manuscript while bringing in some needed family paychecks. And thanks to my at-home (but soon college-bound) son Marlon, for occasionally sharing the second computer (dad bugging for the Internet), and for delivering great musical scores on two DV features. I'm lucky to have such a helpful and talented family!

On the publishing front, my editor Caroline White deserves triple thanks, this being our third book collaboration (Caroline edited the last two revised editions of *Feature Filmmaking at Used-Car Prices*). I'm very thankful for all the work you've done—what I'm aware of and what I'm not. For guiding the book through all the editing hurdles and remaining a cheerful person besides, thanks again!

My agent, Carol Mann, helped inspire this new book by indicating that I should have a proposal ready in six months (I took her lead and did it). You've been supportive all through the last decade as we've kept my books in print. Thanks again for being everything a great agent can be.

And I can't forget Lisa Kaufman, former Viking Penguin editor, who first got me into this business of being published against all odds. Thanks again, Lisa, for picking my manuscript out of the slush pile, and supplying all that enthusiasm. Jayne Walker, editor, agent, and professor, was the core helper behind the first draft of the original used-car filmmaking book, so thanks must also be given to her for all that time and consideration, bringing my writing up to professional standards.

ACKNOWLEDGMENTS

I hope others have been as fortunate as I was to receive your editing wizardry and early career encouragement. Thank you!

My University of California, Santa Cruz (UCSC) nineteen-day DV feature collaboration, *It's Not About the Shawerma*, wouldn't have happened without professor and Ant Farm artist Chip Lord, who somehow worked my unorthodox moviemaking activity into the system. Thanks, Chip! And it was the persistence and determination of the student collaborators that made it happen in an impossibly short period of nineteen days (actually even shorter, considering the loss of the long July 4 weekend in the middle). Thank you, Pedro Avila, our hardest-working collaborator and editor, who put in the final 24-hour stretches to complete the cut in time. And thanks to Andrea Ament, Aaron Anderson, Vaughn Blake, Tavon Boldurchi, Daniel Boynton, Jaron Burnett, Christine Corrigan, Glenn Douglass, Adeline Fong, Ryan Gallagher, Peter Galvin, Timothy Graham, Laurel Graydon, Daniel Harbin, Nicholas Johansson, Chris Jones-Marino, Kathleen Lindenmuth, Anish Patel, Nicholas Philbrook, Philip Rashkovetsky, and Grant Richards, for conceiving, scripting, shooting, editing, doing some acting and real-life storytelling. And thanks, Peter Hazard, for keeping the equipment running smoothly and giving us the access we needed for our off-hours, pressurized production. Thanks also to Eleanor Watson and her daughter Diane Wright for supplying living quarters during my Santa Cruz stay. I couldn't have had more gracious hosts or a better, more restful temporary home. (Thank you, Al and Jaime Hindle, for helping me get settled there!) Also, thank you, Eli Hollander, for the early e-mail contact that got my visiting lectureship organized and rolling. Again, thank you all for such an astonishing experience!

For our Port Townsend, Washington, Feature Workshops production of *Release the Head* (© 2004), I first want to thank participant cowriter/codirector, actor John Barnum, who flew in and brought story development and heart to the project. And Stephen W. Gillard, now a veteran of two features (see him in *Chetzemoka's Curse*), was brilliant in his ideas and acting, helping us shoot 13 hours of keeper footage in less than ten days. Your commitment *made* this one happen! Thank you! During the shoot we were gifted with many people's real-life stories and acting help. Thank you, Sue Gillard, Joe Gillard, Jessica Gillard (Steve's great family of troopers!), Christa Cesmat, Katrina Eggert (all grown up from when she appeared in *American Orpheus* in 1991), John Sheehan, Anchalee Sheehan, Susan McKinney, Jabez Richard, Silas Holm, Roger Cesmat, Michelle Cesmat, Chris Hook, Janice Streitler, Kip Hubbard, Sarah Sweet, Wendy Erickson, Mary Hewit, Theresa Carpenter, Kaiya Lynn Hubbard, Gretta Gohn, Jodey Shepherd, Benson Davis, Tim Heritage, Monica Urichurtu, Samantha Stewart, Delores Jarvi, Vernon Jarvi, Thomas E. Swanson, Cheryl Berry, Margaret Rickard, Jennifer Rickard, Joe Ahladis, Elizabeth Ahladis, Bob Varteresian. And thanks to Marc Gizzi for such heart-stirring original music. Your singing and guitar on "Second Coming's Coming," with Todd Fisher (bass), Brett Pemberton (drums), and my son Marlon Schmidt (keyboards), made the movie come to life. Thanks, Marc!

And for my Portugal-based *Bear Dance* (© 2004) production I have many people to thank as well. José Vieira Margues, director of the Figueira da Foz International Film Festival for over thirty years, receives my most warm appreciation for encouraging me to conduct a Feature Workshop in Figueira da Foz during the festival. The movie was shot in and around the festival office with most of the festival staff contributing real-life stories and key roles. Thank you again, dear friend Willie Boy Walker (lead actor and an official guest of the festival). And thanks to Diana Tavares (first one to show up, and a hard-working collaborator—thanks, Diana!), Sandra Isabel de Jesus Oliveira, Sandra Maria Perestrelo Olim, Ana Isabel da Silva Pereira, Aida SilviRosa Margarida Balreira Prazeres, Joao Miguel Abrunhossa de Limh Moreira, Pedro Miguel Candeios, Ana Luisa Homem Campos Heitdr da Fonseca, Yves André Delubac, Andreia de Jesus Alves, Pedro La, and longtime festival supporters Charles Hedges from London and critic Alfons Engelen from Belgium, for all your acting and assistance.

A few more groups of people must also be thanked, for helping as collaborators on movies produced in the new millennium. *Chetzemoka's Curse* (Dogme No. 10), shot in Port Townsend in January

2000, relied on the talents of a group of local actors, foremost being Maya Berthoud, the lead and a cowriter/codirector collaborator. Thanks, Maya, for telling real stories from your life, jumping in to make the movie happen! Our other cowriter/codirector collaborators (not directors, but "signers" according to the rules of Dogme 95) deserve great thanks. They include my sons Morgan Schmidt-Feng (DP) and Marlon Schmidt (then age 14), Dave Nold, Lawrence E. Pado, and Chris Tow. The entire Gillard family (Steve, Sue, Joe, and Jessica) first graced our scenes in this production, so thank you all for the great impact of your family on our movie! Thanks also to actors John Sanders, Matthew Pickard, Alta Gonzales, D. Jean Gilliland, Levi Ross, and musician/actor Robert Rutledge. And thank you, Paul Baker, for your amazing song "Your Name Has a Story," and Quincy Griffin, for your haunting sax solo that accompanies the end credits, performed right there in the editing room in accordance with the Dogme 95 Vow of Chastity. My daughter Heather also gets big thanks, for helping us screen the results of her brothers' and father's activities at Pixar's world-class theater. Thanks again for giving us such a classy landing pad.

Our 2001 FW Production of *My Bounty Hunter*, shot for us on DV by Morgan Schmidt-Feng at Marta Becket's Death Valley Junction (Thanks, Marta!), also had help from a lot of people. Thank you, Molly Ainsley, Dave Duffett, Lloyd Francis (sound recordist and supplier of DV gear—Thanks, Lloyd!), Stephen King, Tim Kolarsick, Stephen Rubin, Jefé, Phil Smy, and Chris Tow. Thanks again, Morgan, for pulling together another movie as my coproducer!

And for *The 5th Wall* (an FW Production © 2001), please allow me first to thank the cinematographer, Lloyd Francis, who was the determining factor for getting the movie shot. Thanks, Lloyd, for believing in me and helping shoot it with your expertise and high-end Sony DSR-500 Pro-DVCAM camera. What a treat! And thanks again to Willie Boy Walker (lead actor) for gracing yet another of my movies (and supplying archival footage from the Walker media vault). Thank you, Carolyn Zaremba, for appearing in yet another of my crazy flicks, beyond your great performances in *A Man, a Woman, and a Killer,*

1988—The Remake, and *Emerald Cities.* Thanks also to prop wizard Todd Horrisberger, for constructing a portable TV station that Willie could buckle into and wear down the street (and for performing as his on-screen sidekick). Again, I must thank Morgan, who helped make *The 5th Wall* materialize with his well-honed producer skills. Thanks again, son!

Finally, allow me to thank all my art-making buddies en masse, reminding you that your names have sailed through the ether in the acknowledgments of my three previous used-car filmmaking editions, and that list will never change. Thanks again for all your friendships.

INTRODUCTION

Hello, digital video (DV) enthusiasts, and welcome to *Extreme DV*. Within these pages I will try to help you push the *extreme* limits of DV, while expanding your own personal and artistic universe. Why "extreme," you ask? Well, if you are considering the move into feature-length DV moviemaking, you probably know that the technology has taken extreme leaps forward. Each month media magazines like *DV, MovieMaker, Videomaker, MacAddict, Film Comment,* and *Filmmaker* announce the arrival of new cameras and computers, along with amazing software programs. While you're deciding which DV program to buy, another entirely new product comes out to replace it! Things are moving at an extremely rapid rate in DV technology right now.

When I looked up the word *extreme* in *The American Heritage Dictionary of the English Language* (3rd edition, Houghton Mifflin Company, 1996), I thought the definition coincided in various ways with our drive to make movies:

1. Most remote in any direction; outermost or farthest: *the extreme edge of the field.* 2. Being in or attaining the greatest or highest degree; very intense: *extreme pleasure, extreme pain.* 3. Extending far beyond the norm. 4. Of the greatest severity; drastic.

Yes, I'd like to *attain the greatest or highest degree* of artistic and technical proficiency (using DV), in my journey *far beyond the norm* (making original works), and I'd be willing to take *drastic measures* (use credit cards, take out loans) and endure *extreme pain* (being in debt, being misunderstood by parents and even friends) to make my dream of writing/directing a movie come true (*extreme pleasure*). And we seem to link the word *extreme* with sports, don't we? Extreme motor cross comes to mind, as does extreme downhill. So we're being somewhat sporting to take on the challenge of moviemaking. That feels right, especially with the newness of DV. It's obvious that we need to take some extreme measures to make our movies, and my book offers useful new methods for telling your stories and helping others to tell theirs.

Along with extreme technological advances come a healthy impatience to get things started, the need to activate more immediate goals, make plans, and realize dreams. How do you begin a career in DV, sorting out all the options and choosing the best DV camera equipment, story line, actors, computer, editing software system? When DV production is approached in a systematic, orderly, step-by-step fashion, it can be understood by anyone with the basic desire to learn.

Please realize that when I say "DV," I'm referring to *all the possibilities* of electronic image manipulation, as well as normal shoot-and-edit real-time moviemaking. These days, almost any effect you see in Hollywood movies can be duplicated on your home computer if you have the proper software and hardware and the patience to work an effects concept through your footage, rendering it frame by frame for as long as it takes to modify a sequence. On the most basic level, you can change a background, paste in other textures, and even add objects that weren't there at the time of shooting. You have the opportunity to work real magic into your creations. Here's a quick summary of the chapters intended to help you reach all your DV moviemaking goals.

In Chapter 1, "No Concept/No Premise Mini-DV Moviemaking," I'll take you right into the fray of DV moviemaking, to the summer of 2002 when I shot three features in three months. Extremely low-cost shooting equals greater productivity. These were all collaborative shoots in one way or another, beginning with my University of California, Santa Cruz Digital Video Production Workshop in July. For that shoot, the challenge was believing that a good movie could be made with a roomful of collaborators just by jumping in without a script and shooting. I explain in detail how that process worked and how it can work for you as well. At UCSC, twenty-two student writer/directors and I worked hard to complete our DV feature, *It's Not About the Shawerma*, by the nineteen-day deadline.

In this chapter I also cover the enjoyable three-person collaborative Feature Workshops August 2002 shoot in Port Townsend, Washington, where I reaffirmed the power of "just beginning." Three hardworking/hard-thinking individuals—collaborators John Barnum, Steve Gillard, and I—used our combined intelligence to churn out ideas and concepts, proving that if you approach life and people honestly, you are bound to uncover the treasures you need to make a worthy DV. Once again, I learned to believe in the magic of going with the flow.

The third affirmation of this improvisational approach was the DV feature I shot while attending one of my favorite film festivals, Figueira da Foz International in Portugal, with actor and friend Willie Boy Walker. Again, we simply committed to doing a DV feature right there on the spot. By sticking with the everyday activities of shooting and gathering ideas, images, sounds, and real-life stories, we were able to create another movie (*Bear Dance*), a multilingual movie completed on Final Cut Pro. A useful result of this kind of production is the step-by-step guide I compiled for using the most rudimentary Final Cut Pro software tools and procedures to complete a feature-length work (see "Down and Dirty Editing with Final Cut Pro 3" in Chapter 7).

Chapter 2, "You Shoot the Works: Taking Your DV Project from Script to Preproduction," puts case study information at your disposal, offering the same basic step-by-step approach I designed into my previous moviemaking how-to guides and now helping to launch you into DV production. You'll learn how to *will* your feature into existence with moviemaking contracts (see the appendixes), gathering together the best actors and crew members who wish to share the hoped-for profits. Next, I cover scripting and story structure (yes, even though I pride myself on being an "improv" moviemaker, I see the place for a more structured shoot with a script in hand).

Chapter 3, "Selecting Your DV Camera, Sound Gear, and Incidentals," offers information about cutting-edge cameras, sound gear, tripods, even Steadicams/steadiharnesses, and discusses ways to replicate Steadicam, crane, and dolly shot moves with hand-held DV cameras. While many of the cameras covered are beyond our budgeted $3,000 digital workstation price range, you'll become informed about which wish list items can be drawn into your moviemaking operation up the road. What's important is that almost any Mini-DV camera can be used to begin a DV feature filmmaking career, as I've proven with the creation of *Bear Dance* and *Release the Head*, discussed in Chapter 1. So don't let the lure of unaffordable gear dampen your spirits or deter you from joining this exciting DV revolution!

Next comes Chapter 4, "Directing Actors." This chapter fills in the blanks about directing actors and nonactors to truthful performances, ensuring no gaps exist in either continuity, cutaways, or shot list assembly during editing. Two books I cite (and recommend you immediately purchase!)—David Mamet's *On Directing Film* (Penguin Books, 1992), and Judith Weston's *Directing Actors* (Michael Wiese Productions, 1996)—should get you thinking about directing on the highest level. Before the chapter ends, you will have accomplished your own production walk-through.

Chapter 5, "Mac or PC Computer Editing Platform?" offers a lively discussion on the pros and cons of going either Mac or PC. Because I have enjoyed the extreme fun and editing ease of Final Cut Pro NLE (nonlinear editing) software, I can't help favoring the Mac platform. Ultimately, you must discover the system that works best with your own intuitive flow, and this chapter will steer you in that positive direction.

Chapter 6, "Going Dogme 95," indicates a path to take if you'd like to shoot a movie on the raw, cutting edge of cinema, sidestepping the typical process of setting lights for interior shots or using the usual sound effects and music overlays that you've experienced in most mainstream movies. The first Dogme 95 movie, *The Celebration*, thrilled audiences at Cannes Film Festival and won the top prize. In this chapter I show how our 81-minute DV feature, *Chetzemoka's*

Curse (*www.lightvideo.com/chetzemoka*), officially certified as Dogme No. 10 by the Dogme 95 Secretariat in Denmark, was set into production without a known cast or story line, and was shot and edited to completion in just ten days. This Feature Workshops production was probably the very first feature—start to finish—of the new millennium, conceived, shot, and edited to completion in the month of January 2000. This example will help you (1) trust other talented people as cowriters, codirectors, and coproducers (you will *all* share in the glory!) and (2) start producing new DV features at a faster clip, accelerating your forward growth as a digital artist.

By following our example of Dogme 95 moviemaking, learning how to make a feature within the strict guidelines of this dedicated Danish filmmaking group, you can feel confident that your DV feature has a good chance of receiving recognition on the international festival circuit. If you want to seek the truth without any phony affectations—adhering to the ten rules of the Dogme 95 Vow of Chastity (*www.dogme95.dk*)— then perhaps the Dogme 95 approach is for you.

Once DV scenes are shot, Chapter 7, "Electronic Editing: Final Cut Express, Final Cut Pro, and More," will help with the nuts and bolts of exactly what editing software you should consider purchasing, and how to begin using it to tell your stories. I offer some Macintosh solutions (in Final Cut Express and Final Cut Pro) and also some crossover PC solutions, naming the best path and best price breaks for each operating system and giving step-by-step instructions on exactly how to edit with these leading NLE products. I'll introduce you to some of my favorite special effects software programs (NewTek's Lightwave, Red Giant's Magic Bullet, Artmatic, among others), to help you decide which animation system best fits your needs. Remember that some of the most subtle special effects can be very powerful, especially when they are perfectly wedded to the core concept of your movie. This chapter is about a return to the basics and the power to change reality within your DV movie's picture plane at a price you can afford.

Next comes Chapter 8, "Guerilla Promotion: A QuickTime Movie Player at Every Web Site," which explains how you can be just as creative at promoting a DV feature as you are at producing one. Ultimately you can deliver your electronic feature to its intended audience and perhaps secure a return on your (presumably) modest investment. If you feel you have a great movie, a DV work that runs between 75 and 90 (or more) minutes and has truth and magic to share, then you'll need to take off your technician's gloves and promote it in every way possible. I recommend everything from the expected Web site launch to renting a digital video DLP (digital light processor) projector and screening your DV movie right onto a street-level brick wall in Manhattan's Soho district at night (please check local laws first!), if that's what it takes to have a New York premiere. It's time to break through the bonds of the system and reject the findings of so-called film festival programming experts. If you can't get your movies seen in traditional ways, then think outside the box: Start your *own* festival. That's what the originators of Slamdance International Film Festival succeeded in doing, as did Feature Workshop alumnus Barry Norman, founder of the D-I-F-F festival (now Rome International) in Georgia. Creative moviemakers shouldn't have to accept defeat at the hands of "important" festival programmers anymore.

The chapter ends with a detailed explanation of how to launch your work as a QuickTime movie on the Web with the low-cost KDX file-sharing server, as well as how to prepare your movie for a high-resolution Digi-Beta mastering and burning to DVD or future holographic disks, for distribution to video stores and subsequent streaming on the Web. Setting up an online theater is the *ultimate* control you can exert over your cutting-edge DV products—having your own box office receipts!

Chapter 9, "Reality Check: More from Ray Carney's 'The Path of the Artist,'" gives me another opportunity to share some wisdom from this astute Boston University professor. Ray's aphorisms and essays are offered here, in this book's foreword, and at his hugely informative Web site, *www.Cassavetes.com*. Hopefully, this chapter will help dissuade DV moviemakers from being seduced by the commercialization of art, wasting their creative life's blood on dead-end Hollywood and inflated "Miramax indie" budget paths.

Chapter 10, "DV Vagabonds—Shooting by Van," discusses alternative ways to live and travel to make shooting DV features feasible. If you're paying a whopping $1,200–$1,500 a month for rent and utilities, with extra travel and food expenditures necessary for just getting to and from a job, then you might want to consider altering your expensive lifestyle a bit. How about buying a cheap van and using it as a roof over your head while saving money for the purchase of a DV camera, computer, monitor, and NLE software? At ProMax, a Web-based, discount moviemaking site (*www.promax.com*), a completely configured DV workstation begins around $3,000. Your van could become an all-service production vehicle to carry your camera and lighting equipment, at the same time giving you a chance to catch some sleep or fix a meal between editing sessions on your laptop. You could find yourself parked at an inspiring location, watching the sunset in Monument Valley, Arizona, or along the warm California coast. In a couple of months you could turn an overstressed, overcharged life around, having reinvented yourself as an on-the-road indie DV moviemaker.

Chapter 11, "*www.vangoghsDV.com,*" interjects more fun into the DV process, showing creative ways to approach production, with experimental methods of shooting video that can yield fantastic results and propel your work into the fine art realm. For media artists who lean toward a nonstoryline/nonverbal means of expression, using mostly abstract imagery and superimposed sounds to tell their story, this chapter encourages innovation for an off-the-grid approach to DV production.

And lastly, in Chapter 12, "Space-Age DV," I alert DV moviemakers to what is coming up on the horizon with regard to new digital equipment. The new holographic disks technology, with 3-D layers of storage that can hold more than a hundred full-length movies on one DVD-sized platter, will certainly help shape the future of DV. I've done my best to give a forecast of what's coming up, so you won't get stuck with outdated equipment or ideas. Of course, since I'm not a fortune-teller and can't foresee everything, you'll want to keep yourself fully informed by reading related magazines (*DV* [*Digital Video*]), *RES*, *Filmmaker*,

MovieMaker, Videomaker, among others), and visiting Web sites and chat lines for pertinent DV information and networking possibilities. Perhaps you'll stumble on a new group of movie-literate friends on the Web who will become able collaborators for future productions. Great things can happen as long as you keep your moviemaking dream alive.

EXTREME DV

AT USED-CAR PRICES

1

NO CONCEPT/NO PREMISE MINI-DV MOVIEMAKING

One of the most radical developments of feature filmmaking with DV is that you can launch into moviemaking without any premise or concept, with no idea of where the story is going. I'll rephrase that: A person can make a feature-length movie from scratch, *just by beginning to shoot.* I know this is possible because I've personally produced more than ten indie features this way, most within a ten-day, start-to-finish crunch deadline, most by working alongside novice moviemakers. On many of the movies, including our Dogme 95 feature *Chetzemoka's Curse* (Dogme No. 10), officially certified by the Dogme 95 Secretariat in Denmark, I've collaborated with untrained people off the street.

Working in this footloose and fancy-free manner wasn't really much of an option with 16mm cameras loaded with expensive film stock; it was too daunting to burn such footage without a roadmap (though I pulled off my 16mm *Morgan's Cake* shoot in just nine 12-hour days with only a partial script). But with the advent of DV (Mini-DV, DVCAM) and its affordable tape stock/DVD, shooting an hour of Mini-DV (or a DVD disk with Sony's new DSR-DVD cameras) equals the price of *attending* a movie. Now a moviemaker can just jump in and shoot a feature-length work, often achieving amazing results. What follows are three examples of creating a DV feature in the free-flow manner, just by having faith, determination, and a positive attitude.

THREE MINI-DV CASE STUDIES: SHOOTING THREE FEATURES IN THREE MONTHS

As the summer of 2002 rolled around, I was scheduled for two large DV projects. The first was a July collaborative feature workshop at the University of California, Santa Cruz (UCSC), where I expected to produce a 70+-minute DV movie within the nineteen-day time frame of the summer sessions class. On the surface that didn't appear to be impossible, since I had been conducting ten-day start-to-finish Feature Workshops productions since 1993. Also, I had a ten-day Feature Workshops session scheduled for August, although there was only one person registered by the time I left my home in Port Townsend, Washington, for the drive down to California. I decided to leave that second summer feature possibility hanging until I got through the classroom production, not being sure exactly how many pounds of flesh that job would demand of me.

The third feature I was to shoot (in September 2002) came as a complete surprise. Who would have thought that I could travel to a film festival in Portugal—Figueira da Foz International—and shoot three and a half hours of Mini-DV with my little Sony TRV-10 camera operating on just one 4-hour full battery charge? (I didn't want to weigh down my carry-on bags with the electrical current convertor needed for charging batteries in Portugal.) The festival had flown me in five times before for various feature works: *American Orpheus, Blues for the Avatar, Loneliness Is Soul, Maisy's Garden,* and *Crash My Funeral.* This time, my new movie, *The 5th Wall,* was set to screen. I was bringing along the star and cowriter Willie Boy Walker (my longtime collaborator on movies such as *1988—The Remake, Emerald Cities, Morgan's Cake,* and *American Orpheus*), by using a Diner's Club credit card that allowed for a free companion economy ticket. Before departing I must have subconsciously primed myself to think "shoot," because I had done the minimal planning of packing one copy of an Actor's Release form, with the words "Portugal 2002" hastily handwritten in the slot reserved for "The Picture" movie title. I had also brought along a profit-sharing Feature Workshops collaborative contract, which I subsequently filled in with the names of all the young Portuguese actors who ended up contributing to the feature. Having that important contractual paperwork along enabled me to approach the idea of a production seriously, each day shooting real-life stories of the people who worked the festival desks, while including Willie's performance in the mix.

Here is an account of how each of those three productions demanded a slightly different (extreme) approach to DV, for shooting a movie in a very short time frame and under diverse circumstances.

DV FEATURE 1: TWENTY-THREE COLLABORATORS CREATE A DV FEATURE IN NINETEEN DAYS

In late spring of 2002 I found myself scheduled to teach a digital workshop at University of California, Santa Cruz (UCSC), where I would attempt my most ambitious Feature Workshops–style collaboration yet: to create a DV feature with more than twenty students in a nineteen-day production window. I tried not to think about all those potentially different points of view, from which I needed to distill a single, cohesive work. But I was aware of serious conceptual and technical minefields ahead. Could the students shoot and edit well enough for us to make a professional product?

Via e-mail, equipment room technician Peter Hazard informed me that we'd have good DV equipment at our disposal: Cannon GL-1 Mini-DV cameras, fluid-head tripods, portable lights, and G4 Mac computers loaded with Final Cut Pro 3 for editing, and that gave me some needed confidence. But I was a bit wary of the dependability of such sensitive media gear, knowing how students can overwork and even abuse school equipment. Fortunately, I discovered that UCSC's strict checkout and return policy helped keep the cameras and other items in top condition.

Along with a fine array of DV gear, the Communications College (where I'd be teaching) also supplied a professional video projection system for screening rushes and works-in-progress. Five DV edit bays would be fully available, night and day. Fortunately, we would be the only production course in July, so there wouldn't be competition for reserving edit rooms, as might happen during the normal school year. This was essential, since I knew we'd be heading into an intense, last-minute editing crunch that last week of production.

Of course, the big production questions continued to loom. Will the students know how to shoot, and can they edit with Final Cut Pro? While most of the students signing up for my class had taken a prerequisite beginning filmmaking class at UCSC that required the production of three short movies (transfer students needed my OK to register), my concerns went beyond technical proficiency. How would the various levels of editing ability blend when trying to make a cohesive feature? Who was merely proficient on Final Cut Pro, and who could create real editing magic, using juxtapositions and transitions to present new ideas from seemingly mundane footage? Who could shoot "OK," versus who was a really talented cinematographer who could create images with an emotional impact that could enter the subconscious mind and never be forgotten? Actually, a teacher who fretted over these differing degrees of talent among students or any fellow collaborators would be defeated from the start. It's all too easy to conclude that it's impossible to produce a solidly professional work under these conditions. But, as with past collaborative productions, I decided again to act on faith, reminding myself that (1) everyone is talented if given a chance (in an atmosphere without fear) and (2) if the students and I did our best, kept searching for truth and understanding at 29.9 frames per second (fps), then the results would have to be worthy of our efforts.

Day One: The UCSC Class Learns They Will Start Shooting in Four Hours

As my twenty-two–member Feature Workshop class assembled at 8 o'clock Monday morning, July 1, the first day of class, I wondered how my no concept/no premise speech would play. It was vital to convince the group that we could actually begin shooting that afternoon, right after class ended at noon, because with the July 4 weekend just days away we could easily lose momentum, see whole days disappear and the production robbed of essential editing time. We would need every minute of the final two weeks of class to forge the footage into a finished cut, adding transitions, music, titles, sound mix, and color corrections—the basic ingredients that every movie needs to be watchable. I figured that I had about four hours to break the ice, help students shed all their left brain thinking, and encourage them to replace preconceived moviemaking notions with my radical approach. According to my calculations, we'd need to have the entire movie shot by that Wednesday afternoon, just two days away.

Twenty-three Collaborative Contracts

As always with my workshops, I started production by handing out the standard Feature Workshops Agreement form (Appendix B) that I sign along with all participants of my ongoing collaborative productions. This contract is as fair and equal as it gets, in that it grants equal *gross* points to everybody who participates. By awarding gross points, I promise that whatever money comes into the production coffers will be distributed after "loans to the production" are repaid. This reimbursement includes the costs of DV tape stock, actor and crew salaries, food catering and craft services, transportation, sound mix, mastering and dubs, and other incidental costs, which tend to be small when shooting DV. "Net points" indicates that money earned will first be deducted to support the numerous costs associated with running a distribution and production office or business, resulting in few dollars, if any, ever going to the actual moviemakers (see *Fatal Subtraction: The Inside Story of Buchwald V. Paramount*, by Pierce O'Donnell and Dennis McDougal).

The 5 percent that I hold back for the operation of Feature Workshops gives me the incentive to advertise the finished DV feature, make festival dubs (often the expensive BetacamSP NTSC/PAL variety), do mailings, pay entry fees and ship cassettes to festivals, search for TV outlets—in short, to do whatever it takes to keep the movies alive after they've been produced. Thinking big, I reserve another 10 percent for an investor to blow up our soon-to-be-released feature to 35mm (it costs around $50,000 to convert a DV feature into a distributable 35mm print). Those two amounts of withheld gross percentages of profit points puts a cap on the "net" aspect of profit sharing, reserving a solid 85 percent of incoming revenue to be divided evenly among all the cowriter/codirectors.

So our UCSC class began with my distributing the contracts, each class member locating his or her personalized Agreement in the pile (I'd already entered the students' names). After the students had returned to their seats with their three-page documents in hand, we settled into a mad session of signing, filling in our names, date, and place of execution. It took approximately 40 minutes out of our precious nineteen days to complete this preproduction task.

OK. There we were, at 8:40 A.M. or so, suddenly bound together legally, set to make a collaborative feature tentatively entitled "Santa Cruz 2002." This was a placeholding title used just for the documents. The final and presumably catchy main title would be determined before the editing deadline.

Teacher or Producer?

For all practical purposes, my role as teacher ended abruptly at that early point on the first day. When a student boldly asked me to clarify whether I was there "to teach anything, or . . . ?" I quickly answered, "No." I wasn't their teacher. I told them my job was that of producer, someone who would make absolutely sure that the feature got shot and completed on time.

Inside I was chuckling at my seemingly ludicrous answer—there I was, standing before them in a college classroom saying I wasn't going to teach. How absurd! Did I really believe what I said? Well, I knew that just by the process of *doing*—without having time to think or worry—everybody would probably learn more about indie feature filmmaking than they could in any other way. Now, I'm certainly not putting down all the excellent technical and conceptual classes they had attended previously and would likely attend in the future at UCSC or some other equally excellent film school or multimedia program. I'm referring to the kind of trial-by-fire, seat-of-the-pants, intuitive plunge such a production workshop as mine called for. Students would need to take full responsibility for shooting and editing at the highest level they could muster. Such a demanding, risk-taking leap into theatrical-length moviemaking would take all their grit to pull off. They would have to shoot for days in a row, convert idea after idea into scenes that somehow fit together, and create a body of footage that constitutes a feature's worth of material.

Back to the question of teaching. In art school, where I'd been a teaching assistant in the foundry, I was shocked to learn from a professor that a few students had told him I was the best teacher they'd ever had. Oddly, I didn't remember teaching anything! All I'd ever said, while trying to get my own sculptures poured, was that if their stuff was ready, it'd get done too (in bronze or aluminum). I guess they saw me working super-hard, taking advantage of the school hours to get as much art done as I possibly could. I knew, as an old undergraduate (I was twenty-six) that time-to-create was a precious commodity, and hard to come by once real, adult world responsibilities took over (I was already married with two adopted kids at the time). So perhaps my hardy work ethic served to "educate" my younger foundry colleagues.

Flash forward to the class at hand. It was time again to *learn by doing* (for me and everyone else). By offering the intense experience of making a feature in an impossibly short nineteen-day time frame—creating a story, casting and directing actors, shooting and editing to completion—I knew I would in fact be "teaching" plenty!

Determining the Amount of Footage to Shoot

One big decision in my preplanning for the UCSC workshop production had been to determine how many Mini-DV cassettes I should supply for the shoot. Ultimately I decided that five 1-hour Mini-DV cassettes would be distributed among groups of students and from these we'd try to cut a 70+-minute movie. With the tight time constraint and minimal 5 hours of "raw stock" (meaning we'd be shooting at a ratio of approximately 3:1), there was no choice for the students but to perform to the best of their abilities, work hard, and make instantaneous decisions. There was no time to contemplate failure. The process left no room for the usual student gripes and excuses for late homework or incompleteness. They would all have to be dependable and rely on each other for everything production-oriented: getting viable story concepts, delivering good acting performances, recording sound ("booming the shots"), shooting scenes in focus and well framed. When it came to editing, the demands would grow exponentially (twenty-three people cutting on one movie, if you included me). If feature-length moviemaking was their dream, then they had definitely signed up for the right class, because they would be fully immersed in that reality very soon. In fact, depending on who was selected for the first production group, they could be shooting as soon as four hours from the moment they'd signed contracts.

Our First "Location Miracle"

Back to class. I repeated that the tight deadline for our DV feature required that we start shooting right after lunch that afternoon. This was probably the second or third time I'd mentioned that we'd be shooting in a few hours, and still there was no audible response. I think the class thought I was kidding. How could we shoot without a script, actors, or even a premise? There was definitely no time to script anything (I thought out loud), and *hardly any time even to acquire a location.* Speaking of location (hearing my own words jolted me), I appealed to the assembled group of students to help solve this problem. Could anyone supply an apartment, workplace, *anywhere to shoot*? No response. "No location equals no shoot," I added. Silence again. Finally a hand went up. A guy named Nick said he might be able to get the place to which he had just moved: "a sort of drug dealer or rich person's house with swimming pool, hot tub, pool room [as in billiards]." He added that he'd have to check with his new roommates first. "Great. We'll take it!" I exuberantly exclaimed, hoping for the best. I told Nick to leave the classroom immediately, grab a phone and inquire. Within minutes he returned with the good news that it was a *go*. I felt huge relief. In less than five minutes, we had gone from having no place to shoot to acquiring what sounded like a world-class location. You have to realize that without the inevitability of actually starting a shoot that very day, of being desperate enough to ask the world for help, this kind of production miracle would probably never have occurred. The *intensity of need* brings good things like this to your production. That is what true indie moviemaking is all about: jumping in, taking a risk, making a feature.

> Consciousness cannot precede expression. If you can storyboard your film in advance, if you know what's going to happen, how your characters are going to react and feel at every moment, save yourself a lot of time and trouble, skip the shoot and publish the storyboard. As Robert Frost said: No surprise in the writer, no surprise in the reader.
>
> —from Ray Carney's "The Path of the Artist," *www.Cassavetes.com*

Supplying at Least One "Known": Great Improv Actors

Did I really show up at the classroom at UCSC with nothing at all set up in advance to make a DV feature in three weeks? Well, I did try to cover myself a little by supplying the project with great improvisational actors: Maya Berthoud, Adam Karagas, and Yahn Soon. These three are among the most intelligent people I know, and I imagine they must enjoy the challenge of entering into a screwy (by Hollywood standards) moviemaking process such as mine, where they have license to express their own ideas, and go way beyond what any written script would provide. In how many movies can they help create the movie's script straight from their own intellect? (More on this later.)

I had received an e-mail a few months before from Maya Berthoud (cowriter, codirector, and lead actress of our 2000 Feature Workshops production *Chetzemoka's Curse*, Dogme No. 10). She reminded me that she was hoping to be involved in my next movie production, and she had noticed the listing of the UCSC movie at my Web site (*www.lightvideo.com*). Maya also mentioned that her then-boyfriend, Adam Karagas (also in *Chetzemoka's Curse*), was again willing to do some acting and was ready to accompany her down the coast from their new home in Marin County. On my drive down from Port Townsend to Santa Cruz, I had called Maya and solidified the arrangement. I also phoned Oakland actor, writer, and director Yahn Soon, who also agreed to participate in the new project. Yahn had starred in several other features, including *Loneliness Is Soul*, *Maisy's Garden*, *Crash My Funeral*, *Sun and Moon*, and *The 5th Wall*. So I arrived in Santa Cruz with the promise of three world-class improvisational talents. For me, that knowledge made the idea of starting to shoot a DV feature on Day One of my Special Topics Digital Video Workshop a little less reckless.

Knowing that my actors were planning to arrive at the classroom between 10:30 and 11:00 A.M. that first day, I decided to set the stage by screening parts of *Loneliness Is Soul* and *Chetzemoka's Curse*. I showed about 15 minutes of each movie, and barely 10 minutes later my trio of indie movie stars appeared in the doorway. What a great moment that was, I thought, to suddenly see movie images come to life as real, breathing human beings! I hoped all the students in that class felt the same tingle I did.

Going Dogme 95?

Since I still had paperwork to attend to with the students, I asked my three actor friends to please wait in the front courtyard of our Media Communications building. They were happy to cool out from their rush-hour freeway drive by sitting amid the redwood trees that adorned the campus. Inside, we voted on whether or not to make our production a Dogme 95 movie (see Chapter 6 for the Dogme 95 ten rules embodied in The Vow of Chastity). The class voted down working within the strict Dogme 95 shooting guidelines (no tripod, no lights, no overlaid music or sound effects, only hand-held camera work, etc.). Thinking about it later, I knew it would have been a mistake to go the Dogme 95 route with this project, given that some members of the class had connections to bands who supplied us with music tracks (used in the opening scene and end credits), and some relished the use of special effects via Final Cut Pro (see Chapter 7). Finally, certain shots demanded the use of solid tripod framing. So this was one of many correct decisions we made that first day.

Structuring Twenty-two Students
into Five Production Units

My student collaborators signed the Actor's Releases included with the contracts (some of them might act in our movie) and began writing their real-life stories (part of the contract handout was also an application form for my Feature Workshops, which requires a half-page personal story). I then pointed out that each real-life handout was printed in a different color, five colors in all. I had realized that I needed to take extra pains in structuring the creative process and divide the twenty-two-member class into small production units. That's when a color-coding idea came into play: The five color-coded handouts represent five different production units, I explained. Before the writing got into full gear, I requested the five members of each color group (purple, blue, green, orange, yellow) sit together. Thus, classmates were thrown together in intimate groups, regardless of their normal cliques and friends. Having no way to determine the level of each individual's talents at shooting or editing, I tried this random intermix, in which some would undoubtedly be more challenged than others. A certain generosity of spirit was demanded; each collaborator would need to be sensitive to his/her group's members.

Selecting the First Group to Shoot

As a final organizational act, I folded up five colored dots representing each of the separate groups and dropped the small wads of paper onto the classroom floor. Recruiting a volunteer from the first row, I asked her to close her eyes and pick one. The Purple Group "won." With different people blindly selecting the dots, I soon had the order in which the teams would shoot. Yellow Group was selected to shoot second, the following morning (Tuesday), working in the 8:00 A.M.–12:00 noon slot. The Orange Group was third and would start after a lunch break, shooting from 1:00 to 5:00 P.M. And finally, Blue Group and Green Group would finish up on Wednesday with an all-day final shoot from 8:00 A.M. to 5:00 P.M. Because these last two groups had only three and four persons respectively, we decided to merge them into one. Sometime during the organization of production groups, an attractive young woman suddenly appeared at the classroom door and announced for all to hear that she was "available" to act in our film. Of course, Piper Corbett was "hired" on the spot.

Adding Five Line Producers to the Mix

As a final control factor, I had drawn an X on one handout for each color-coded group, indicating the person responsible for securing and returning the original Mini-DV cassettes to me after each group finished shooting. This person would also have to get signed releases for actors and locations if I didn't. So I had my "lieutenants"—my line producers—on whom I would depend. Yet I didn't want to grant them an additional title, because it was important that all the collaborators have equal status, each having to pull his or her creative weight as we proceeded. It seemed that if each five-person group had a "big boss," some less assertive members might take a creative back seat, which wouldn't help our cause. Still, the students who drew an X certainly earned big applause for taking the extra responsibility and coming through for us all.

The Role-Playing Aspect of Production:
Screening Footage as We Go

Looking at my notes there in the classroom, I found another important topic to cover (this was a very complicated early morning production meeting; I would have been lost without a "points to cover" list). I needed to explain to my fellow collaborators that, as soon as each group's half-day shoot was completed, the students were responsible for screening their results (the hour-long Mini-DV cassette) in the classroom on the large projection screen. In that way, each new group would see the footage previously shot and be up-to-date on the movie

> We have a mistaken notion that you make a movie after you've decided what you want to say. It's actually the reverse. You learn what you want to say by making the movie—like conversation, which would not only be more boring, but stupider, if we tried to plan it out in advance. Use film to learn.
>
> —from Ray Carney's "The Path of the Artist," *www.Cassavetes.com*

in progress. We'd all see the direction of the developing story, experience the basic flow of scenes, watch character development, etc. This was how we would build on what had already been accomplished.

Think of it as a kind of role-playing game, I told the class, where we add to what came before, exercising our abundant intelligence and savage wit to thrill and mystify the noble opponent. In this way, we can forge ahead without concerning ourselves with backward steps or unnecessary worry and concern. Of course, this routine demanded that I be present at every shoot and available each day, twice a day if necessary (way beyond the official class hours), to unlock the room and operate the video projector.

Scheduling the Screening of Cassettes to Build a Movie

So the schedule was set for Group One (Purple) to screen their hour-long Mini-DV tape for Group Two (Yellow) the following morning (Tuesday), at 8:00 A.M. Once the second group understood where the movie was going, it would be their turn to create new story threads, further develop the characters, and add more action, drama, or comedy—without any real limitations on their creativity. Then, around 1:00 P.M. Tuesday, Group Three (Orange) would likewise view the accumulated footage, by then two hours of Mini-DV, before heading back mid-afternoon to our "drug dealer" location atop a hill overlooking the Santa Cruz skyline. Their shooting schedule would have to extend past the normal 5:00 P.M. deadline, to make up for the late start. Lastly, all three hours of Mini-DV footage would have to be screened for Group Four (Green) and Group Five (Blue) at 8:00 A.M. on Day Three (Wednesday), before they departed from campus around 11:00 A.M. to wrap up the movie, finish the various plots and subplots, and conclude the action in some way.

Since our actors had to return to the Bay Area (for real jobs!) that Wednesday night, and all the equipment had to be checked in to the UCSC equipment room by 5 P.M. at the latest (the university would be effectively closed July 4–8), there was really no wiggle room in the schedule. We had to go for a weekend-style shoot of two and a half days. (In equipment rental house terminology, a weekend shoot rental fee covers picking up the camera and gear at noon Friday, returning it Monday morning before 10 o'clock.) Before the class broke up, we exchanged cell phone numbers in case people had setbacks traveling to or from the location, or had any last-minute emergencies.

> Hollywood movies tell us what to think. But they forget that explanations kill involvement. When people and events are explained, a viewer ceases to care about them. In being brought into our minds, they leave our hearts. When you watch Tarkovsky's *Stalker* or Cassavetes's *A Woman Under the Influence*, you *feel* things precisely because you can't quite *understand* them. Explanations make us passive. Following directions is the opposite of thinking. Real thinking can take place only when we aren't told what to think.
>
> —from Ray Carney's "The Path of the Artist," *www.Cassavetes.com*

Shooting in the Restaurant During Lunch— A Tight Schedule Dictates!

The stage was set. After loading up equipment (Canon GL-1 Mini-DV camera, tripod, lights, and sound gear), the Purple Group, three actors, and I departed the campus in three cars, heading downhill to a local falafel cafe where our people said good, inexpensive food was available on the way to our hilltop location. Sitting around the cafe with our actors and student collaborators (GL-1 in a suitcase at our feet, since we didn't leave expensive DV equipment in cars), after placing our orders and getting our beverages, I suddenly realized that we were drifting into a time wasting lull. My God, I thought, We need to be shooting right *now*! So I put out the alert, and the Purples responded positively to my suggestion. But who and what to shoot?

Looking at the three young women behind the counter (one had bright red and yellow hair), I was happy that we had selected that particular restaurant, because if the clerks and chefs would agree to sign actor's releases, we would be off to a colorful start.

No Releases Equals No Shoot

The young women cooks said they'd have to wait to ask the manager, due back shortly, if shooting was OK. Fortunately he did return soon and was happy to oblige a moviemaking class, saying that he had hired several other UC "movie majors" in the past, pointing to photos of several young men and women on his bulletin board. So I got a location release signed as well, while the women of the kitchen, along with the one male helper, signed their acting releases. Meanwhile the students broke out the camera and sound gear and started to form a concept.

Getting a Concept and Building on a Present Reality

By the time I collected the releases, we had determined that actor Yahn Soon would be a guy named Mikey, who had placed an order for chicken shawerma (that's what he had actually ordered, so we went with it). While collaborator Tim got the Canon GL-1 ready to shoot and Glenn assembled the boom pole and mike, first-up writer/director Andrea (she had asked to shoot and direct first since she had to leave in 40 minutes for another class) was offered an idea from actress Piper. "Why not have me steal the chicken shawerma before Mikey can pick it up off the counter." It was decided that Piper would lurk there near the gumball machine, about six feet from the pickup counter, watching for an order that wasn't collected so she could take it. When Mikey's name was called and he didn't immediately respond, she'd grab his bag of uncollected chicken shawerma, quickly leave the premises, and run off down the street. (No one knew at that early stage in the shoot, as we struggled to initiate a movie, that the title would become *It's Not About the Shawerma*.) As soon as Yahn heard the details of the shot he began creating his mindset (as any good improvisational actor or non-actor should do). Sitting at a table far back from the counter, he figured he'd be wrapped up in the process of tearing out classified ads, searching for a job. That's how quickly scenes can be envisioned and blocked out, with the framing, camera angles, and cuts figured out on the spot and recorded on DV. Someone later mentioned how "the actors had made the scenes." That's what usually happens if you surround yourself with intelligent, creative people who get a chance to use their imagination during the scene-making process. This is different from what happens on Hollywood sets and even in most indie features, where a written script must be religiously followed. At any rate, we had that series of shots pretty much "in the can," including an impromptu dispute between Yahn and the flaming-red-haired cook arguing about his missing order, before the Purple Group and I finally sat down to eat.

Sizing Up the Main Location and Getting the Action Rolling

It was about 2:00 P.M. by the time we rolled up to the hilltop Santa Cruz house that Nick had secured for us. It didn't take more than a second to realize that we had hit a location gold mine. The house was impressive, sprawled out in a wide U shape, so that the vast backyard and swimming pool were privately enclosed, the view opening wide toward downtown Santa Cruz and the ocean far in the distance. Inside, we had access to a room totally devoted to a large pool table, the picture windows looking out toward the diving board, hot tub, and hammock beyond. In addition, a large, pedal-type Hammond organ was tucked into the corner near the pool cues case. (Fooling around on the organ one day, actor Adam Karagas played a strange, repetitious dirge that became part of the movie's actual soundtrack.) Several large fish tanks set into the wall of the same room held exotic species, including a lovely Tiger fish that floated gracefully as eels swirled around it (another shot captured for *Shawerma*). Before anyone thought to have an idea for a shot, Maya and Adam started a pool game. It was out of that activity that the first scene at the Red House developed.

Building Characters Through Their Attitudes

A new student director, Glenn, jumped in and began shooting the interaction between the actors. It didn't take long for Maya (Yvette), Adam (Dean), and Yahn (Mikey) to set up some threads for our quickly evolving story. It was soon made apparent through Yvette's dialogue that she had an affinity for Mikey, even had knowledge of Mikey's attempts at writing, to the surprise of Dean, his best friend, who knew nothing about Mikey's creative side. The more Adam interjected his cynical overview, picking on his "lazy drifter-dude" buddy, the more Maya came to Mikey's defense. We milked this discussion between the principal actors, getting some good shots. Since we had Piper along with us on that first day's shoot, someone suggested that Piper, the shawerma thief, should be Maya and Adam's new roommate, the irony being that the thief lived right there in the house. It was then decided that Mikey would show up first, entering through the front door, to tell the couple his amazing and irritating tale of shawerma theft, followed a minute later by Piper herself entering with the bag of shawerma in hand. Before her arrival, Yahn would describe all the slights he'd endured at the falafel cafe, including the argument with the punkette. Just to push the envelope a bit further, I suggested to Yahn that he get deeper into analyzing the legal aspects of the shawerma theft. Maybe he could wonder out loud to his friends just where the liability of the restaurant began and ended. He ran with the suggestion: Did they relinquish their ownership and legal responsibility when the bag lost contact with the counter surface (was picked up by someone, anyone), or when the customer's name was called for pickup? Suddenly there were three brilliant

Knowingness is the curse of our art. The director knows what his characters are; the characters know what they themselves are; and the viewer knows what everyone else knows. Watch your mind at moments when you *don't know* something: when you meet a new person; when you hear a loud sound at night but don't know what it is; when you're running out and looking for your wallet or keys. How does your mind function differently from when it is on autopilot? Most of the important parts of life are lived not in the state of knowing, but of not-knowing. Get that into your work. Let your characters experience it, let your viewer experience it. Look at the scene in Tarkovsky's *The Sacrifice* in which a loud sound is heard off-screen and a pitcher of milk spills. Why is it more powerful than if the cause of the sound were shown or explained? Don't explain more than life does.

—from Ray Carney's "The Path of the Artist," *www.Cassavetes.com*

improvisational actors hashing out the shawerma dilemma, making mountains out of mole hills, compounding fact and fantasy.

To further the drama, it was decided that Piper should arrive through the front door during Yahn's story, placing the shawerma sack right down on the edge of the pool table for a brief second (the most visible spot in the framing of the shot), while greeting Maya, before walking around the table, greeting Adam (off camera), and disappearing into her room (beyond the fish tanks).

That, of course, would lead to Yahn asking, "Did you smell that?" Maya and Adam would ask, "What?" and Yahn would say he believed he smelled shawerma. OK. Sure. "An obsessed Mikey," a cynical Adam would rib. By the time we left the pool room to shoot new roommate Claire (Piper) bouncing on the diving board (Yahn watching), we had our movie up and running at the central location.

Actors Piper Corbett and Maya Berthoud (seen behind) are videotaped by Anish Patel on a GL-1 Canon Mini-DV, while across the pool, Grant Richards shoots actors Yahn Soon and Adam Karagas with the second Canon camera. Both shots were used simultaneously for a Final Cut Pro dual sliding screen special effect.

Real-Life Stories for Editing Juxtaposition

It was now time for me, as a cowriter/codirector collaborator (and producer) to request a student tell his real-life story to the camera. In my last ten features I've encouraged the inclusion of real-life stories in the fiction mix. The inherent honesty of real stories adds an important element to these mostly experimental works. Depending on the kind of life the viewer leads, there's often at least one story in these workshop-style movies that can supply him/her with new and interesting information. (All stories are told in a static-shot, locked-down tripod framing.)

Vaughn, who joined our class as a transfer student from the East Coast, supplied the first of seven great stories for our DV feature. He agreed to tell about how he was riding on a Greyhound bus one night as a kid on a school excursion, when his buddy got himself locked into the bathroom (this was the story that Vaughn wrote in class that morning, on his purple-colored handout). He went on to explain that when his friend gave a hard kick to the door while braced against a window atop the sink, the glass gave way, propelling the boy out onto the dark highway at 60 miles an hour (he miraculously survived, though it took six months of hospital care). We included Vaughn in several other background shots, with Maya and Adam playing pool in the foreground, just to have Vaughn appear in the movie beyond his storytelling sequence. In the final cut, Vaughn's story comes after the stolen shawerma sequence (at the falafel cafe) and before Adam and Maya playing pool and Mikey's and Piper's arrival at the Red House. If you're resourceful and persistent in the editing room, you will discover how this kind of adventurous juxtaposition can add an exciting dynamic to the cut.

Believing in the Flow

In this kind of improvisational shooting, when scenes are created in order without any roadmap, the moviemaker must be able to let the movie feed organically on itself without blocking the path—just let it flow with new ideas. As soon as you make that first decision, start shooting some kind of narrative concept, a wealth of brand-new ideas appear out of nowhere. Again, try to imagine role playing. Don't become rigid and frightened when you can't foresee later scenes. Just have faith that they'll be there for you when the moment arrives. Live in the present and honor the special miracles—scenes, shots, sounds, accidents—that suddenly present themselves. Functioning in a state of terror won't help you identify these gems when they occur, so try to stay somewhat relaxed, but attentive. The process of actually operating your own DV camera helps you remain in this state of high awareness without becoming too frightened. You're too busy working, building concepts, planning your cuts, framing shots, placing actors, blocking out action, and supplying lines of dialogue to become distracted by unnecessary thoughts or irrational worries.

The *Shawerma* movie was my tenth collaborative feature in about five years, but I continue to be amazed and thankful that this freewheeling, present-tense moviemaking process can deliver such meaningful material. As I've told students, the day may come when blockbusters like *The Lord of the Rings* and *Titanic* are only remembered as entertainment, while indie flicks with honest real-life stories become required viewing for audiences who need *reality-based* input to improve their real lives and make more informed decisions.

Pickup Shots to Cap Off a Story

By the time our Wednesday evening 5:00 P.M. deadline arrived, the five production groups had shot their cassettes to good effect. During the shoot I had decided to get some additional footage with my Sony DCR-TRV10 Mini-DV camera. Using Night-Shot (night vision) mode, I recorded some green-tinted shots of the house from a distance with framing that was purposely loose and unsteady, as if someone was watching, conducting surveillance. Often, with fully improvisational shooting and story building, you need to shoot "pickup" shots to tie the structure together. But you usually won't be able to determine what's missing from your movie until you try to edit it into a cohesive work. (Up ahead you'll read how these night shots led to an ending sequence for the movie.) So I wouldn't recommend waiting too long before starting on the edit; jump on your Mac/Final Cut Pro or

PC/Avid/Adobe Premiere editing workstation (see Chapter 5), capture DV in good-sized chunks, and see if your footage delivers a full movie experience others can understand, appreciate, and enjoy.

Why do we think film should be easier, purer, more Idealized than life? Don't spoon-feed the viewer. Don't give him or her pre-digested bits of knowledge. The experience of a good film should be as demanding and raw and unassimilated as the experience of life.

—from Ray Carney's "The Path of the Artist," *www.Cassavetes.com*

Twenty-three Collaborators in One Small Editing Cubicle

Before we started editing, we screened all the footage so that everyone could see all the different parts of the movie in progress and understand all the contributions their fellow classmates had made as co-writers/codirectors/cocinematographers and sound recordists. Then, with each group having its own one-hour cassette in hand, the class dispersed into five separate Mac G4 Final Cut Pro editing suites, where someone from each color-coded group took the initiative of capturing footage and beginning the two-week process of editing their portion into a usable rough-to–fine cut.

It was, first of all, a relief to see that we had created enough interesting scenes and had some hope that a finished 70+-minute movie might exist somewhere within the raw footage. But I had no time for self-satisfaction. We were five blinks away from a production disaster, I explained to the class that assembled after that July weekend, because with only five class meetings left (a sixth class would be lost to screening the movie on the final day) we had a tremendous amount of editing to do in a very short time.

All during that second week I visited editing rooms, viewed cuts, made suggestions, and screened various sections of the movie during scheduled class times. But there was no escaping the pressure of the crunch deadline. As producer, I had to question the progress and improve work flow at every turn. Halfway through the two-week editing stretch, after a particularly weak screening of some rough-edited footage, I got tougher. I announced that everyone must give at least 30 hours' editing time outside of class, if they wanted to get a good grade. I tried not to apologize for terrorizing them during this "easy" summer session workshop, but as producer with only seven production days to final cut, I had no other option.

At the beginning of the final week I went around with our most highly motivated student editor, Pedro, and collected all the separate sequences from the five digital workstations onto his external hard drive unit, so we could incorporate the parts into a cohesive whole. Surprisingly, we soon had something to screen that ran in the 70-minute range—but it was clear that some re-editing was needed. Thinking as an editor, I knew that changing the cut of any of the groups' work would be "stepping on toes." And I certainly didn't want to alter students' precious cuts behind their backs. So at our second to last class meeting I had everyone, all twenty-two students (with some girlfriends/boyfriends along) squeeze into Pedro's editing cubicle. I explained that those who had a complaint about the cut—didn't like something they saw or heard on the monitor—should write a little note (I passed out two-by-three-inch notebooks) and send it forward to me. That way, I wouldn't have to deal with everyone talking all at once. I told them Pedro would be operating Final Cut Pro and making changes for us. We'd try to clean up the cut in one edit session, making all the parts contribute effectively to the whole before it was too late.

Within five minutes of starting the movie rolling I had a criticism. I told the class that a few dissolves were adding unnecessary confusion to the first moments of getting to know a lead character. The dissolves were set into the movie between when Yahn entered the pool room and when he kneeled down at one end of the pool table; since I had seen the raw footage I felt that the original shot, without effects, was fine for just letting the scene play. He needed to be seen just *in present tense*, I explained. So I told Pedro to remove the dissolves and roll it again for the class to see. It was immediately clear to me that the straight-forward scene worked a lot better.

But the student who had edited in the stylistic extra-dissolves effect was upset. He was emotionally connected to his editing work and wasn't as yet prepared to "kill his baby" for the good of the entire movie. This is the hardest part of editing: to remove a great shot or fancy effect you love for the betterment of the whole. Still, it had to be done, and I was the son-of-a-gun producer to do it. I'm sure that some other toes were stepped on that day (some of my student evaluations reflected this). But I knew it was better to get the movie into a cohesive state at that point (my job) than fall prey to oversympathetic placating that would result in a faulty final product. I had to protect *all* the good work. Surprisingly, this edit fixing went pretty well overall, even as the room got uncomfortably hot from all the people squashed inside. We tightened up cuts, repositioned a few real-life stories, reset sound and picture transitions, adjusted volume and music levels, everyone working together to make the cut as clean as it could be.

Shooting a New Ending (with Night Vision)

With only a few days of class remaining, I realized that our ending was unsatisfactory. It involved guitar playing by actor Yahn Soon and intercuts to his character's first meeting with the Piper character. This musical interlude seemed more like introductory than ending material. I came up with the idea of shooting a raid on the hilltop house (by DEA agents) again using the night vision setting on my little Sony TRV10 camera. The concept was the result of several story threads already in place: the first reference to the hilltop house ("sort of a drug dealer's place . . ."), Yahn's drug-overdose dream sequence that one of the groups had shot and edited into the cut, and the unanswered question of how the Maya and Adam characters could afford to live in such an expensive rental. Piper and another student, Dan, who would play an agent, agreed to do the scene. The three of us were able to stage (1) a discussion between Dan and Piper about how she'd be paid off and allowed to leave the country if she followed through with the plan, (2) a point-of-view raid on the house concept (the camera creeping through the high grass front lawn, side yard, and watching the house from behind the pool), and (3) camera shooting agent(s) as they rushed through the back and front doors. In less than an hour, between 9:00 and 10:00 P.M., we had shot a new ending, thanks to the portability and ease of operation of DV.

The Important Final Screening

Regardless of your type of DV production, all the work sooner or later boils down to a moment-of-truth screening, where family and friends, along with cast and crew, assemble to see the movie they've worked on or heard about. That climactic event contains plenty of suspense (you're throwing a party *and* screening your masterpiece!), but for moviemakers it's just another test to see how the cut performs, if the pace and content are correct or need further work. All these usual things were at stake for our UCSC movie screening that last Friday of class. There was a final all-night editing session (even though I would later mix the sound a final time with Scot Charles of Blue Charles Productions in Seattle, for $600, to further tighten the cut). Then, as students started to arrive about 10:00 o'clock, our movie *It's Not About the Shawerma* was still being printed from the computer to a master DV-CAM tape. I had the students fill out the teacher's evaluations and hang in for the next hour until the 75-minute DV feature was ready. At last the lights went out and the feature was projected as digital video to the screen overhead. And it worked! There was an audible gasp of surprise in the screening room when the new ending hit, followed by

Rouse the viewer to the same state of curiosity that he is in when he experiences things outside the movie theater. The work we do when we negotiate Henry James's syntax or puzzle out one of Jesus' parables is not something to get beyond; it is the value of the experience. Because we create it, the knowledge we arrive at is different from knowledge handed to us. Each viewer feels that Cassavetes's films speak to them alone, because they must exert themselves to master them. When you make things easy on your viewers, when you tell them what it means to you, you deny them ownership of their own experience.

—from Ray Carney's "The Path of the Artist," *www.Cassavetes.com*

resounding applause when the final credits rolled. I took orders for VHS copies (at my cost of around $10 each) and felt a lot lighter as I emerged from the building out into that lush redwood-forested campus.

NOTE: Without a 24/7 Final Cut Pro editing whiz like our Pedro Avila, a three-week college-based production probably won't get completed by the deadline. To you future DV workshop teachers, I recommend you identify that motivated DV student editor as soon as your production class commences. And make sure there is an available external hard drive (nice to have 120 gigs) to collect the various edited sequences for compilation at a central DV workstation.

DV FEATURE 2: THE PORT TOWNSEND FEATURE WORKSHOP, AUGUST 2002

As I said earlier, I hadn't been sure whether I should conduct a Feature Workshop with just one paying customer, but let the record show that the last time I decided to go ahead with a one-participant production, the results were one of my favorite FW productions: *Chetzemoka's Curse* (Dogme No. 10). So, notwithstanding the logic of trying to earn a living, the urge to make a movie with a modest budget was again irresistible. And the twenty-three-year-old man, John Barnum, who had applied after I met him at a one-day workshop I conducted at the Ozarks Foothills FilmFest (*www.ozarkfoothillsfilmfest.org*) in Batesville, Arkansas, seemed like a very positive and highly motivated person. Aside from my favorable first impression of John, it was the super-personal real-life story he had sent as part of his application (about how the death of his father had shattered his normally complacent life) that ultimately won me over. If John could get that personal and truthful in print, be that open with his emotions, I felt that together we could create something just as personal and enduring in DV.

During the shooting of our movie together, I was to learn more about his father. It turns out that John was given life by a sixty-four-year-old man and his much younger wife. John's father died twenty years later. And this wasn't just any man. His ethics and high moral standards were reminiscent of the Frank Capra–style, *It's a Wonderful Life* ideal. From what I learned, both off screen and in several stories John told before the camera, his father stood for "telling the truth, no matter what the personal cost." The man truly believed in and lived by the Golden Rule: You must treat others as you yourself wish to be treated. The finished movie contains several references to John's father, along with a real-life story about him. It refreshes the soul to have such a high level of common decency held up as a measure of a life. At any rate, I decided to go ahead with the production, alerting John in early August that it was a go for our August 18–27, 2002, dates. Once again, I tried not to worry about having no actors, no locations, and no story.

The Subconscious Mind as Scriptwriter

As you probably already know, the subconscious mind is an active and resourceful tool for moviemaking, especially when you're highly "focused" on (i.e., worried about) something you need to solve in order to survive. My subconscious mind has always been a great editorial problem solver. When I go to bed wondering how to reorder a feature's worth of real-life stories set in a fictional backdrop, I often wake up with a surprising solution. Well, this subconscious channeling occurred again for the August 2002 workshop movie-to-be. I fell asleep with no story in mind and dreamed about a guru-type religious figure who told his congregation he expected them to complete three exercises before he saw them again two weeks later. Upon waking, I remembered he ordered them to (1) *say* something new, (2) *do* something new, and finally (3) *be* something new. In the two-week countdown to the start of the shoot, I'd recite this dream when people asked me what the workshop movie would be about. It's hard saying "I don't know" when asked about the content of an upcoming movie because most people believe in starting with a script or at least a concept; they need the security of a blueprint for making movies, building houses, living, etc. Most people became quietly contemplative after I gave my dream-derived response. When it came down to it, "Be something new" sounded to me like a good adventure—for anyone! So my subconscious had delivered just what I needed.

Repeating those three phrases a few times led me to consider including my friend Steven Gillard in the cast and creative part of the process. Steve, a practicing attorney and a talented writer working on a novel about a bartender/guru, is the most well-informed person I know on the subject of alternative religions and new age philosophies. The combination of my friend's expansive, all-inclusive belief system colliding with the direct simplicity of John's father's traditional Golden Rule philosophy gave me confidence in our no-script movie-to-be. I now knew the movie would be about basic belief systems, with a proselytizing Steve spreading the word of his own new religion. And somehow Steve would hook up with John (who, in an e-mail, offered the possibility of performing an acting role for the movie in addition to cowriting and codirecting) and attempt to recruit him for his new venture.

> Ever notice how much more interesting a movie is when you channel surf into it ten minutes after it has begun? Or how fascinating even a dumb movie is for at least a few minutes before the idiot plot kicks in? It gets boring the minute you figure it out, or as soon as the characters are given a road map to follow. How can you keep that openness in your movie, that state of uncertainty in the viewer (without, of course, relying on Hitchcockian tricks to stoke up fake dramatic interest)?
>
> —from Ray Carney's "The Path of the Artist," *www.Cassavetes.com*

Since John, it turned out, had taken a vow of celibacy until marriage, we decided to also explore that issue in the movie. Steve's teenage son, Joe, and his present girlfriend, Christa, both wanted very much to act in my movie, so, as they say, the plot thickened. Teenagers talking about virginity was suddenly in the cards. For a no-script situation, we were suddenly involved in a rich tapestry of ideas.

That All-Important First Scene:
Starting the Moviemaking Flow

Because there was only one person flying in for the Feature Workshop, I decided to drive to Seattle, pick up participant John Barnum curbside at SeaTac Airport, and get to know him a little on the drive back. On the trip across Puget Sound by ferry, and the hour drive to my house, John reconfirmed his intention to contribute whatever talents he had (acting, concept building, etc.) to our production. Back in Port Townsend I helped him get installed at the Water Street Hotel, a stately Victorian building that houses the old Town Tavern at street level. In the nineteenth century, sailors were often kidnapped from the place—drunks woke up the next morning to find themselves hung over and out at sea. The bar had become a famous haunt in the 1960s, when hippies worked as bartenders and dishwashers in trade for a room in the then-unpainted (since yuppified) flophouse above. So a lot of interesting history was available for future moviemaking concepts. Before John and I parted, we agreed to meet with Steve at 8:00 o'clock the following morning at the Salal Cafe across the street.

At breakfast I enjoyed seeing John and Steve hit it off, with some good intellectual "buddy" chemistry percolating. We got our paperwork quickly completed (only three signatures, rather than the twenty-three for the Santa Cruz collaboration). Then, when the conversation moved into a discussion of the mechanics of starting a new religion, Steve reminded me that a local group had begun holding religious meetings in an old building recently vacated. That spurred further scripting ideas, most importantly about how vital it was to legitimize a business, rent a space, put up a sign, and lay down roots for the new religion. After paying for breakfast, we walked outside and, within a few steps, noticed an empty Victorian storefront on Water Street with a FOR RENT sign taped to the inside of the glass. Our first dream location had materialized!

I immediately unpacked my Sony DCR-TRV10 Mini-DV camera, hooked an AudioTechnica Pro 88W/T lavalier mike on Steve's lapel (the transmitter was out of sight inside his coat), adjusted the camera's exposure and focus settings, framed Steve in wide-screen (format set to 16:9), and started recording. Steve launched right into an impassioned case to John about how they must secure that particular storefront for their new religion. (I had them stand closely together so that the one mike could pick up both their voices while I shot from a distance.)

And as with any good improvisational actor, Steve responded to what he saw and heard while giving the opening speech. In the two panels over the door of the vacant storefront were designs that Steve identified, "One for Sol, the other for Luna . . . Sol-Luna, Sun and Moon, Male-Female, the new religion." Before we moved on, I asked John to tell about being recently tempted by a teenage girl, despite his vow of chastity (a story he'd shared on the ride in from the airport). As he talked straight to the camera, John's face revealed the intensity of his inner struggle to stick to his pledge of no sex before marriage. It was barely 11:00 A.M. on Day One, and my second DV feature-length production of summer 2002 was already in full swing.

Moving to a Hotel Room in My Own Town

I have to laugh when I think of the look on my wife's face when I explained that I needed to rent a hotel room for myself ($46 per night) during the shoot. She had to question why I needed *another* bed, given that I lived right there in the town where I was shooting. I explained that I was so tired after each day of writing on the fly, directing, shooting everything, handling sound with the lavalier mike or the directional mini-shotgun mike aboard the Mini-DV camera, and controlling lighting and exposure with my framing, that, as soon as I parted from my collaborators each day, I simply needed a pillow to faint on. I further confessed that I was totally unprepared for dealing with the everyday real-life moments of being part of a family—phone calls, paying bills, talking about issues unrelated to DV moviemaking. I couldn't talk, couldn't think beyond the shoot, and couldn't stand to be kept awake for even a second longer than necessary. That's how it is when you're in production if you give it everything you've got. It's an exhausting affair, whether you're in your twenties (as I was on my first feature shoot) or older. You may need to isolate yourself from everyday realities to do your best on a feature-length work.

When my wife gave her blessing, I packed up fresh underwear, a T-shirt, and toothbrush, and checked into the Water Street Hotel where my collaborator John Barnum was lodging. I was fortunate to get the large, second floor corner room, with its six huge windows that gave a panoramic view right down the main street of Port Townsend. I collapsed gratefully on one of the two beds and was asleep as soon as my face hit the pillow.

Awaking the next day, I found myself drowsily staring at the other unused double bed. Then I noticed the six curtains glowing beautifully in the early morning light, and my scripting faculties took over. This room should be where the two characters first stay in town, I realized. Two beds means two people. And the room's six heavily draped windows could be used in the story. The Steve character could stop John from pulling back a middle curtain, explaining that on each new morning they would open the curtain corresponding to the counting of days, starting with the one at the far left. Six curtains, six days. Each morning they'd scope out the view for signs of how to proceed toward

Actor/cowriter/codirector collaborators Stephen W. Gillard (sunglasses) and John Barnum, from *Release the Head*. (FW Productions, ©2003)

their goal of starting a new religion—and on the seventh, they'd . . . It all fit! The money I'd spent for a nightly crash pad hadn't been wasteful at all. Not only had I been responsible to myself in preserving my moviemaking energy, but I had also lucked into a very special location—a real script builder. I'm always open to being reminded that we poor humans don't always know what's really going on. The important thing in feature-length moviemaking—and in life—is to follow your intuition.

> Your interactions with others are constantly on the move—playful one instant, serious the next; surprised a second later, bored the next; impatient one instant, apologetic the next. Put the liveliness back in life. Watch your mind for five minutes, even when you are doing nothing. Notice how your feelings shift and shimmer, surge and subside. Look at any scene in Tom Noonan's *What Happened Was . . .* or Cassavetes's *Faces*. The shifting tones and moods flicker like schools of tropical fish; the inter-actions vibrate with continuous, mercurial changes, adjustments, and unresolved possibilities. Put the motion back in emotion.
>
> —from Ray Carney's "The Path of the Artist," *www.Cassavetes.com*

Ex-Wife Showdown: How Scenes Lead to Other Scenes

From what Steve Gillard said in his improvisational dialogue outside the storefront that first morning, it was clear that he would have to visit his "ex-wife," played by his actual wife, Sue Gillard, also a performer in *Chetzemoka's Curse* (Dogme No. 10). Steve's character would try to convince Sue's to let him stretch out a support payment; the money, he had explained to John, could be used for a rental deposit on the storefront. So our first scene of the movie had inadvertently led to the next because of dialogue that had naturally evolved during the videotaping. That's how a movie can be magically built without a script. If you pay close attention and listen to all ideas as they emerge, you'll discover the next signpost. Follow each new lead and move on.

A phone call alerted Steve's wife that we were heading over to their house. And, as it turned out, Steve's daughter Jessica was also there, along with Sue's older daughter Jennifer and her four-year-old daughter Margaret. Once there, we tried to figure out ways to use everyone present for our movie. Here's what we came up with: The scenario was that Steve had been an absentee father, gone for at least five years, so he would hardly recognize his own daughter, who had grown from a young teenager to a twenty-year-old woman. I also figured that, after I shot a bit of Sue and Steve arguing over the money (and old disputes), Jessica could march up to the backyard picnic table where they were seated, her "daughter" (Margaret) in hand, and throw deadbeat dad Steve off kilter. ("Why didn't you tell me I have a granddaughter?") We had fun playing with the cinematic possibilities at hand.

Before we were done, Sue's other daughter Jenny also performed in a scene in which John iterates his vow of having no sex before marriage in the face of her questions about where their relationship is heading. The moviemaking pot got stirred in good fashion with these hot topic domestic scenes.

Can You See Your Head?

Following the natural leads as they cropped up in the previously shot scenes, it was clear that we should take the two main characters, Steve and John, and shoot something at Chetzemoka Park. Again, we'd been directed to a location because of dialogue in the early storefront scene, where the Steve character fantasized about having a "rock concert-worth" of audience for his future revivalist meeting. As we stood on the lush grass and viewed the sparkling blue water of the Strait beyond, the options seemed endless. But what brought the shoot down to earth was spotting a picnic table where four elderly people, two men and two women, chatted away happily while nibbling on a picnic lunch. "Maybe we could include them in our shot?" I wondered aloud to Steve and John. "Wouldn't it be great if they could listen to your [Steve's] rap about a new religion? I'll see if they'd be willing to sign releases."

> **NOTE:** It always comes down to the release. If a person off the street or any nonactor will sign an Actor's Release, then you have a chance of getting footage for your movie. If they won't sign, then just don't bother shooting, because *if* you record something good

on DV you won't be able to use it in your cut legally. A distributor will demand that that scene be deleted from the feature before it can be released, sold, or broadcast.

We were fortunate that the retirees who had ventured into Chetzemoka Park that morning were friendly, game for signing releases, and perfect at looking deadpan about Steve's fairly outrageous religious spiel. Their mute expressions (I had told them not to talk because I couldn't mike them and Steve at the same time) made Steve's pronouncements all the funnier and insightful at the same time. Again, we had approached a location with nothing except a desire to do *something* in a nice setting. We were letting the story tell itself by following whatever leads we found along the way—going with the flow.

Wrap Party Luckout: Getting the "Big Song" for the Movie

The third location lead that arose from the storefront shots came from John mentioning that he'd learned about the rental from a friend of a friend somewhere in town. This "fact" had just popped out of John's mouth during the improvisational discussion between the two men. So it seemed wise to shoot a short scene with John and someone who could be that friend. When we heard that local musician Kip Hubbard was having a housewarming party, we called to see if he'd be willing to appear in a scene with John during his party preparations. Being the great guy he is, Kip said OK. Kip had done the L.A. industry scene—he knew the trials of making movies and was ready to help by letting us invade his party. So we got our pickup shot connecting Kip and John. And after a week and a half of constant videotaping, that was our last shot for the movie. All at once we knew we had covered almost all the leads from our material, buttoned up the beginning, middle, and end on that day. Steve came up to me and said, "Nice wrap party!" Of course, it wasn't for us that all the guests were showing up, bringing delicious looking potluck contributions of salads, desserts, pastas, and beverages. It was Kip's and his wife's celebration. But we *were* there, and we *were* wrapped (and we didn't have to make even one phone call, worry about the beer kegs getting there on time, or sweat the live band showing up). Ah, the glamor of moviemaking!

As it turned out, another final moviemaking gift lay in wait for us there. As I was chatting with one of my son Marlon's musician friends, singer/songwriter Marc Gizzi, telling him what our movie was about, I heard him say, "I might have just the song for you." Marc's comment eventually led to several heavenly weeks in a recording studio, taping and mixing his original song "Second Coming's Coming," with Marc singing and playing guitar, backed by Marlon Schmidt on keyboard, Todd Fisher on bass, and Brett Pemberton on drums.

The moral: Gifts will rain down on you when you place your life in the risk-taking situation of making a feature-length DV movie. It's happened to me in amazing ways throughout the twenty-plus features I've written/directed/produced so far. Somehow we artists unknowingly tap a source of positive energy when we do our heartfelt work, whether it be writing, painting, sculpture, or moviemaking. For this reason, nothing compares to the spiritual high derived from such creative endeavors.

DV FEATURE 3: FIGUEIRA DA FOZ INTERNATIONAL, PORTUGAL

It had always been a dream of mine to make a movie while lounging at a film festival. I remember being in Park City, Utah, for the Sundance Film Festival, making an effort to at least throw myself in a snow bank before returning to sunny California. That simple desire to enjoy the special mountain surroundings was a far cry from actually shooting a movie. I could only wonder back then about the exact mindset and ingredients (available actors and equipment) that would be needed to pull off such a thing at an unfamiliar and exotic location. It hadn't seemed at all possible in the past, when I visited festivals in Florence, Rome, Berlin, and Belgrade. Only with the advent of DV did this dream suddenly become a reality.

Bring a Good Actor Along to Shoot a Movie

On my sixth trip in as many years to the Figueira da Foz International Film Festival in Portugal, I finally made proper use of my time (usually a 10-day stay) and shot a DV feature. Probably what helped the most was having along my actor friend Willie Boy Walker, one of the supreme acting talents it's been my privilege to record on film and video over the years (see *www.lightvideo.com*, "Films" link, for a full list of Walker appearances). We were set to show our collaborative feature, *The 5th Wall*, and with a free companion ticket compliments of Diner's Club Card, I could share the European premiere with the star of the movie. While I had shot a bit of footage with my earlier Mini-DV Canon ZR the previous year, I hadn't delivered the necessary flow of ideas, connection of concepts (creating beginning, middle, and ending material) that it took to turn a disparate body of footage into a feature. Now, with Willie Boy Walker at the festival, I figured it would be a shame not to at least attempt something. Willie would be my coproducer, cowriter, and star, that is, if we could get something rolling, and if the anti–jet lag diet—about which I advised Willie by phone—saved us. I told him not to drink *any* coffee for two days prior to the long flight. We'd slug down several strong cups the morning we arrived in Portugal, which was meant to help reset our human clocks to their time zone (Portugal is nine hours ahead of West Coast time). Travel fatigue and jet lag are serious concerns for anyone traveling overseas, but the diet worked and we at least had the energy to attempt a movie in that foreign setting.

Most Minimal Mini-DV: Traveling Light

On this trip I brought my Sony DCR-TRV10 camera and only one fully charged 4-hour battery (I was unwilling to pack heavier stuff like the voltage adapter for Portuguese electrical outlets), and I had with me just two hour-long and one 80-minute Mini-DV cassettes. Along with the minimal gear (I didn't even bring a lavalier mike), I had just one Actor's Release, to copy as needed, and one contract to fill out for actor's profit sharing. I guess I *sort of* wanted to do this movie, but wasn't quite ready to make the full commitment. Maybe I should be partying in Portugal, celebrating having survived two feature shoots in the past two months and having a new movie to screen in the festival. Did I really want to jump into shooting another? I decided that if something did get started, it would have to be a real easy flow.

So there was Willie, a very affable presence who, without trying, could bring out the best in people, make them laugh, become more alive. And I was scheduled to run a one-day Feature Workshop with Willie in attendance, something I'd set up in prior correspondence with the festival's director, José Vieira Marques. It was out of this very basic workshop that yet another DV feature magically got under way.

The shoot effectively began when our sole workshop attendee, an attractive and personable young woman named Diana Tavares, showed up at 10 o'clock on September 6. Within minutes the three of us were joking around, Willie interviewing Diana, and just being his normal fun-loving self. Then an old friend from past festivals, Alfons Engelen, happened along. Alfons is a well respected Belgian critic and author of an ongoing, self-published edition of original fairy tales. In the 2000 edition of *Feature Filmmaking at Used-Car Prices*, Alfons reminded my readership that we know only maybe half of "the film alphabet," and that the only way to approach moviemaking is to "do something new, say something new, be original in your approach to cinema." This holds true more than ever with the elastic media of DV. So, though a serious thinker, Alfons could be playful and join our game. Within minutes he was teaching Diana something he called the "bear dance," a simple two-step, back-and-forth children's movement in which the participants tip from side to side, lifting their right foot, then left foot. At any rate, it was a delightful and funny moment for all, and I wouldn't have guessed then that months later, back in my editing room in the States, the main movie title that would emerge from reviewing, assembling, and fine-tuning the footage would be *Bear Dance*.

Connecting Concepts to Visualize Your Full Movie

The idea of the bear dance being some sort of weird therapy cropped up somewhere in the conversation, leading to an important thread for the ongoing movie. Then, as I shot real-life stories on the day that followed (almost all the young members of the film festival staff told their personal stories to the tiny Sony TRV10 Mini-DV camera), the more it seemed that some "doctors" could be applying therapy, using real-life storytelling to discover the emotional and psychological ailments of their "patients." The ever growing question in my mind was who are the patients and who are the doctors? Willie and Alfons had shared real-life stories as well; were they and the other older people doctors? Or were the others, the young festival assistants who could easily pass for young medical school graduates with knowledge of the latest, cutting-edge techniques in abnormal psychology? Yes, the young doctors could certainly be the promising leaders in their field, trying new and unusual methods of healing the sick and distraught. As a storyteller I could run with that.

As the doctors idea gathered momentum, I kept enjoying my European vacation, making new friends, including a local woman, Rosa, who

Rick Schmidt (straw hat) shoots a gathering with his Sony DCR-TRV10 for the Portuguese DV feature *Bear Dance*. (Note the back-of-head earphones, $60 Sony ECM-HS1 directional mike, and framing with hand-steadied, fold-out LED screen.) (Photo by Willie Boy Walker, ©2002 FW Productions)

quickly became a buddy and helpmate to the production. We continued shooting stories, such as Anna's, about how the small act of eating a special kind of chocolate helped her remember her deceased grandparents, and Pedro's, describing a guy arrested for dropping bricks from a twenty-story window and nearly hitting a baby on the sidewalk.

The fallacy of most film performances is that characters respond to each other, when in life we are mainly responding to ourselves, engaged in continuous course corrections, constantly readjusting our trim tabs to counteract the previous trim tab movement. In any case, most speech is not about revealing, sharing, giving—but the opposite. We talk for every reason except the one we give. We talk to cover up, to hide, to evade scrutiny, to defend ourselves against imaginary attacks, to pretend we care, to dust our tracks, to deflect attention away from the real subject. Rent a copy of Harold Pinter's *The Homecoming* or *Betrayal*. Get those zip-zapping tonal laser beams into your characters' relationships.

—from Ray Carney's "The Path of the Artist," *www.Cassavetes.com*

Sony TRV10 Mini-DV camera's 9:16 aspect ratio view of Portuguese restaurant group (as seen by Schmidt on the fold-out LED screen) shows the good effect of wide-format framing.

Next, we learned that Rosa's mother ran a medical clinic (Rosa herself is a psychiatrist) and, yes, we could shoot a scene there. *Wow!* As it turned out, Rosa, Willie, and Alfons were there, talking about their various therapy sessions, wearing official doctor smocks Rosa readily supplied from the closet. In the scene, there is the mention of over-drugging patients. We then decided to have our original workshop participant Diana (also in a doctor's smock) approach, requesting that the "doctors" hand over their smocks to her and Dr. Hawk (played by a London Cineclub official and many-time Figueira da Foz International jury member Charles Hedges). Round and round the ideas swirled, connecting real-life storytellers with the structure of "doctors" offering "therapy." For this movie, the real-life stories would be the scaffold from which to view the ever-evolving human condition.

BUDGET FOR THREE DV FEATURES:
$215 OF MINI-DV STOCK

After a whirlwind summer of DV production I had to look back at the budgets of those instant shoots and laugh at the difference between shooting in video and shooting in film. Of course, the bottom line was that if these had been film shoots they wouldn't have happened! The instantaneous flow required to make these movies would have been completely frustrated by the processes and high expenditures related to using motion picture film. Because I shot on Mini-DV, at about $10 per 1-hour cassette, the UCSC movie cost five cassettes ($50), the Feature Workshop production cost thirteen cassettes ($130), and the Figueira da Foz Portugal feature cost three cassettes ($35, one being the more expensive 80-minute variety)—basically next to nothing. I worked out the math of shooting that same 21 hours with film: six 11-minute rolls of 400-foot color 16mm film stock at $140 per roll came to $840 for 66 minutes, minus the head and tail leaders, for a net total of 60 minutes. I would have spent more than $17,000 on just the film stock.

Of course, for each of the three features there were production expenses beyond the cost of Mini-DV cassettes, such as buying food for actors and crew, and giving actors a token fee. I paid the UCSC workshop actors Maya, Adam, and Yahn a token $100 each to help cover the costs of travel and housing while they spent three days in Santa Cruz for the movie (you always need to offer amenities to your actors to keep production spirits up). Of course, if you are producing your DV feature with friends and colleagues, then housing and food are already taken care of (people eat in the cafeteria, return to their homes or dorms each night); maybe just buying beverages and snack food or refilling gas tanks will suffice. At any rate, with DV you can shoot with intuition and abandon, at a cost you can afford.

By taking advantage of special locations, like film festivals, vacations, or simply the back alleys of your own home town, you can "flow" your movie. Maybe you'll even embark on a feature shoot without *any* idea where it is heading (as I did with these three features I describe here) and then edit at your leisure while maintaining your everyday job. If your computer is equipped with great editing software like Apple's Final Cut Pro (or the more affordable Final Cut Express at $299), Adobe Premiere, or Avid Xpress DV, you can work on the movie when your schedule dictates, slowly getting to know your footage, discovering the best cut points, and adding music as you explore your local music scene. For a token payment of between $250 and $500, you should be able to buy several songs from an up-and-coming band. In other words, you can make your moviemaking dream come true without the pressure of carrying a huge debt on your shoulders.

Beyond all the obvious advantages of DV feature filmmaking, the most exciting development is that you'll be creating *new* movies with new forms of storytelling and expression. You may produce an entirely new type of movie like no one has ever seen before. The moviemaking mold has been broken. With DV (Mini-DV, DVCAM, direct-to-DVD), you can follow your heart, virtually *thinking* your movie into existence without resorting to conventional Hollywood moviemaking techniques. If you just use your instincts, shoot however it feels best, you're bound to make radical shots reflecting your own particular way of seeing. And you'll probably invent unusual transitions to make all those unusual shots work in the editing room, so ultimately you can

Rick Schmidt's digital video moviemaking workstation, powered by a Mac G4 with 933 MHz/60 gigs. A Sony Multiscan 200ES Trinitron monitor (a garage-sale find for $40!) connected by a $30 Apple-to-VGA cable to a second monitor supplies two-screen viewing. (Courtesy of Apple and Sony Electronics Inc.)

emerge with a ground-breaking work. At least that's what I'll be expecting from the new DV moviemakers. I hope my description of three DV features in three months of production has demonstrated some of the possibilities, and shed light on how to role-play a feature into existence. So, instead of giving your production power away to the Hollywood coffers, use that $10 (a movie and popcorn) to *make a movie!*

2

YOU SHOOT THE WORKS:
TAKING YOUR DV PROJECT FROM SCRIPT TO PREPRODUCTION

I hope I've conveyed the pace and magnitude of the continued effort it took to produce three DV features in as many months. Now I want to give you a closer look at the increments of feature-length storytelling in the next several chapters, from selecting helpful scripting software to purchasing affordable DV equipment and learning writing/directing techniques that you'll use as a digital moviemaker to produce your own work. You could just grab any old copy of the three editions of my *Feature Filmmaking at Used-Car Prices* (find them at *www.bookfinder.com*) and apply much of that information. But there is a decidedly new approach to making a movie using DV that goes beyond the difference between loading hour-long Mini-DV cassette tapes or DVDs and loading 400-foot rolls of film stock. The immediacy of shooting broadcast-quality digital video, its ease of shooting (for no-lights-equals-Dogme 95 shooting style, see Chapter 6) and electronic editing (Chapter 7), coupled with the advantages of the Internet for vast research and resources (downloadable plug-ins and products for editing and animation, etc.), all add up to a completely new brew of artistic possibilities. With these new approaches to solving the classic problem (making an interesting movie that embodies important truths and sparks the imagination), I offer a step-by-step guide for making an electronic feature. The first step is to have a story you're burning to tell, or at least the desire to enter into other people's stories with your DV camera.

SELECTING A VIABLE CONCEPT
FOR YOUR DV FEATURE

Given the established ease of digital shooting and editing, the DV moviemaker may be more likely than any filmmaker ever was to just jump in—load an hour Mini-DV tape or DVD (a bit more pricey than a tape at $12 per disk) and start shooting as I've demonstrated in Chapter 1. Of course, I sympathize completely with this level of excitement, having done this very thing the moment I first got my hands on a DV camera. But it takes practice and experience to make this giant leap of faith and get good, structured results—to produce a sturdy, feature-length work that merits recognition and distribution, one that can break through the wall of the Sundance Film Festival or at least get selected for major digital film festivals. [Smaller showcases like The Digital Room, started up by moviemaker Sujewa Ekanayake in Washington, D.C. (*www.wilddiner.com*) may be a more reasonable launch pad.] To do all this, your DV movie must have powerful and well-crafted elements. So, for the sake of including everyone's dreams here (with regard to making DV features), I'll backpedal a bit from my brash, just-jump-in, build-as-you-go approach to shooting, to celebrate the scriptwriter's craft and support those visionaries who wish to translate their preconceived ideas and dialogue to DV. There is certainly more than one path to making your moviemaking dream come true.

Probably more important than anything else is the initial concept. Before you start shooting without a roadmap, ask yourself if your kickoff idea is good enough to spend several months of your life rendering it into a digital video product. It is easier to abandon a DV project than it ever was to walk away from the pounds and pounds of film rolls and sound track of an expensive 16mm feature film project. In a sense you can just quit or change direction if things aren't working out as well as you'd hoped. When a DV concept doesn't deliver quickly enough, you can just take those few little three-by-five-inch boxes of DV tape you shot (five tapes per box equals five hours of moving images) or those thin plastic DVD disks, and put them into a shoebox for your grandkids to discover someday.

The downside to being so casual with DV movie footage therefore is that your willpower isn't put to the test, as it was with filmmakers of old, when there was no direction to go but straight ahead after the shoot. We were stuck with all the footage and related lab debts, and we simply *had* to make that movie work, come hell or high water. We had to bear down on existing footage in editing rooms until we edited together a minimum of 75 minutes' worth of movie viewing experience. Only then was there hope that we could get back the production monies, or at least move forward in the world with a completed movie. What I'm driving at is that it's not necessarily to the advantage of the DV moviemaker to take on a project lightly, shoot frivolously, and edit dispassionately. You should try your best to operate on the notion that the movie you decide to shoot must be *very* meaningful to you. A story tied into your own personal history would be the *most viable* place to begin—a story you are willing to devote long periods of your life to tell, without quitting midstream.

Have you ever considered how you literally give up an hour and a half of your real life when you sit down in a theater to see a movie? That's the trade-off. You sit there in a darkened room and let someone else's story temporarily supplant your own. *Making* a movie is a much bigger trade-off. But it's your life and you're spending it making a dream come true, and that's got to be as good as it gets. So the narrative you shoot must be a great one, not necessarily grand in commercial terms, but perhaps gigantic in heart, explosive in information, and magnificent in the kind of sublime images and sounds you can create using the new digital video medium.

Let's get started, identifying an idea that will bring all that excitement to your life.

Family Stories

As I previously mentioned, the tighter the relationship is between you and the story you are telling, the more persuasive your movie is likely to be. If you are suffering the horrible fate of having a family member close to you dying of AIDS, then turning the lens on your family and *yourself* might be the movie concept you're looking for. *Silverlake Life*, a feature that screened at the Sundance Film Festival Documentary

Competition in 1993, was such a tribute to two gay men trying to survive the heartbreak of AIDS (see *http://www.filmstransit.com/silver. html*). Of course, hearing that a movie like that has already been done (and done beautifully and effectively) might dissuade you from repeating that theme, but this is commercial logic talking. If you have the fire to tell the story from your perspective, then you should definitely proceed and, using the DV camera as a tool for surviving hard nights and impossible days, apply your energies to shooting images and sound that can result in a movie that shares your particular experience.

I firmly believe there is at least one great movie concept hidden within the pages of every family history. The hundreds of real-life stories I've received as part of the application process for my Feature Workshops, as well as the ones I've shot to include in the FW features I've produced, have affirmed this hypothesis over and over again. Reading even the short, half-page stories about an applicant's personal history, I'm always surprised to discover the variety of strange and profound experiences "normal" people have. And half the time they don't realize just how special their stories and lives really are! Try this yourself. Take a blank sheet of paper and, without thinking too hard about it, spend about 15 minutes writing the best real-life story from your own family history. Get your sister or brother to do the same. See if your parents or grandparents will write something as well. Apart from actually devoting your time to making a movie using this material, I believe you'll be amazed at the things you discover about your own family members. If nothing else, this exercise will open your mind to the narrative power of small personal stories, the kind from which the most heartfelt indie movies evolve.

Newspaper Articles or Internet Search

While you may have enjoyed learning about your family's history, let's say that you didn't hit any moviemaking pay dirt with regard to a suitable feature concept. Then perhaps it's time to use other sources to stir up your interest and curiosity, fuel your mind with raw material that might suddenly catch fire. Your local newspaper will supply an ongoing parade of potential movie concepts, as stories appear on a daily basis. And, of course, with the Internet offering literally thousands of online newspapers and periodicals from around the world, you aren't limited to just your hometown paper or library reading room anymore. Maybe you'll be as fortunate as screenwriter Nicholas Kazan (*Reversal of Fortune, Matilda, Fallen, Dream Lover*, etc.) who became aware of a newspaper story about a murderous family, his script the basis for *At Close Range*. Another notable movie, *Boys Don't Cry*, was based on stories about a transgender murder in the Pacific Northwest. (Public-domain novels published before 1922 could yield good stories as well.) So, if you are persistent and thorough in your research, you may have the kernel for next year's indie hit.

After you've done solid research into current newspaper and magazine stories, maybe you'll get playful and insert a few keywords into a search engine like *www.google.com*. Try any two words in combination. Use nonsensical words, such as "musty gravy." I followed my own advice, typed this in, and one of the sites on the Google list was *www.newmeyer.com/essay_template.php?id=166*, a fun and fascinating history lesson on how food might have played a role in a 1821 treaty between King Louis XVIII of France and King George IV of Britain. (For those who shy away from another "history lesson," you'd be surprised at this good read!) If I had what I'll call a "food fetish," if I loved food, cooked a lot, believed that there was some grand importance to the culinary arts, then this article might have spurred me to create an entire DV feature about the historical role food has played throughout the centuries. Believe it or not, food and cooking, when combined with the socializing that surrounds it, can result in a truly great moviegoing experience (rent *Big Night* or *Babette's Feast* and see if you agree).

So almost any combination of words will connect you to interesting sites, and somewhere within that set of random links could reside your spark of inspiration, a topic or magical phrase that leads to the exhilarating moment when you realize you've latched onto the subject of your future DV feature. If that happens, go ahead and yell out loud. Scream "Hooray! Yahoo! Bingo!" or something in a vernacular that your buddies will better understand. Who cares who's listening? Your life is now aligned to a whole other way of being, and you are ready to tackle the vital work of moviemaking that lies ahead. Now you can set out on your DV adventure, ready to devote great energy and determination to the quest, for however long it takes to be successful. That's "feature filmmaking."

Literary Options

If an original idea isn't forthcoming and no viable DV moviemaking topic is in sight from scanning the Internet, maybe consider using other people's writing as a source for a movie. Of course, you can't just take somebody's book or short story and shoot it without first clearing the rights of that literary property. But if you are truly in love with a story, just can't let it go, then you should at least learn the current asking price for "buying an option," the legal arrangement by which you are granted use of the property for a specified period of time (one year, two years, plus extensions) as the basis for a movie (see Appendix C, Literary Purchase Option Agreement). For those who have proceeded in this fashion, their life is set on a course that first requires detective work. Who represents the book in question—a literary agent, the family estate, the author or spouse? How can you get in touch in the most effective way to acquire the rights? And what will it cost—$5,000, $25,000? Now you'll be stuck raising money just for the option—all that spending before you raise additional funds to actually shoot the movie.

Of course, with some known, well reviewed literary properties that have undeniable appeal and staying power, the funding for the movie arrives quickly on the heels of the option purchase. That's probably because the topic of the book you acquired is so hot and current (even if it wasn't when you first approached the author and bought it) that businesspeople and studio executives can easily recognize the guaranteed return on their investment.

When you go the option route, you're moving away from the low-key DV moviemaking realm, leaping into the big-time, Hollywood/Miramax "indie" production matrix, where properties are seen as key

PR factors with regard to the movies produced. A new Tom Clancy best-seller will consistently draw his fans to the theaters. *Lord of the Rings* certainly has its assured followers. Even Wayne Wang's less widely known *Anywhere But Here* had its built-in audience. Wayne's more brilliant *Smoke* had its beginning when he happened to read a one-page newspaper article in *The New York Times* by novelist Paul Auster. Wayne then got in touch with Auster through his literary agent and persuaded him to expand his piece into a full-length script. The result of that collaboration proves the viability of the literary option approach: using the moviemaking process to make a concept reach its full potential.

When you adapt a book, you're always faced with having the movie version compared to its literary original. Was *The Joy Luck Club* (also directed by Wayne Wang) as good as the book? Actually, in this case they were both heart wrenching and unforgettable. But that's the big time. It takes years and good luck to get into the position to be trusted with a major literary property. Wayne was recommended by the book's author, Amy Tan, to direct *The Joy Luck Club* because she had admired his sensitive treatment of women in his previous feature, *Dim Sum Take Out*. He had to prove his worth as a moviemaker first, on several successful indie productions, beginning with his breakthrough, *Chan Is Missing*, before he got the opportunity to transform a best-seller like *The Joy Luck Club* into cinematic terms.

Beginning with a literary property was the rocket Robert Evans (*The Godfather*) rode to success, and is the route my Los Angeles producer friend, Mark Yellen, has chosen for several movies. Recently Mark and his wife, along with his business partner, were invited to the Texas ranch of author Robert James Waller (*The Bridges of Madison County*) to discuss a proposed option in person. Mark and his party left three days later with some gigantic hangovers, and the option for Waller's 1995 novel *Puerto Vallarta Squeeze*. The option process has already helped Mark produce some fine, low-budget indie features in the past, including *Where the Rivers Flow North* (1991) and *Shiloh* (1997), which Roger Ebert called, "One of the most overlooked films of 1997."

While I've supplied the standard Literary Purchase Option Agreement in Appendix C, you should still review contract papers with an entertainment lawyer to make sure they have been properly designed for your particular option.

SCRIPTING (OR NOT . . .)

Before we get to the or-not options, it's obvious that something needs to be written down before a moviemaker leaps into the making of a feature-length work. In earlier editions of my feature filmmaking book, I suggested that writing a script could be compared to scrawling out a recipe for chocolate chip cookies. I thought it was worth quashing the idea that you have to spend years rendering a professional script, because such a long, drawn-out process can divert you from your original determination to create movies. Under duress, the mind will come up with just about any excuse not to begin, from lack of funds ("There's not enough money") to those eternal doubts about your value ("I've never written anything before, so how can it be any good?"). When you've spent several years on a script, it's easy to imagine it might attract major funding from a Hollywood studio or major indie production house—the "Miramax syndrome," I'll call it. So you get sucked into submitting the script all around Hollywood, waiting for responses, eating the costs of mailing and copies, and losing valuable time (another two years?) and energy. My complaint is that too much youthful artistic energy can be eaten up in this waiting-to-be-chosen game. And it may be the entirely wrong game to play.

But don't let me stop you from shopping a great script to production companies and investors if you're determined to do so. Although the odds aren't really in your favor with this approach, I applaud your gambling spirit. Miracles do happen. Your script *could* get picked up, right off the bat, like hitting the bull's-eye in *Star Wars* by believing in The Force. Every life has its special miracles awaiting, once the appropriate risk is taken. I'll add that I sold my first *Feature Filmmaking* book to Penguin Books like that, on my first try, just by following my intuition, though the odds were something like twelve thousand to one against an unsolicited manuscript reaching publication. So I'm living proof that you should definitely travel your own path, taking the gigantic leap of faith that may seem completely nonsensical to others. But if you really want to sell your script to Hollywood or a powerful indie producer, then I'd say establish a realistic deadline, selecting a specific date by which you will feel satisfied you've given it a good shot. Beyond that day you'll be mentally and emotionally free to produce the work *yourself*, on low-cost DV.

A final word of advice: Don't tell anybody about your extreme dream, unless you are prepared to let their left-brain logic shoot down the effort and pull the rug out from under your good intentions. The few times I've talked about a movie concept prematurely (before it was in script or outline form), I've found that immediately after airing my dream in public I experienced a big energy drop. When people didn't fall all over themselves complimenting the brilliance of my concept, when they instead became silent and noncommittal, I felt discombobulated. And that confusion and uneasiness made room for self-doubts. So don't take the wind out of that special project by speaking about it out loud. If it's that great, it needs to get made. Save the surprise for the screening.

THE IMPROV SCRIPT

In my particular improvisational moviemaking style of combining in-experienced nonactors with professional actors in a free-flowing , un-scripted story, I get impatient for the shoot to begin. For me, almost all the good ideas are waiting up ahead, in the process of shooting. Once I actually begin, the pressure of the shoot helps me think better and stay focused on what's important to include in my movie. I'll start out armed with just a bare-bones outline in hand (my "script"), confident that I can start making a movie simply by creating a few navigational pointers (the middle and end of my story will become evident later, as the shoot progresses). I believe in process and feel that I don't need a script to get something rolling. I'm more inclined to build an entire movie with improvisational events, digging into reality as I record it, and then edit the material down with an analytical eye, asking what the footage is really about. Occasionally I'll work off a full script if time and money permit, but shooting on the fly is my preference.

Over time you, too, can develop your own creative style, in a direction that your own personal flow dictates, just as many other artists have done. Check out Picasso's early realistic Blue Period paintings and then compare them to his final, fully abstracted masterworks. As time passed, he gravitated toward the reduction of realism, ultimately focusing on the juxtaposition of form and color. Let your natural inclinations lead the way. The important thing is to be true to your central interests and to follow your instincts about how to make *your kind* of personal movie. It takes some courage to hold out against naysayers, friends and professionals alike who think that they know the correct way for you to proceed. Your resolve will be thoroughly tested, if you are an original talent of this new DV age.

Develop a scriptwriting process that aligns with your natural talents and style of working. You may find that your DV moviemaking style requires a combination of partial scripting and impulsive shooting. Or you may end up prescripting, storyboarding, shooting, writing some more, storyboarding and shooting again, on a production that stretches out over several months while you test and change edits. The trick with this long process is to keep all the central actors involved while the production meanders along, so that you can shoot additional footage if needed. Sometimes it takes an out-of-town location shoot to keep the production team intact.

When Wayne Wang and I shot our first feature, *A Man, a Woman, and a Killer*, we decided to script for two weeks and shoot the following two weeks, getting it all done in a month's time. (Of course, the editing took longer—another year and a half!) We had already learned how hard it was just to get people together for a half-day, short film shoot and decided we'd have a better chance at shooting a feature's worth of footage (eight hours in this case) if we got everyone out of town and shot the entire movie on location (Mendocino, California). That way we'd be less likely to lose our actors and crew to daily real-life concerns (jobs, families, etc.). And the tight schedule ensured that some kind of script would have to be created by the two-week deadline *and* actually shot.

Murphy's Law dictates that workload will always expand to fill whatever time period you've allotted to accomplish your goal. And it's true. Surprisingly, workload will also shrink to fill a limited time frame. Our success with producing DV features start to finish in ten-day marathons in my Feature Workshops shows that even when the production schedule is impossibly tight, quality work can be accomplished. In any case, as a DV artist you must take control over your limitations and use that inherent energy to get work done.

The bottom line is that you need to figure out the best framework for moving your movie from initial concept to scripting and on to the actual process of shooting. If you're not a born writer, then abbreviate the scripting process to reduce that challenge. Maybe partner with a writer/collaborator friend, or speak your ideas into an audio tape recorder and have the results transcribed. If you're fascinated by real people's stories, jump into a method of presenting that truth in your movie by making the scripting more of an outline/note-taking process. (See "Final Draft" and "ScriptWerx" software later in this chapter, for two-column image/audio scriptwriting.) However you proceed, writing your ideas down *is* critical, at least to make sure that nothing is left out of your shooting recipe—the shortening, the flour, or even the chocolate chips!

Ultimately there is a deep satisfaction in being able to cross off scripted pages from the list when they've been shot. The writing process orders up the brain, snaps it into a more efficient producing entity, and allows ideas to be fully fleshed out for the screen. So spend some time evaluating the special scriptwriting combination that best suits your particular needs and abilities.

HOW TO WRITE SPECIFICALLY FOR DV

A local videographer/producer friend, Chris Johns, once encouraged me to write an outline for our proposed DV movie *Lemon Law*, using a method he had learned in a scriptwriting class. Chris told me his scriptwriting instructor recommended laying out a movie using a twenty-point outline. He said that penning five beginning scenes (each just a couple sentences long), then adding ten middle scenes, and concluding with five ending scenes would help to build a sturdy foundation. The trick is to jot down ideas as fast as you can, spending little time rethinking anything. In that way, your mind isn't filled with questions and doesn't have a chance to become fearful about your scripting abilities. With things listed by the number, Chris and I were easily able to split up the jobs. He selected scene 6 to script over the weekend while I took scene 4 from the first section, and so on. There was enough variety in our list to allow each of us to choose assignments that were personally more interesting than others and work up to the harder parts. And even though he was on a PC and I used a Mac G4, we were able to share files across the platforms by e-mail using Scriptware software, converting scenes first to "rich text files" (as an rtf export), then sending them as attachments. In this way we could flesh out spoken dialogue, build descriptions of action and locations, and accumulate the complete script on both our computers for the DV movie we planned to eventually shoot.

DV seems to beg for a more relaxed scriptwriting approach, but in the end your movie must survive the comparison with fully scripted, major Hollywood and indie features—in richness of dialogue, convincing character development, and storytelling verve—if it is to stand a chance of being accepted at major festivals like Sundance. Ideally, the full-out experimental approach (working without a script, building a story on the fly, with a role-playing approach as described in Chapter 1) should produce more unusual storytelling results, centering on the kind of truth-telling dialogue you or any scriptwriter could never write in a million years. But if you aren't delivering this kind of strong and interesting material with an improvisational approach, you'd better take stock of your DV feature-in-progress. If the good improv stuff isn't forthcoming, then it would be wise to restart the production with more of a fully developed script in hand.

SCRIPTING SOFTWARE THAT HELPS

While we're on the subject of scripting, I want to recommend several very helpful software programs to get you started. These products format your writing so that you don't have to waste your time adjusting your margins to conform to the usual script template. Once you've used a certain character's name, or a transition label (such as FADE OUT or DISSOLVE), most software offers its repeated use with just a click of the mouse. These tools allow you to write scripts at a much faster speed than ever before—all you need are great ideas and a great ear for dialogue!

Final Draft

Final Draft (*www.finaldraft.com*, 1-800-231-4055, $199.95 or $124 with academic credentials) is one of the most respected and widely used scripting programs. It advertises itself as "the only scriptwriting software with an authorized agreement to integrate with WGA

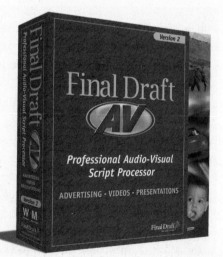

Final Draft's AV2 helps nonwriters script by listing audiovisuals in two columns, text automatically realigned during changes. (Courtesy Final Draft Inc. All rights reserved)

(Writer's Guild of America, West, *www.wga.org*) online script registration." Their list of testimonials from famous moviemakers is a long one. Daniel Myrick (cowriter/codirector of *The Blair Witch Project*) says, "Thanks to Final Draft the right side and left side of my brain are finally getting along." If a software product can do that, I'd say it definitely deserves a look.

Aside from supplying its well appreciated scriptwriting software to professionals, Final Draft offers a Syd Field Scriptwriting Workshop on DVD (only $29), and also Final Draft AV (cheaper at $149). Using a two- or four-column breakdown of shots, with video images on one side and audio on the other (scenes stay aligned across the columns), Final Draft AV2 helps the DV moviemaker be less of a traditional writer and more of a compiler and choreographer of images and sounds. And if you want to get started promoting your finished work, Final Draft also sponsors an international scriptwriting contest. So start checking out this fine product by signing up online and downloading a free demo.

Scriptware

Scriptware by Cinovation (*www.scriptware.com*, 1-800-788-7090, $229.95) is another fine alternative and must be pretty good if *MacAddict* magazine called it "Freakin' awesome!" They also offer a free demo so that you can test their tab-return system and see if it fits your needs. By pressing Tab and starting to type a character's name you've already used in your script, the remainder of the name is automatically filled in when you hit Return. This autocomplete action saves some of the repetition, helps make scripting a lot less painstaking (most of the top scriptwriting programs offer this particular timesaving option). And like Final Draft, Scriptware offers the writer the ability to shift scenes around and test different scene assemblies, whether you're working in regular script text or with "scene cards." The *X-Files* series and the movie *Leaving Las Vegas* were created using Scriptware.

Scriptware (*www.scriptware.com*) is a user-friendly scripting software program that can help you get the job done. (Courtesy of Cinovation Inc.)

Movie Magic Screenwriter, Story View, and Dramatica Pro

Another player in the scriptwriting software field is Movie Magic Screenwriter (*www.screenplay.com*, 1-800-84-STORY, only $99 if your purchase is an upgrade from any other scriptwriting software program). At their Web site you will find a free downloadable demo that allows you to save your work (though a watermark will be visible if you print it out). Their online literature says that only Movie Magic lets you edit the text while in index card mode, but you can be sure that, if any of the scriptwriting software products makes an advance, all the others will catch up soon.

The parent company, Write Brothers Inc., also offers Story View ($99) for help building a structure and story outline [*scr(i)pt magazine* says, "For writers this program really rocks!"]. Dramatica Pro (*www.dramatica.com*, $269 or less—look for ongoing special discounts online) is a program that builds a screenplay (or novel) on facts and character descriptions in a role-playing type of process. Using this product is sort of like having a sympathetic and encouraging writing coach on your team.

ScriptWerx

To top off the list, a great new scriptwriting product, ScriptWerx (*www.scriptwerx.com*, 1-845-355-1400, $129), has come along to pair scriptwriting templates with your existing Microsoft Word program. With ScriptWerx you can choose to work in any of the eleven standard industry scriptwriting templates, from the typically indented script text to a two- or four-column image and audio worksheet (compiling images and sounds without needing scriptwriting mastery), while still using all the usual Word commands and procedures. That means if you're used to Word, there's virtually no learning curve to deal with. *Saturday Night Live* went from buying one copy of ScriptWerx to licensing its use for all the show's writer/performers. You might just follow their lead, download a free demo, and start writing a movie.

ScriptWerx (*www.scriptwerx.com*) is Word-based scriptwriting software that uses all the attributes of the time-tested Word text processing program, making it particularly easy to master. (Courtesy of Parnassus Software)

■ ■ ■

Yes, I know you've already probably budgeted yourself out of affording one of these scriptwriting programs (there's always something new to buy for DV moviemaking). And it's true that with patience you can duplicate the traditional script indents with just about any computer writing program. Still, it's nice to have a new writing toy, new bells and whistles, a template that helps you get started with the difficult process of hammering out a script. So visit these various scripting software Web sites, test the demo versions, select the one that's best for you, and put the winning name on your wish list.

Computerized Notebook Cards

Most scriptwriting software programs can print out your script onto four-by-six-inch cards, which become handy items for shuffling scenes around, remembering scenes and shots while scouting locations, and in general keeping a good mental handle on the movie you are about to make. It's comforting to know that your entire movie is literally in your hands—a manageable pack of cards you can hold together with a rubber band and stick in your pocket. Having a script in card-collection form gives you the opportunity for a read-through while sitting relaxed in a coffee shop, away from the hum of a computer. If reviewing your written work in a new setting helps you to better understand the subtle problems you've set for yourself, then the cost of the software is money well spent. Of course, if you don't mind typing on something as archaic as a typewriter—or if you've got good, legible handwriting—you can create your index card pack without an additional expenditure. But you'll be missing out on what computers best supply: instantaneous rerouting and reordering of information.

> **NOTE:** Make sure that the software you buy can make changes on the index cards and then translate the information back to traditional indented script form. You can't afford the extra time to

reformat your writing, especially when this is the perfect job for a computer.

Printout for Cast, Crew, and Investors

Once you've finalized your script, it's easy to print out the results from your computer, enabling you to supply all the interested parties with their own copies. Certainly, investors are assured by seeing a neatly printed script, believing that you've got things well under control. But be prepared to answer any questions people might have once they read your written descriptions and dialogue. Sometimes, by supplying your written script or plan to everyone, you create more questions than you answer. If you find that you must continually reexplain yourself after scripts have been distributed, you'll need to do damage control. Other people might not understand what your movie is about, won't get what you're trying to say with your odd moviemaking style. That's nothing unusual when it comes to original art.

Often the artist (whether sculptor, painter, or DV moviemaker) is the *only one* who can see any merit in the direction his or her work is taking. Maybe thirty years in the future it will be fully understood, but not now, not at the beginning of an exploration. So watch out that your enthusiasm isn't dulled by the distribution of scripted material. There is no rule that says you have to hand anything out. On my *American Orpheus* shoot I waited until filming began before distributing scripts to cast members (cinematographer Kyle Bergersen did take an early look, which helped us get the movie shot in a tight ten days). I didn't want to risk diluting my positive energy before the shoot was underway.

SHOPPING YOUR SCRIPT AND BUILDING A MOVIEMAKING TEAM

If you have opted to use a script to raise money and/or convince certain actors/stars to participate, you will need to print out several pristine copies of your script and contact actors' agents and movie companies you think may be interested in your venture. Thanks to the Internet, you can track actors to their agents by going to *www.whorepresents. com*. It seems to work best if you use just last names at the fill-in slot. Again, I'd dissuade a beginning moviemaker from going this route—that is, holding out for a star—but don't listen to me if you have your heart set on this bigger dream. I do believe, however, that the focus of DV moviemaking should be more inventive, more radical, and as much under your control as possible. This means you need to be free of commercial concerns. Only when you follow your heart, trusting your intuition, can you succeed on your own terms. And when it all gels, then your work will suddenly *be* commercial (shown at Sundance, IFC, etc.). Maybe on a second or third feature it might be appropriate to take the big-time commercial approach, but please consider taking the chance of defining your own style first.

As you probably know, it starts getting expensive when you need ten copies of a 115-page script, so make duplicates at Kinko's or some other discounted copy center. If you can send out your script as a CD or e-mail attachment, that will be a substantial savings. If you're a member of Costco you can purchase 50 blank CDs (with cases) for under $40. It's worth learning early how to cut corners with related moviemaking costs, so that your overhead doesn't far outrun your indie income.

FUNDING BASED ON SCRIPT

If you receive funding based on a full and detailed script, your backers will probably expect you to follow it religiously, since that script represents the precise movie they want to see realized. That's why your project was selected over many others. Of course, there are exceptions. Some filmmakers have even been funded with hardly more than a story line, but that kind of trust comes only with a strong track record of high artistic achievement. Veteran writer/director Jon Jost (*www.jonjost. com*) was able to get the quarter-million-dollar funding for *All the Vermeers in New York* this way (and its Two Thumbs Up rating certainly justified its relatively low-cost investment).

Until you build a reputation, though, you need to understand that you might have to stick carefully to your game plan in terms of dialogue, scene breakdown, and story structure when it comes to actual shooting. Certainly that will be OK in 98 percent of the cases. But if you are one of those intuitive writer/directors who constantly responds to new things as you shoot—suddenly framing shots in unusual ways, pulling in a new character (the waitress at the restaurant, the musician busking across the street), jumping to a new and, in your opinion, vital location—then you may run into some very big difficulties. If this is your first feature outing, you can't possibly have a full idea of how it will feel to be occupying the set when shooting finally commences. But maybe you can venture a guess about your personal creative preferences. Ask yourself if you will be satisfied just shooting your script, without adding scenes, characters, dialogue, or locations as yet unknown. Perhaps at the outset, you should request some leeway from the investors and producers for shooting extra material, to see how they react. Let them know that you will probably continue to be a fully observant person, someone who may see new possibilities as you shoot. You want to make sure you don't miss these important new scenes, should any come to mind during shooting. Certainly there is nothing wrong with having a few more options in the editing room (you explain). You need to make sure you can do your best without interference, so clear up this issue before the shoot begins.

DV SHOOTING SCRIPT

Certainly, for moviemakers who like to nail everything down, a shooting script is essential. This differs from the initial script in that it contains many notes detailing how the scenes will actually be shot, including what type of framing (close up, medium, wide), movement (dolly, pan, hand-held, and so on), and perhaps duration. Each scripting software program I've checked out enables you to make notes in the margins, with the option of hiding or revealing them during printout. Thus you can make notes as you proceed through the first draft of the screenplay, to keep the writing aligned with the logic that the movie will indeed get shot and produced with your own pocketbook if no suitable investors are found.

When I was hired to codirect *Prospects*, a movie set in Colorado starring actor Curtis Imrie, I wrote a quick shooting script for the opening bank scene, where his "Everett" character would apply for a loan against his ranch. Notice the camera directions and detailed-shots entries, giving a sense of what needed to get rendered to film within a few days of when this was written.*

FADE IN:

EXT. DUSTY STREET IN FRONT OF BANK, MORNING.

EVERETT, the main character of this movie, is looking at the bank and its sign, trying to psyche himself up before going in to talk to the loan officer. If he can't get a loan to cover his last BALLOON PAYMENT on his ranch he's in BIG trouble, may lose the homestead he's supported and bought into for the last 20 years. The problem has been TAXES. Ever since his area has become a playground for the rich his taxes have doubled every few years.

EVERETT (AS HE FLIPS A SILVER DOLLAR HIGH IN THE AIR)
Damn you . . . I say . . . HEADS.

Shot in slow motion, the coin flips slowly past his head on the way up . . . and comes down past his face before hitting the ground. EVERETT has pretended to shoot the coin in the air with his pistol-shaped hand and fingers, just like in the OLD WEST (cut in sound of bullet shots here). The coin hits . . . comes up TAILS.

EXT. BANK ENTRANCE, MORNING.

EVERETT walks toward front door of bank, in a series of slow-motion shots. We watch his face bouncing, hands swinging, feet shuffling, to wide shot as he finally enters the building.

CUT TO:

* ©1997 by Rick Schmidt, for *Prospects*, a film by Curtis Imrie and Rick Schmidt

INT. BANK, MORNING—SAME TIME.

EVERETT is seated across from a man, JOHNSON, who is obviously going over his loan application. No one is saying anything, so we take this time to look EVERETT over more closely. His face is weathered, eyes attentive, but shaded with a sense of upcoming pain in the discomfort of the situation, like a mustang penned instead of running free. LOAN OFFICER JOHNSON is on friendly terms with EVERETT, but the background is that they went to high school together, and now JOHNSON the nerd has the power over his popular old buddy.

JOHNSON (LOOKING UP FROM THE PILE OF PAPER)
So, Everett, let's just double-check all this before I make a final decision, OK?

EVERETT (A LITTLE TRICKLE OF SWEAT ON HIS LIP)
Sure, partner. We've been down this road before.

JOHNSON
Your ranch . . . currently worth $250 . . . a quarter of a million . . . if it's logged, landscaped, cleaned up to sell. You owe us $22,000 on this third mortgage balloon payment.

(PAUSE)

JOHNSON (CONTINUING)
You raise burros. How many do you presently have barned up there?

EVERETT (JUST HEAR V.O. AS CAMERA STAYS ON JOHNSON)
Four . . . well five when you count in Chelsey Whitewater . . . when she gets born. I think it'll be my best bred jenny yet. If she's a coal-black one I'm back in the money. Should bring in over $4,000 minimum, given her sire. Oscar Democrat won the Nationals you know . . . riding

high on that. Plus got the big race coming up...a purse of over $5,000...over in Fairview...we're all set to...

JOHNSON (INTERRUPTING)
How can you guarantee if she'll be black? It could be white...or grey...right? What's a white-skinned or light-skinned one worth?

EVERETT (TIRED...RESIGNED TO THE NIT-PICKING)
$1,400.

The more unusual and original your shooting notes become, the better you'll be doing at creating a unique movie, something that may be of interest to an eager young moviegoing audience in places like New York, Chicago, and San Francisco (historically good cities for limited indie runs). It is this newness of story and execution that has prompted so much attention to the Dogme 95 movies (see Chapter 6). If you shoot improvisational DV, as we did on our *Chetzemoka's Curse* (Dogme No. 10), then there wouldn't be a formal shooting script—no script of any kind, in fact. Maybe you'd have only notes jotted down for possible scenes, then create a dialogue list transcribed after the shoot, like this subtitle text used for our screenings of *Curse* at Kino Centre Skalvija in Vilnius, Lithuania.

Where's the adventure?
I mean what would you do?

What do you want to...what
adventure do you want to take?

Well, the thing about adventure is
you don't always know ahead of time...

...what it's going to be. I've
wanted to write...

In fact, I'm probably 50 pages into . . .

. . . a novel that really comes from
my gut. You know what I mean?

But I can't seem to get it quite
right. I don't know . . .

What would you do? Wouldn't
you see that your husband . . .

. . . needs a change. That he needs
to be doing something that's . . .

. . . that's really coming from
inside him, that's really him?

(Excerpted from *Chetzemoka's Curse* [Dogme No. 10] ©2003 FW
Productions, USA, *www.lightvideo.com/chetzemoka*)

Of course, for these listed subtitles you need to be watching the
actual movie to understand which two characters are talking. But you
can at least sense a flow of ideas in dialogue form. If you used Final
Draft AV, ScriptWerx, or one of the other scripting software programs that offer two-column Video Production templates, then dialogue (prescribed by the moviemaker) could be set in column two
(audio) and attributed to certain characters, with images (video) in
column one.

If your Mini-DV tape and your gas money get you around to the
various locations (and it's your out-of-pocket production), then you
can feel free to mix the scriptwriting forms, add camera and audio
notes, use whatever template best fits for your particular moviemaking
style.

LOCKING IN: FINALIZING THE MOVIE SCRIPT AND CONCEPT

How do you know when your script (outline, essay-style production notes, audiovisual matching) is good enough to shoot? Throw it on your bed. Does it look real? Test it in a bookcase alongside *Moby-Dick* or some other enduring work. Sign the cover page and date it. Now it's a collectible—if your movie turns out to be a classic!

But what's inside? There are a few techniques for "seeing the forest for the trees." For one thing, you can just leave it alone for a few weeks and then read it again. That helps you to see the material from a fresh standpoint. Or maybe mail it to one or more trusted friends whose opinions you respect. Also, is the final copy beautifully clean, without punctuation problems or typos that distract? Are the margins and the font suitable for easy reading? Don't send out an inferior copy and expect to get quality feedback.

To feel ready to shoot, you probably need some kind of input, some words from family or friends, who can give you the heads-up you need. If several people report they can't read past the halfway point, then you need to take that response to heart. Better they say it than your lead actors! You'll want to figure out why the story drops dead at page 50. Or if your consultants say they have trouble following the locations, or mix up the characters, you need to rework the scene descriptions, write more clearly. Everyone, no matter how savvy in the ways of scripts, will give you *some* feedback, and it's up to you to decipher the various comments and make the appropriate improvements. If your script is contained in a software program that allows cut and paste, then major changes can be made in a matter of hours.

Some will decide not to give their script a public airing, protecting themselves from any chance of negative feedback. If you go this route, keeping your script a secret and unread by anyone else until you, cast, and crew take the set on Day One, either it better be very good or you better be ready to withstand some powerful opposition. You might need to field some direct criticisms as you try to continue shooting, and that situation could get ugly. Whatever your decision, the one thing all approaches will have in common is that the written script or complete outline should be registered at Writer's Guild of America, West so that your copyright can be protected.

At *www.wga.org*, you can register your script ("intellectual property") online for just $20 ($10 for members). Their preferred files are ASCII, PDF (Adobe Acrobat), Word (ScriptWerx), Final Draft, and Movie Magic 2000, but they do accept all file formats. To register, fill out the forms with your name, address, and social security number, and pay the fee with Mastercard or Visa. When you click to submit your script, keep in mind that you may submit only one file per project (with a limit of 10 MB, zipped files prohibited). With the large volume of more than forty thousand pieces of literary material registered each year, WGA will not correct, reformat, read, or in any way intercede with the registration process. So make sure you have your script in the final order before submission. Only when you receive your confirmation page can you be assured that your project is fully registered and legally protected.

If you've done a thorough job, paid close attention to all the aspects of the scriptwriting process (content, style, format, a clean presentation), and registered your script at Writer's Guild of America, you should now give yourself a big pat on the back. Finishing a script is a big deal. It's said eight thousand scripts are completed each year by just the inhabitants of Los Angeles alone. What you need to do now, to separate your feature-length digital project from all the unfulfilled scripts, is "green light" it. DV gives you that production power.

And if you still need a little nudge toward actually moving your own script into production, then I'd say go directly to *www.interactivefilmschool.com* and check out "How to Make Your Movie," a terrific program created by Rajko Grlic (available for $49.95 with a free ninety-day home trial). Not only is it fun to wander around this virtual film school, but as a learning tool it comes as highly recommended as it gets. Legendary editor and three-time Oscar winner Walter Murch calls it, "The best, most complete and innovative filmmaking guide I have ever seen, in any format. Endlessly informative and amusing. I would highly recommend it for students and professionals alike." It even includes a helpful *Production Notebook* (a free download at Web site) with an array of important tips for casting actors, rehearsing scenes, improving scenes with improvising, and other advice. So check out this great instructional, interactive program, which is an art form in its own right.

COMMITTING TO A SHOOTING SCHEDULE

Once you've decided that the script you've written is the final draft, you can set a shooting date. Of course, the beginning date of principal photography depends on your having the camera and sound gear ready to shoot images and record sound in a professional manner (see Chapter 3 "Selecting Your DV Camera, Sound Gear, and Incidentals"), as well as having the people available for that work. Whether you have bought a good DV camera (Mini-DV, DVCAM, DVD), scheduled a camera rental, or borrowed equipment through friends or DV classes you're attending, you can now send word out that you'll be shooting for, say, eleven days, from October 10 through October 20, between the hours of 8:30 A.M. and approximately 6:00 P.M. (going later requires a dinner break, which needs to be factored into the food budget). Because your people have commitments that go beyond the time they'll be involved with your project, you must let them know your precise schedule.

It's smart to break up the shooting day into four- or five-hour segments, and your planner, Palm Pilot, or production calendar should reflect this before you get the word out to cast and crew. Lay out the schedule so that you find yourself shooting something like 9:00 A.M. to 1:00 P.M., with an hour lunch break, then resuming 2:00 P.M. to 6:00 P.M., plus a little time to clean up before a 6:30 P.M. dinner. If you then feel the need to put in a third segment for that day, you can shoot 7:00–11:00 P.M., but I'd be reluctant to enact this extra four-hour nighttime stretch except when access to a location is only possible after dark. The point is, *don't burn out your cast and crew right off the bat, with eighteen-hour days.* Inflict the 15-hour-or-more day only when there is absolutely no other alternative. If you do go late, toward midnight, set the next day's gathering call for a later time (at least 10:00 instead of 8:30 A.M.). This length-of-workday advice is *so* critical that I'll repeat it again.

NOTE: Do yourself and your production a favor and keep your shoot limited to a maximum of twelve-hour days. Beginning with an eighteen-hour day will be unnecessarily debilitating to your cast and crew. You certainly don't want to pay for sloppy work later in the editing room.

Because so many different things have to happen for a shoot to start up and keep its momentum—a gathering of equipment, rehearsals, location confirmations, food ordering and preparation, actors and crew schedules cleared for the production—you need to be very careful that the dates you select are pretty much written in stone. Don't hedge on this unless you want to seriously undercut your ability to make a movie. Like the boy who cried wolf, you'll be in trouble if you repeatedly revise the announced schedule. You're asking for a big commitment from the people you bring together; get the dates right so that you don't lose the support of those necessary to the success of the project.

Also make sure that there is enough money to take care of people who are helping you with this dream. You will probably need to use a credit card (a debit card from a business account loaded with money is best) to keep up with meals and unexpected incidental costs. You may need to think more generously than you ever have before. If there is a series of nighttime scenes, be prepared to buy the entire cast and crew dinner before continuing for that long day's shooting. If you and six helpers can dine on Chinese food for around $75, you're doing OK. And you'll, of course, cover gas and breakfast for whoever gets you out the door each morning—*is that them honking?* You need to be in charge, with your wallet in hand.

NOTE: Schedule your shoot at least a month in advance after making sure that paperwork (contracts, release forms, partnerships, incorporation) is in order, and that all your principal players and crew members can commit to the dates.

PAPERWORK

Without your legal papers in order, any success your production may experience will be for naught, because once money (or even the idea of money) enters the picture, you'll get twenty different versions of "what's fair." Longstanding friendships can be ruined, your life a chaotic mess, if you don't have all the legal protections in place. So the best way to proceed is in an orderly fashion, completing each paperwork requirement for a good, healthy production. The paperwork process can begin with either a movie company name, a movie's title, or even a Web site name.

A while back, when I was considering distributing my movies on the Web at a new site away from my main home page, I decided to call the distribution outlet Xbrandfilms.com. I was thinking of the 1950s advertising campaigns, in which there was a promotional product (for instance, Tide laundry soap) and a comparison product, often referred to as brand X. Perhaps that's what my movies had come to represent. There were the mainline Miramax indie flicks, and then there were mine. So I spent the $70 to register that domain name for two years. Of course, someone later brought it to my attention that having an X in the title might lead the public to think that my movies were pornographic. As yet, I haven't had the time to build the site and learn just what kind of traffic it attracts. The point is, in this computer age your paperwork can begin with the purchase of a Web site name, with no real "paper" involved. The important thing is that you create new positive energy by assigning a descriptive—and original—title to your DV moviemaking activity.

Registering Your Movie Company Name

The initial step you need to take before drawing up contracts, incorporation papers, Actor's Release forms, and other paperwork is to determine the name of your movie company. The selection of this name is very important since it will figure in the value of your movies (think "Goldwyn Presents"), a moniker with which you will be associated for years to come. Matthew Biancaniello, who created Dogme No. 29, calls his company My Way or the Highway (*www.mywayorthehighwayfilms.com*), which is a big step, I'd say, toward letting others understand his particular attitude about making movies *his* way. You want a company name that appeals to you on many different levels. I've used L. L. Productions, based on the words "Living Legend," since my graduate school days when I stated in my graduate proposal in sculpture that "I want to create enough elegant works of art to become a living legend before I graduate." Yes, I put my foot in my mouth—didn't make it to legend status—but I believe it was psychologically helpful to publicly state my determination to work hard toward that goal. And I was right about hard work being the correct path of the artist. Hard work always gives birth to new ideas.

"Light Video" started out as a name under which my friend Jon Jost and I, along with moviemakers William Farley and Liz Sher (*ivstudios. com*) distributed our videos back in the last century. The name has been kept alive, first at my Web site and later by legal incorporation (as Light Video Inc.). I certainly didn't realize at the beginning that my prime moviemaking business would be in video instead of film. At any rate, create a name that shouts your commitment to doing things your way, making your movies with an uncompromised vision. The name could be as personal to you as Miramax is to the Weinstein brothers who run that operation, using their mother's and father's names intertwined. So keep rolling names around in your head until you come across one that you'll be proud to fly on your masthead.

Incorporating to Control Expenditures and Write-Offs

Before you proceed with getting a profit-sharing agreement together (see Appendix B), it may also be appropriate for you to consider legally incorporating your moviemaking operation, transforming your production company into a corporate entity that can make use of all the expenditures of moviemaking. Once you have paid the usually modest $200 to $300 registration and filing fees for your corporation, you will need to keep very accurate books on all expenditures and income for your yearly tax accounting. It will require that you balance your business checking accounts to the exact penny each and every month.

I know that sounds scary and perhaps even impossible. But I've learned this extra work and attentiveness can be satisfying, a blessing in disguise, when you get tax credit for equipment purchases of a camera, computer, and sound gear, and you can itemize the actual costs of shooting your movies, all the while knowing exactly how much cash is left in checking. When you write checks or use a business debit card to pay production costs—your phone service, cable modem company or Web site provider; travel, food, or lodging; mailing scripts; buying Mini-DV/DVCAM tapes or DVDs; purchasing equipment (camera, computers, software); actor's and crew's salaries; photocopying scripts, contracts, reviews, and articles (PR for the finished movie); your salary—it all falls under one or another heading in your business ledger.

When money comes in from tape sales, in-person screenings, TV sales, and festival prizes, you balance that income with the costs of every element of your moviemaking business. Suddenly there is a logic to spending all that money. Once your moviemaking activities fall under a corporate umbrella, there is more of a method to your madness, a financial structure that establishes the legitimacy of your efforts, however experimental they may be. Even if a movie doesn't earn any money, all your neatly penciled-in account book entries (use pencil, not pen, so you can correct math errors) will be summarized at tax time, when an accountant will compute your losses and gains. You may find that your business deductions counterbalance the income tax you normally would have paid on your day job income, making your moviemaking venture a less foolish economic risk in uncertain financial times. Suddenly your DV moviemaking is grounded in solid business practices.

Although the corporate filing fee of around $200 in most states is reasonably low, you should be aware of other costs and deadlines regarding doing business as a corporation. You'll want to have your corporate taxes (due March 15, not the usual April 15) done by a certified public accountant. That service can cost between $200 and $500, depending on how well you've kept the books. And there will be state revenue taxes due quarterly at first, then more likely yearly, if your income is somewhat low (under $10,000 annually). Again, this tabulation requires the help of a CPA (the fee is usually under $100).

If you're not used to balancing your checkbook, I promise you that this corporate process will quickly shape you up, making you a more precise and careful person regarding your assets and liabilities. This is a good thing. Ultimately you'll be making better choices regarding spending your money, and get the same benefits that every other registered business enjoys when it risks capital to provide goods and services to customers. Welcome to the adult world.

Investor's Limited Partnerships

For my *American Orpheus* production, dealing with four investors who made different-sized payments to get the movie shot, cut, and promoted, required that I set up a limited partnership in Washington state for their taxation purposes. Fortunately, I found a motivated young lawyer who created the paperwork for me at the base price of just $800. So there's hope, if you search long enough, of finding an attorney who's fascinated by the digital video movie business, or even believes he or she could be an actor! Try the person out in a role; Bay Area attorney Michael Bolgatz acted in our *Maisy's Garden* and *The 5th Wall* productions, both times to great effect.

To be prepared for the limited partnership registration in your state, you need a company name, address, and telephone number, along with the full proposed budget so a monetary value can be attached for each share unit. On a million-dollar movie, shares might be 100 units of $10,000 each. For a section of the partnership papers entitled "Compensations and Fees to the Manager," you'll need to indicate the salary you propose to receive for your various jobs as writer, director, producer, and editor. And you'll need to supply a short description (synopsis) of what the movie is about. The entire partnership form is usually about fifty pages, a pretty extensive contract (see my 2000 edition of *Feature Filmmaking at Used-Car Prices* for the complete document).

NOTE: Please let me restate that you'll need an attorney to review your final legal work, even if you use a preexisting copy of any contract. Laws change continually and each state has its particular requirements for limited partnerships.

THE CONTRACT

The key agreement between yourself (your movie company) and all the participants of your DV venture is the contract, which details the jobs to be accomplished and the exact amounts cast/crew members are to be paid upon completion of their jobs. You must determine beforehand which participants receive cash up front and whether the cash is paired with percentages and deferred salary. Don't forget that *you* must also be included, so you receive something for all your hard work. The contract should state in clear terms how the investors are to be repaid (what profit point amounts, with annual interest) and what "loans to the production" (deferred salaries, money you personally invest) must be repaid before profit-sharing checks can be written. You may partition the contract so that you are repaid at the exact same time your investors receive their first returns, as an act of good faith. At any rate, all these determinations are accomplished through the use of a *profit-sharing movie contract* (see Appendix B).

With each person's signature, date, and place of execution entered on the lines provided, you are more assured that the production will move forward on its own accord, pushing against the inertia that can take hold when venturing into uncharted territory. A contract at least dispels the notion that the movie is all in your head (i.e., you're the crazy one). A contract says that someone is taking care of business, and that the venture is serious. Also, the contract forms provided in the appendix state that whoever signs up for profit-sharing agrees to release the moviemaker and the company, as well as "agents, licensees, successors and assigns," from any and all claims, liabilities, and damages arising from their participation in the production of a motion picture. The contract thus becomes your shield against being sued. Why should you have to risk your house, car, and possessions when you're risking everything else—your money, time, reputation—to make a movie?

Collaborative Contracts:
Cowriter/Codirector Collaborations

The Feature Workshops Agreement (Appendix B) enables everyone to share equally in the profits of a DV feature-length movie. This is the collaborative moviemaking contract I've used at my Feature Work-shops/FW Productions where up to ten people join me to write, direct, shoot, edit, and produce a DV feature in ten days. (For a collaboration contract for eleven or more participants—usually a college course with little or no overhead of rental cameras or other equipment fees—check out the Multiperson Collaborative Contract, Appendix A). At Feature Workshops, 10 percent is set aside for an investor to help us afford a blowup from digital video to 35mm film if the need arises, and 5 per-cent is reserved for expenses that Feature Workshops incurs during promotion. The remaining 85 percent is to be equally divided among the writer/director creators, less any half-points given to actors (see page two of the contract). And often the lead actors' fees are raised con-siderably, up to 2–5 percent, sometimes even to a full writer/director/ collaborator equal partner status, as lead actress Maya Berthoud was given for *Chetzemoka's Curse* (Dogme No. 10).

What I like about this equal profit-sharing arrangement is that it shows everyone's contribution is important and that no one person is more important than anyone else. By democratizing the process you have access to the best ideas and motivation of everyone on your set (my cinematographer and sound/boom person are usually included as equal profit-sharing partners). The atmosphere is purely positive, the best working conditions you could ever hope to achieve.

If there is a downside to sharing the hoped-for wealth, it might be that, with everyone in for a full and equal slice of the pie, some partic-ipants may become too focused on the idea of financial success, and convince themselves the production will fail if some great idea of theirs isn't respected and immediately implemented. They may actu-ally come to believe that anyone who thinks differently is trying to rob them of their future grubstake and potential fame. So by all means in-vite everyone to share in your movie's financial and public success, but maintain the final control (legal and otherwise) by keeping it a movie by your production company, with you "doing business as." Keep con-trol over not only the artistic direction, but also the hiring and firing. You, the central moviemaking force/writer/director/producer, must re-main the final determiner (read "terminator"!) for what is shot and what ultimately stays in the cut. Then, even if you are generous to a fault, it's still your movie.

Actor's Release

Along with the contract, you must have photocopied Actor's Releases available (Appendix D), which is another crucial piece of paperwork that must be completed if you are to protect the production from possible lawsuit and estrangement. Before handing out the form for signing, add your company's name and the movie title (or the name of the city and date when the title is not final). No person should appear in your movie in recognizable form (their speaking or singing voice included) without their having signed a release for the use of that audible or visual material. Only after the individual has signed the form can you safely include him or her in your movie. And because the release mentions "for valuable consideration," it's wise to pay each person some small token amount, $5, $10, $20—whatever your budget can afford. On my 2001 shoot *The 5th Wall*, I asked several people sitting in their cars parked at the Berkeley marina if they wouldn't mind commenting on our lead actor Rohanna Kenin's strange appearance as she walked by. After they agreed I handed them an Actor's Release to read over and sign. Some looked confused at the document, but all eventually signed. If they hadn't I would have had to scrap the concept of having various real people watch and discuss our actress in her "meltdown" moment.

The Actor's Release has a small paragraph at the bottom, which parents or guardians should sign if a minor under 18 years of age is involved in a production. Don't think that children don't need a legally signed release form. You'll need to hunt down the parents if you want to include a jump rope scene at a local grade school. You must get every actor and nonactor who appears in your movie to sign a release.

Location Release

A Location Release (Appendix E) is also vital to the legal well-being of your production. Wherever you shoot, it is important to get this permission signed (again, pay a small, affordable fee "for good consideration") to reduce the chances of legal and financial backlash if the project becomes a hit. Once the movie is successful, one recalcitrant landlord looking for a windfall can hold the entire production hostage until his or her inflated "location rent" is fully paid. How would you like it if you had to scrap your most important sequence of scenes because you or the distributor couldn't meet the $50,000 fee for shooting in a hotel lobby?

Sometimes, if you are afraid to break the mood when you shoot, or are too stressed to approach an owner (or you just hate dealing with authority figures), you will let this slide. If you return just a few weeks after your shoot, there is still a chance that you can get the signed location releases you need. I'm not recommending this risky path, just explaining that if you don't protect yourself by having the forethought to obtain a release for certain locations, you might still get them in the early stages of postproduction. For our collaborative 2000 movie *Chetzemoka's Curse*, I returned to the four main locations after the feature was completely edited. Since the movie was created start to finish in ten days, this meant that I returned just shy of two weeks after shooting. I asked all the nice people to read over the release and please sign it. I must live in a friendly town because everyone readily complied! You may not be so lucky. Please, take care of this legal requirement before you shoot! Be precise and painstakingly thorough in getting all your legal moviemaking affairs in order.

NOTE: Always have several copies of the Actor's Release and Location Release forms on your person during the shooting process, just in case an unexpected opportunity arises. No releases means don't shoot.

Music Rights

Of course, you must also come to a mutually agreeable legal arrangement regarding any songs or musical arrangements you use in your movie (see Music Rights Agreement, Appendix F). You'll want to be able to use original music in your movie for an affordable fee (say $250–$500 for several songs), while making sure that the musicians or band members retain their copyright and full ownership of their copyrighted material. The Music Rights Agreement grants you a one-time usage, the ability to use their songs in your movie without owning the copyright. You can, of course, make a separate arrangement to share the rights to a movie soundtrack album put out on CD, which will be advantageous for all.

So, unless you try to gain the rights to "Happy Birthday" from Michael Jackson (yes, he owns that song), you should be able to afford a few hundred dollars to enliven your movie with fresh, new sounds from your local, cutting-edge bands. Over the years I've had music rights agreements for songs composed and performed by Oakland, California's Paul Baker, the band Mermen of San Francisco, jazz songstress and composer Diane Witherspoon (her hauntingly beautiful "Thanking You," out on Tonal Gravity Records of Berkeley, was the title track for my feature *American Orpheus*), Marc Gizzi, Sylvia Heins, and "The Art of the Dulcimer" album's Robert Force and Albert d'Ossché (for *Release the Head*), punk bands Flipper and The Mutants (*Emerald Cities*), and music by my teenage son Marlon Schmidt, who composed and performed twelve original songs for *The 5th Wall*, using Sibelius software.

Again, let me caution that you must have musicians sign the contract before finalizing music in your movie. Wouldn't it be a bummer if, due to legal problems, you had to remove great music that worked perfectly in your final cut? Why put yourself in such a potentially negative situation? Approach the band or musicians as soon as possible, tell them how much you love their work, and see if they're willing to grant you the one-time usage rights to their music for inclusion in your DV feature. If one song in particular will be the title track or heard as the front credits roll, let them know that. They may be delighted to learn that some of their music will be prominently displayed in an indie feature.

PEOPLE WORK

After the paperwork comes the people work. As you get all your legal forms and script in order (maybe you did everything on computer and no real paper was used—good for you!), you now need to call, e-mail, or text-message various people who will be involved in your project to inform them of production details and schedule. Like it or not, you need to be a combination cheerleader and coach, keeping their enthusiasm stoked with periodic calls and contacts, letting them know that you are indeed moving forward on making a DV feature. If you are paying little or no salaries to your actors and crew members, consider your attention to them all the more important. You may be forced to match someone's salary at their job, if that person is crucial to your production. I paid $100 per day to get twins Mary and Margaret Craig away from their beauty shop for four days during the shoot of our 1997 Feature Workshops production *Someone Like Me* (each of them also received several gross points of profit for their lead roles). When I produced *A Man, a Woman, and a Killer* with Wayne Wang and Dick Richardson, I paid the lead actress, Carolyn Zaremba, $125 per week (1973 dollars) to match the salary she would have gotten from her secretarial job. If you want good people, you need to take the real world pressure off them temporarily, so that they can perform at their best for your production.

Gathering Production Energy and Spreading the Word

As the shoot date approaches, you must keep your people happy, let them know that you're thinking of them and their best interests. Make them aware of the fact that you've listed them in a contract for profit sharing and a small salary, and show them something in writing—script, outline, pages of action and dialogue—that reveals your deep commitment to the upcoming shoot. Keep them constantly updated. Let them know that you will have a great cinematographer helping you, and express excitement about his or her terrific equipment, high-end DV camera and lights, sound gear, tripod, and grip truck. Even if you yourself are shooting with a tiny Mini-DV camera, 1-chip, without lights or other equipment aids, you can make that a positive if you're committed to making that system deliver a feature. Whatever excites you can be transferred as positive energy to the others who are part of your team. When they also have ownership in your venture through the profit-sharing contract, they can't help but be delighted as they hear the chances are increasing that a good and potentially salable movie might be forthcoming. So, short of driving your friends and associates crazy with gratuitous updates, let vital people know biweekly what's happening, assuring them that you are on the case, preparing for the shoot.

Certainly, if you air your moviemaking dream to others outside of the production loop you will be greeted with some skepticism as well as encouragement. A few of those around you may applaud you, but others who are not doing anything so adventurous with their lives may express negativity about your project. If you deeply yearn to be accepted by your peers (a subconscious need we all share), it might be unwise to even broach the subject of the production-in-progress, because the slightest expression of doubt from a best friend could derail you. If all your friends think you're crazy in your extreme moviemaking quest, can you go it alone, maintain your focus? If you're swayed too easily by public opinion, I'd recommend letting it be your big secret—hold the energy tightly inside—until the DV feature is unveiled at the premiere screening.

On the other hand, it's the excited blabbing about a movie that sometimes helps form a great moviemaking team. Think of Kevin Smith's *Clerks* and how he got help from the various people around his convenience store job to make his hit movie. He happened to be surrounded by friends who were obviously ready to contribute their youthful energy and savage wit to their own brand of creative enterprise. So, although there is substantial risk in voicing a moviemaking idea aloud, you might decide to use that verbal communication among trusted, artistic-leaning buddies to get your DV feature started.

PAID ADVERTISING TO MAKE IT REAL

It may even be worth using the power of advertising to make your production more real for cast and crew members, investors, and family members who aren't exactly sure what's going on with the movie. A well-placed local ad in your hometown newspaper might be just the thing to get that last bit of support you need. It wouldn't have to cost more than $100, possibly as little as $5 in the classified section—just a line or two letting people in your town know that a movie will be shot there and thanking them ahead of time for any considerations they may give. If you advertise you will surely hear from local actors and extras eager to participate. Of course, if you live in a big city like Los Angeles or New York, you may not want the authorities to hear about a no-budget production, especially if the city is known for rigid enforcement of filming permits. Stay "under the radar" if this is the case—or at least be discreet.

In Arkansas, where I recently appeared to help kick off the first Ozarks Foothills FilmFest for festival director and longtime friend Bob Pest, support for moviemaking seems wonderfully positive. I met the director of Arkansas's film office, Joe Glass (*jglass@1800arkansas.com*, 1-501-682-7676), who is based in Little Rock. Because Joe will do anything and everything to ensure your movie gets made, he could become your greatest asset (a good reason to plan a shoot in Arkansas). Joe Glass has himself been a successful indie producer of low-budget feature films, long before the "indie" word was brought into play. So he knows all the ins and outs of the movie production process and can help you get the job done. Almost every state has a state film commission, so check out what level of support is available where you live.

INVESTOR PRESENTATIONS

Some investors like to attend a kind of presentation party, with the filmmakers showing a clip or two, making a speech about the content of the movie, dropping names of actors, and prophesying which festival circuit will premiere the final work (Sundance, New York, Berlin, or Cannes). While this kind of public display may be outside your personal abilities or interest, it could be a good opportunity for you to test your public relations skills. Your mother, boyfriend/girlfriend, or significant other might enjoy throwing a shindig a month or so before production is set to begin, preparing a festive-looking buffet, hors d'oeuvres and champagne, or simply guacamole, chips, and a keg of beer. A lot can actually be accomplished on a limited budget. Of course, if there isn't any potential investor interest, then save your cold cuts for the shoot and/or wrap party after your feature's shot.

MANAGING FAMILY AND FRIENDS

As the day of the shoot approaches, your moviemaking antennae will be up and scanning any and all experiences, people, and places for more needed actors, helpers, and locations—anything that might serve your movie. Those closest to you may see a new person emerge, someone whose focus is laser-sharp, who is suddenly operating with a one-track mind. It will be apparent to all that you have an important mission, maybe even a missionary's zeal, and it may cause them a little confusion at first. They thought that they knew you so well, that you were a such and such kind of person (slacker, easygoing). Well, not anymore. You're going for it, deadly serious about making the greatest movie that you can, creating the most amazing thing that they or anyone else has ever seen.

Part of your job therefore will be to understand and handle the reaction from close friends, family, and associates, who think you're anything from "too full of yourself" to "distant and cold." We all know the cliché about the person "in a world of his own," the daydreamer, like an Einstein, who doesn't seem to hear what others say because he's so deep in thought at the dinner table that he seems to be somewhere else. Well, you may get a little like that when your feature filmmaking dream seems within reach. You're on a real and valuable productive path, ready to make a contribution to world cinema using your highest level of creativity.

It is probably time to recognize the fact that you are possibly an artist—a DV artist, that is (why else would you have bought this book?)—and that your life is special in that regard. Learn a little about the lives of other artists, past and present. Read biographies like *Lust for Life* about the fiery friendship between the nineteenth-century painters Paul Gauguin and Vincent van Gogh. All artists have something in common as they struggle to bring their creations into existence. Imagine Leonardo da Vinci alone in his studio, applying oil paint to the portrait of Mona Lisa. Think of the thrill—and possible risk—attached to the process. Making art is exciting and demands that every cell of your body focus on solving the immediate and long-term problems associated with the creation.

So, as your personal universe shifts, you will need new people skills to reassure family and your significant other that you are still the same old pal and lover, but that you need to be singularly focused so that you can remember the myriad details necessary to make a good movie. You're sorry (you tell them) if you seem to come across as too confident and demanding one second, too emotional and desperate the next. Making a movie can do that to a person (you explain). Understand that some of your friends may be envious of your new, high-energy persona, jealous that they don't have something meaningful and exciting going on in their lives. They may not be artists like you, which makes what you do something of a mystery. While they'd like to sample for themselves your suddenly electrified life, they just can't. The closest they and others can ever come to living and feeling the artist's life is hanging around the set or later on attending the parties, perhaps becoming patrons and owning what the artist creates.

Understanding works two ways. Everyone feels a tinge of jealousy at some point in their lives, so don't fault yourself if some of your friends—not you—embark on the great adventure. *You'll have your turn.* Just give them the space to go about their (crazy) business of making movies the super-indie way (without Miramax or other studio backing). Only their ego is telling them this is an OK and worthy process, so maybe they're a little fragile under that gruff exterior. And they'll need your help to get through the production. Be as supportive as you can, and when you need *them* for assistance on a project, they'll be happy to reciprocate. At this moment, sitting here at my desk in Port Townsend writing this book instead of making a movie of my own, I confess to feeling some jealousy myself, thinking about you first-time DV hotshots preparing your movies while I sit here off the front lines. But I'll soon be back into the moviemaking trance, sometime before you pick this book off the bookstore shelf!

Now that you have an idea—according to my experience, anyway—of what you and those around you may encounter emotionally when you take the plunge, it's time to consider the best DV equipment to buy or rent to produce the highest-quality DV feature, on a budget you can afford.

3

SELECTING YOUR DV CAMERA, SOUND GEAR, AND INCIDENTALS

One of the most critical decisions you make while assembling your DV moviemaking workstation is selecting the right DV camera for purchase or rent. This choice determines not only the quality of your pixels but the very style in which you deliver images to the screen. The heavier, bulkier cameras demand on-shoulder or on-tripod framing (traditional shooting), while the smaller, lightweight Mini-DV handicams with fold-out screen allow a freer approach to framing and movement (by hand, Steadicam). Here's a whole new challenge: determining a balance between cost and portability.

Before you purchase a DV camera, you may want to try out some models under the fire of actual production by renting. That way you have valuable insight into the inner workings of a particular camera over a few days' time (while you perhaps get a movie shot . . .). While you're at it, you want to be extremely thorough before you pair a certain DV (Mini-DV, DVD, DVCAM, Pro-DV CAM) camera to a shooting effort.

BUDGETING DV EQUIPMENT FOR A $3,000 TOTAL

A crucial set of decisions on any production is what equipment to use under the imposed limitations of your budget. For our examples, let's work within the $3,000 budget I've described on the cover. Why $3,000? That amount is the least you'll need to spend to obtain a complete, professional digital moviemaking workstation, with a fast computer, the necessary DV editing software, and a fully manual (adjustable focus and exposure) Mini-DV/DVD camera that is up to or approaching broadcast quality. The cost of special effects software like Lightwave, Combustion, Adobe's After Effects, and Magic Bullet exceeds this bare bones budget, but if you end up with a Mac platform and Final Cut Express, that NLE software includes enough effects to satisfy most first efforts. Let's try to operate on a budget that can be reached by almost anyone with a credit card, a car of some sort, and/or a part-time job. (I mention the car because, if you need to sell something to finish your movie, your used car will come in handy.)

The $3,000 is broken down roughly as follows: something like $1,500 for the computer (the basic G5 price), $300 for NLE software (I'm talking about Final Cut Express for now, not the $1,000 Final Cut Pro 4), a $200 monitor, and $1,000 for a Mini-DV/DVD camera. With a big bite from sales tax (unless you purchase your items in a state like as Oregon or Montana that has no sales tax, saving 8 percent or $240, almost what Final Cut Express costs!), you have to budget your computer very carefully. A $1,500 computer can cost you $1,750 with tax and a few incidentals added (roller mouse, cheap auxillary computer speakers, etc.). Make sure that your budget is working out correctly.

If you are a beginning moviemaker, maybe you'll be satisfied with a computer that includes some kind of basic DV editing software (iMovie comes free with Macs), allowing you to purchase a slightly better DV camera. Later, after you've shot some footage and successfully cut the results, you can jump to the next level, perhaps purchasing Final Cut Express new for another $299. Your total investment in digital moviemaking would then reach $3,300. Or you can perhaps settle for a used but fast, media-friendly fully loaded Mac G4 computer with monitor for under $1,000 (see Computers at *www.ebay.com*) along with a used Sony TRV900 3 CCD Mini-DV camera (winning bids around $1,000), paired with top-of-the-line Final Cut Pro, found on eBay for $300–$500 (see Chapter 7 for detailed instructions on cutting with both Final Cut Pro 3, Final Cut 4, and Final Cut Express NLE software).

NOTE: Our $3,000 budget doesn't include the cost of Mini-DV, DVCAM, or DVD stock, since it is relatively cheap and can be purchased as need dictates. Mini-DV cassettes run about $10 per 1-hour tape; six 1-hour Mini-DV cassettes (six hours of shooting) should run about $25 at Costco or comparable discount stores. DVCAM costs about $15 for 40 minutes of shooting. The DVD disks for the new Sony DVD cameras are in the range of $8–$9 for DVD-R (60 minutes of footage), and $10–$12 for the DVD-RW rewritables, which supposedly can be used up to a thousand times; that's a hundred DV features if you shoot 10 hours per movie!

Now, work the budget backwards. If the Mini-DV/DVD camera you want is $1,000 (plus tax) and Final Cut Express is $299 (plus tax), what is left for the computer platform and monitor? If sales tax is around 8 percent you easily end up losing about $100 on the combined purchase of camera and editing software, edging the total spent by this point to approximately $1,400. Can you obtain a suitable DV-editing computer and monitor for $1,600, tax included? With a $1,400 G4 or G5 (watch for discount rebates at *www.macmall.com*), that would leave you with less than $100 for a monitor (maybe not even that, if tax is factored in). Of course, if you're resourceful anything can be acquired through determination (and luck). I found a perfectly good $400 Sony Multiscan 200ES Trinitron monitor at a garage sale for $40. So don't give up when you're this close to getting a full DV workstation together.

RENTING OR BUYING A DV CAMERA

The selection of a DV camera is critical to your first production and perhaps even to your entire moviemaking dream. If you make a wrong choice, and (1) fail to accommodate your individual style (hand-held vs. eyepiece shooting with a tripod), (2) exceed your budget (it's real easy to overspend), and (3) forget your technical needs (broadcast quality or not), you can derail yourself right at the start. The first thing you need to consider is how to juggle cost with compatibility. Here are four possibilities:

1. Buy a Low-Level, 1-CCD Mini-DV/DVD Camera You can obtain a Sony Hi-8 1-CCD Digital Handicam with 500x digital zoom, Super-Steady shot, and FireWire connection, for around $500 (probably the Hi-8 digital model, which records digital images to Hi-8 tape), and pair that with a $200 wireless mike kit from Audio Technica. You should be able to find affordable DV handicam cameras at discounted Web sites like the huge B&H in New York (*www.bhphotovideo.com*, 1-800-947-9939), and maybe even Costco, which has occasional good deals on DV cameras. I bought my Sony DCR-TRV10 Mini-DV camera at Circuit City for $699 (now around $300 for used units on eBay) which is the camera I shot two features with during the summer of 2002 (see Chapter 1). If you can afford a Mini-DV camera over a comparable Hi-8 model, I'd say make the stretch and go for it.

Another good choice is the new Sony DVD cameras, of which the DCR-DVD300 model falls into our budget range of under $1,000. What's great about shooting directly to DVD is that you don't have to

The JVC GR-DV500 Mini-DV camcorder (*www.jvc.com*), costing as low as $378 at *www.beachcamera.com*, has a 1:33 megapixel CCD that delivers 540 lines of resolution/1600x1200 still pictures, making it a great "first camera." (Courtesy of JVC Americas Corp.)

worry about Mini-DV tape disintegration, crimping, or aging. The images you shoot are forever deposited onto the DVD for easy computer loading and transfer to your NLE program. And if you use the $12 rewritable DVD-RW disk you could conceivably keep shooting and capturing the results to a computer for a full feature's worth of taping and not spend a cent more on stock. Certainly when the next generation of holographic disks comes into play (see Chapter 12), with their multilayered storage, the DVD cameras will be even more viable. At that point you'll be able to shoot 10 hours on a single disk with room to spare. For now, though, these breakthrough Sony cameras are an excellent way to get your DVD movies shot on a tight budget, and in a nonperishable medium.

NOTE: Sony doesn't include a FireWire connection in their line of DVD cameras, but supplies a USB 2.0 port, which they say is just as fast for transferring footage to computers for editing. Check out their claim during your return policy period, and return the unit if you're not fully satisfied. (Always read online feedback/reviews posted at amazon.com, etc., *before* buying a camera!)

With camera gear covered (a relatively cheap accessory microphone, like Sony's $60 ECM-HS1 for my TRV10, is a must for any low-cost camera package), all you need are some cheap photoflood bulbs or rented lights. Of course, if you opt for shooting Dogme 95 style, where artificial lights are forbidden (see Chapter 6), you'll be spared the extra expense of lighting kits. By adding a few inexpensive gels to the most basic light kit—see-through, colored plastic sheets of varying density—you can control mood and dynamics with different tints, all the while seeing exactly what you're recording by looking into the lens eyepiece or at the LED screen of the video camera. A color-corrected Sony field monitor would be another fine asset to your on-location shoot; maybe you can borrow or rent the $1,000 item from a fellow moviemaker.

Some people prefer the more-grain/less-razor-sharp video images these under-$1,000 cameras deliver because the images more accurately resemble filmstock than what's recorded by the high-end 3-chip

DV units. There is actually a "filmmaking" movement in this direction, so don't sell your little 1-CCD Mini-DV camera short just yet. I find that some of my most creative images result from using such "low-quality"cameras, like windows being blown out from overexposure, image tracking (tails of light), and "dirty" grain appearing in low-light situations.

2. Rent a Top-of-the-Line Mini-DV/DVCAM/Pro-DVCAM Renting can put in your hands the best equipment available; it's the approach I took for my first four 16mm features. By having to nail your entire movie in a limited period of time before the deadline for returning equipment, you suddenly raise the stakes and naturally increase your mental focus. You have to think more clearly and be more highly organized, while still taking improvisational chances and exerting the power of your intuition. A firm, nonstop shooting schedule almost assures that you'll deliver a feature's worth of footage to the editor before the time is up and the cast and crew return to their normal lives.

Having made such a large commitment by renting expensive DV gear, you'll have no time to second-guess yourself. It's surprising how much of a burden we all carry in daily life, when most decision making is open-ended and subject to endless discussion. On a movie set, with a looming deadline, there's just no time for messing around. Success requires you take only forward steps. It's all positive action. Perhaps that's why we moviemakers feel so mentally refreshed (albeit physically exhausted) after a wrap. For once, all our desires are acted on; all our thoughts and decisions, by definition, are "correct." This is not to say we don't pay for our lapses in the editing room, where "mistakes" must be turned into "original effects"!

(Whether you rent or not, don't be set adrift for months of shooting actors and friends every weekend, trying in vain to get the production team assembled again and again. I recommend a tight, condensed, week-to-ten-day shooting schedule [and an extra eleventh day for pickup shots if needed], even if you shoot with your own Mini-DV camera and don't have that rental deadline pressure to contend with.)

On the high end of rentals, if you truly feel you need and deserve the best—perhaps the $50,000–$75,000 Sony HDW F900 24 frames per second *Star Wars* camera—you must hold out and raise more money to get a great camera. This HDCAM camera package (including lights, tripod, Sennheiser mikes, field recorder, and monitor) will cost you approximately $1,400 per day, with an extra fee for an operator (available at *www.rule.com* and elsewhere). The rental facility will require a technician be present, unless you're personally certified to shoot such high-end HDTV units. Maybe you can shoot an entire feature in just one day, using the less expensive Sony DSR-500 (Pro-DVCAM camera with 700 lines of resolution), a high-definition field monitor, professional lighting and sound equipment package, and on-site technical assistant to match (see Lloyd Francis information in the next section).

3. Collaborate with a DP (Sharing Gross Profit Points) I was delighted and thrilled when director of photography Lloyd Francis decided to enter into a profit-sharing arrangement with me for the production of *The 5th Wall*. Both Lloyd and lead actor Willie Boy Walker, along with my coproducer (and son) Morgan Schmidt-Feng, entered into a fully collaborative agreement by which each of the four principal participants owned equal shares of gross profit points—85 percent divided four ways. Lloyd's usual $1,200 per-day camera package fee included a Pro-DVCAM Sony DSR-500, plus full light kit, radio and assorted directional mikes, Sony field monitor, tripods, and numerous incidentals that a professional director of photography must have on hand. (Contact Lloyd at *lloyd81@hotmail.com* for his current DP and equipment rental rates and schedule of availability.)

If you go online to various moviemaking support Web sites, like the great and helpful *www.indieclub.com*, *www.dv.com*, *www.filmarts.org* (for the Film Arts Foundation in the San Francisco/Bay Area), Chris Gore's *www.filmthreat.com*, or *www.Moviemaker.com* magazine site, you're bound to find classified ads for DPs, as well as people with DV cameras to rent or sell. Maybe your timing will be just right for making a new friend while gaining a DV production partner who happens to have the equipment you desire. If you have a vital moviemaking concept you can put into words, something you can energetically communicate verbally to a cinematographer, then perhaps he or she will take up your cause and help you make your feature with cutting-edge Pro-DV equipment.

4. Reconsider the "Little" DV Camera When I refer to a "little" DV camera, I'm testing how you feel about using less-than-top-of-the-line equipment. The fact is that even an inexpensive 1-CCD single-chip Mini-DV camera can do the job. My first Mini-DV camera, the hand-sized Canon ZR, which originally cost $1,200, is attainable now for under $300 (if you can find one on eBay.) It can shoot over 500 lines of resolution and go from 1/60th to 1/8000th of a second shutter speed; it has manual exposure and focus controls, as well as lots of arty transitional effects (mozaic, strobe, fade, dissolve, B&W settings), shoots 16:9, and works as a VCR (like most DV cameras), playing back the Mini-DV footage to a computer via a FireWire connection. My current "little" backup camera, the Sony TRV10, also sports all these important manual options.

Again, if you feel deep inside that you simply can't tolerate anything but the best-quality camera that money can buy, you should face that fact now, rather than fooling yourself and realizing halfway through the shoot that you have somehow undermined your production.

NOTE: Don't limit yourself to a 1-chip DV camera if you are intent on selling the results now to a network or cable TV station. If the possibility of a big-time sale is a vital ingredient to your moviemaking plan, then dig deeper into your bank account and purchase a $2,000+ camera with 3-CCD (Canon GL-2, Sony VX-2000, Sony PDX10, and the like) that meets current broadcast-quality standards. But be realistic. Don't get sucked into the purchase of an overly expensive camera at the early stages of your moviemaking career; debts can weigh heavily on future artistic endeavors.

CAMERA EQUIPMENT OVERVIEW:
GOING INTO DEBT FOR ART?

If you forgo purchasing your own camera, your next production will require another rental of similar cost, which means that you'll be stuck in much the same financial merry-go-round that I had to endure with 16mm filmmaking. I was always in debt, stuck for years owing thousands for lab costs from previous shoots, while trying to raise funds for the next. I would spend a week and a half shooting a feature's worth of 16mm film stock (usually about 8 hours of material, though *Morgan's Cake* was just over 3 hours' worth), and then not touch a camera for the next two years, being too busy editing shots into scenes and finally forging scenes into a cohesive story. Editing took the major amount of my filmmaking time—still does. So, I reasoned, why own a camera and tie up all that money? Now, though, it *does* make sense to purchase a DV camera, given the virtual no-cost expense of tape stock.

I like to think that the DV revolution helps to alleviate that brutal, debt-ridden moviemaking dance. After an initial $3,000 expenditure, DV moviemakers are free to make feature-length works for a mere $100 dollars' worth of stock (if they own the camera and computer/software editing gear!), without burdening themselves with constant debt. Wouldn't it be nice to replace extreme agitation (those credit card payments!) with extreme equanimity?

THE BEST DV CAMERA FOR YOU

While many of the cameras I am about to cover are out of our present $3,000 budget, costing much more than the $1,000 allotted for a DV camera, please don't pick up a mixed message. I still believe it's crucial that we stay with the $3,000 overall moviemaking workstation budget, for reasons already stated. We'll all certainly be tempted again and again by new and fantastic DV cameras advertised in the coming years. In the future, after you recover from this initial $3,000 outlay, it will be time to select one of these expensive professional cameras to move your moviemaking career ahead. For now, you need to become aware of what's available and learn on what basis any camera selection should be made.

Cost Factors

I recently discussed DV cameras with a moviemaking friend who was considering the purchase of some new gear. I found it impossible to recommend any single camera without first knowing her exact budget ($1,000–$4,500), professional needs (3-chip/broadcast quality, XLR sound outlets, etc.), and particular shooting style preferences (hand-held, like the Sony DSR-PD150, PD101a, VX2000, Cannon GL2, Panasonic AG-DVX100a, or over-the-shoulder with only eyepiece access, like the Sony DSR-200/500, Canon XL1S). If she was set on spending $2,200, the Sony DSR-PD101a or PD150 and Canon GL-2 came to mind. Once she reached $3,800, the Canon's XL-1S was in sight, along with the new Sony DSR-PD170. Hitting $4,500, she'd be approaching the price range of Sony's, Panasonic's, and JVC's Pro-DVCAM models. The point is, once a precise budget is established, it's easier to review the DV cameras available and make an informed purchase.

Portability

Who cares that a 3-CCD DV camera is affordable if it feels too bulky and heavy for a digital moviemaker who likes to float her shots hand-held, like an arm-manipulated Steadicam? If you like to shoot below eye level, watching the action and framing on a fold-out screen, then the Canon XL-1S may not be suitable for you, but perhaps one of their smaller units is, like the GL-2 (about $2,000). Choosing the right camera, one that best supports your particular shooting style, can make all the difference between developing new skills as a DV shooter and ultimately getting frustrated and bored with the whole thing. A first feature, by definition, is where you will discover your shooting preferences. You don't want to get stuck with a camera that you don't fully enjoy.

Broadcast Quality (or Not)

Most people who read the video production magazines (such as *Video-maker*, *MovieMaker*, *DV*) will get the idea that if they don't shoot 3-chip they have forfeited the broadcast quality that their fine work deserves. On this issue, all I can say is that I've been shooting features with the "substandard" 1-chip/500+ lines of resolution Sony TRV10 with excellent results. My video-making buddies have been astounded at the sharp images, which look more like film than video, and the top-quality sound I've been able to achieve with just an onboard mike. (I interchange an onboard $60 EMC-HS1 Sony mike with an Audio-Technica Pro wireless lavalier when I need to record clean dialogue from actors several feet away).

Am I worried that what I shoot may not be viable for regular TV screenings because it may fail to meet industry broadcast standards? The quick answer is no. If the movies are well done, having good stories and energetic shots and framing—in short, have the necessary magic that makes a movie move and remain interesting to an audience—then I can't be bothered by what the industry dictates. If, up the road, the work is important enough to earn public screening at film festivals, on the networks or cable outlets, the price of distribution can include an up-res process, where the pixels are doubled or tripled to meet certain criteria (see "After Effects and Magic Bullet" in Chapter 7). By then, the occasional washed-out exposures of brilliantly lit windows, the distinctive framing resulting from my hand-held methods, the unusual cuts that I've used to keep the story rolling—all these eccentricities will simply add to the originality of the work.

Regarding the issue of fine-grain, 3-chip technology versus 1-chip consumer video: Remember that most 1-chip cameras have 500+ lines of resolution—most home TVs have only 330 lines. One of the most intriguing and powerful movies I've ever seen, *The Celebration* (Dogme No. 1), was quite grainy on the movie screen, but that technical aspect detracted nothing from—and may in fact have reinforced—the incredible hyperrealism of the film's human drama. Though it looked (and felt) like no Hollywood product (it was shot with a Sony PD7, a lower-resolution unit than my Sony TRV10), that didn't stop this unique movie from winning the highest honor at the Cannes Film Festival in 1998 (shown as a 35mm video-to-film blowup). If a movie is great, offering a compelling human experience,

By constantly adjusting the direction of the swivel microphone to catch the best sound from actors (you monitor audio with earphones), you can record CD-quality tracks, even with a consumer-grade Mini-DV unit like the Sony DSR-TRV10.

I don't care if the grain is as big as basketballs. If it's a must-see movie, we'll be glued to our seats, riveted to the screen with the rest of the audience, regardless of which camera was used for its creation.

Physical Handling

Obviously any book will fail to deliver a suitable hands-on experience when it comes to testing DV cameras. What you probably want to do is spend a few hours actually handling cameras in a full-inventory shop, like B&H in New York City (420 Ninth Avenue, at the corner of 34th Street) or at the NAB convention in Las Vegas (National Association of Broadcasters, *www.nab.com*), where the latest DV gear is trotted out each April. After a bit of testing, examining images through the lens or on an LED screen, switching modes, checking exposure, changing manual controls to watch built-in transitions, arty settings, then monitoring audio (bring your own earphones), you will probably start to gravitate toward a few of the cameras offered in your price range. But be careful a salesperson doesn't woo you into buying something beyond your means. A thousand dollars should be enough to spend on your first Mini-DV camera (especially if you consider used DV cameras on eBay!).

The final consideration—your personal shooting style—is something that can't really be determined until you have a camera in your possession for a while and start adapting a personal shooting method to your particular storytelling needs. It is imperative that the camera can create "Time Code" and can be operated through your computer's FireWire connection, so that your editing software can operate the camera as a VCR (rewind, fast-forward, stop, and play scenes by clicking of the buttons shown on your NLE computer screen). Also essential is that you make sure your DV camera is compatible with the editing software program you are planning to use. For iMovie compatibility with your DV camera, check at *www.apple.com/imovie/compatibility/camcorder.html.* For Final Cut Pro (FCP) compatibility, check at *www.apple.com/finalcutpro/qualification.html.* Strangely enough, some DV cameras, such as my Sony DCR-TRV10, aren't listed as compatible with either iMovie or Final Cut Pro (perhaps because it's a discontinued model), but can still import and export DV footage smoothly to FCP3/FCP4. So the final test for compatibility must ultimately occur when you hook up the camera to your computer via FireWire and see if the Camera Connected message appears on the screen. If you can't import the camera's footage, immediately return the unit to the store while it's still under its fifteen-day return warranty.

NOTE: Regardless of which DV camera you finally select, it must have a built-in FireWire connection to allow its digital images and sound to be captured by a computer for electronic editing. (The exception is the Sony DVD models, which allow for the transfer of images and audio via disk or USB 2.0.) Also make sure every possible feature on your DV camera can be set on manual as well as fully automatic mode. Only with *full manual controls* for focus, exposure, and white balance, plus an accessory slot for an external mike, can you satisfactorily shoot a DV feature.

The great, now-discontinued Sony DSR-PD100a, with its 3-CCD broadcast-quality image and compact frame, makes it worth a trip to the Web (*www.ebay.com*) to locate and purchase this ahead-of-its-time DV moviemaking marvel. (Courtesy of Sony Electronics, Inc.)

Ease of Shooting with a Mini-DV Handicam

For the record, the Sony DSR-PD100a (a discontinued model), with its 3-CCD and nearly broadcast-quality electronics (priced about $2,000, if you have the budget), is a great choice for shooting lightweight, low-key, and portable. David Lynch uses this camera for his *www.david lynch.com* Web site and online moviemaking, as does artist Chip Lord of Ant Farm, *http://arts.ucsc.edu/faculty/Lord/*. And Kirk Lohse, director of the Fest-EYE-ful film festival in Texarkana, Texas (*www. festeyeful. org/*) also sings its praises, using his unit in a professional DV-production capacity when he isn't teaching, completing scripts, or keeping his festival alive through sheer willpower (see more information about DV festivals in Chapter 8). So if you have extra camera money to spend, this 3-chip camera is definitely worth your consideration. With a small, "tourist-sized" consumer DV camera like this one, you have more access to the impromptu personal moments. This became very apparent when I shot with my TRV10 in Portugal, taping real-life stories in the

For many DV "filmmakers" this 24-frames-per-second Panasonic AG-DVX100a digital camera, at around $3900, is a dream come true (shooting film-like images with inexpensive DV!). Just realize it takes some extra time to adjust its many settings for different shooting situations, making it less of an "impulsive/improvisational" unit. (©2004 Panasonic Broadcast & Television Systems Company)

film festival office of Figueira da Foz International Film Festival and elsewhere (see Chapter 1), setting up shots at a moment's notice. Since my little DV camera fit in a small belt bag, I kept it on me at all times, which helped to generate a new kind of flow.

Imagine this. You're sitting in a restaurant or other public place with your small DV camera easily concealed in an average-sized, over-the-shoulder camera bag, when suddenly the moment seems right to shoot *something*. You unzip the bag, remove the small unit, click it on, manually adjust the exposure and focus, lock down those settings, don your low-key earphones for monitoring audio, and make your shots. With a larger unit, something approaching the news broadcast size of Betacam or other bulky DV cameras, you're bound to attract attention. You'd change the ambience of the room, altering your subjects' mental focus with the mere presence of your big camera.

Mulling over Your Final DV Camera Choice

So back to the initial question: Which camera should you purchase? On what specifications should you base your decision? In my case, I wasn't ready to plunk down $3,800 for something like the Sony PD150 (closer to $2,500 now as a discontinued unit), with the XLR ports for quality sound connections and great image production. Actually, I just didn't want a serious, truly expensive camera yet, one that might be sitting around a lot as I spent months editing, all the while trying to pay off my credit card bills for that costly purchase. I felt it was OK to have an inexpensive Mini-DV camera, get used to the routine of shooting and importing images, learn the ropes before making a major investment (watching while new cameras made current ones obsolete!). And I could use my DV camera as a cheap VCR deck to import the Mini-DV footage into my computer, making it play, rewind, fast-forward, and so on with the cursor on the computer. While I'd read, as you probably have, articles in various moviemaking magazines about how repeated use of a DV camera as playback deck will ruin the heads, I figured that a careful approach to capturing footage wouldn't appreciably cut into the life of my little, inexpensive, "temporary" DV camera. If I captured footage directly into the computer's editing program on Final Cut Pro, the first time maybe in 25-minute chunks, then I certainly wouldn't be damaging it beyond the expected wear and tear. (Note: Batch capturing like this can't be accomplished with Final Cut Express.)

And as with filmmaking, I would shoot steadily for a couple of weeks, amass a large amount of images with sync sound, then capture all the footage that seemed usable. Calculating that I needed a gig of storage per each five minutes of captured video footage (or 12 gigs per hour), I could load something close to five hours into the 60 gigs of my 933-mhz Mac G4 and start cutting. I'd get to know my footage in the capture window of Final Cut Pro, let the computer play, and rewind the loaded images and sounds during editing, instead of wearing out my camera.

Shopping Online for a Mini-DV Camera

On eBay recently, I spotted the online auction of a complete Sony DSR-PD150 camera package (batteries, cables, charger) with accessories like a Bogen tripod with fluid head, Canon WD-58 wide angle lens, professional mikes (shotgun and radio lavalier) and microphone stand, lights (three Ianiro 650s, softlight, stands)—the whole lightweight production package. The entire set of equipment went for a little over $5,000. Supposedly, the camera had been used for only one professional shoot. So there are buying opportunities if you're ready to take a calculated risk that comes with obtaining used gear.

> **NOTE:** If an online store sells a *new* Sony product (or other name brands), there should be an active, one-year warranty—inquire! For used Sony cameras, you can still buy a service manual (call 1-800-488-7669) if it's unavailable for free on the Web.

Before purchasing any DV camera, it's certainly worth using the Web to comparison shop for new equipment, especially now that there are some very creative sites built by dedicated videomakers who are enthusiastic about their thoroughly tested gear. Check out the long list of links for comparing various DV cameras at *www.bealecorner.com/trv900/cats/cats.html*, conceived to honor Sony's DSR-TRV900. This extensive Web site includes links where you can read reviews, get specs (download camera manuals), compare images shot on the TRV900 with other DV cameras, even hear QuickTime audio playback examples from several built-in camera mikes. Of course, if you've purchased a Sony TRV900, this is a gold mine of helpful support as you shoot your movie.

You can see it's pretty easy to become an equipment junky, loading up on all the latest gear, until you wake up one day with $30,000 worth of DV stuff and realize it isn't really being used for anything. My advice once again is to start small, buy an affordable Mini-DV camera that's compatible with current Final Cut Pro software, and start shooting feature-length movies. Get them cut, and then screen them for family and friends on your home TV. Just get started making some movies!

NOTE: Regardless of which DV camera you buy, I recommend purchasing a separate microphone so that you are not recording directly off the body of the camera. For some examples on how to use an onboard microphone, see the section "Shooting Without the Pro XLR Outlets" later in this chapter.

GOING PRO-DVCAM

For some, the acquisition of an inexpensive little DV camera—something lacking the 3-CCD top-quality chips for "true color and sharpness"— will not supply the needed quality or the psychic energy for their full-out moviemaking and movie-directing fantasies. The urge to be thoroughly "professional" will drive them toward the major purchases of Pro-DVCAM gear, ranging from $5,000 to more than $20,000—

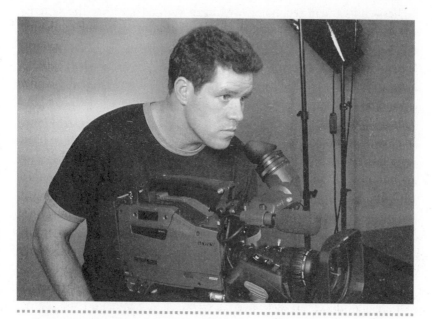

Morgan Schmidt-Feng at the helm of a Sony HDW-750, a top-of-the-line HD camera he used to shoot in-house interviews of George Lucas and others for the *Star Wars* behind-the-scenes DVD. (Contact him at *www.filmsight.com* to learn more about the high-definition, 24-frames-per-second DV approach.) (Photo by Tina Mills)

way beyond the kind of "used-car" moviemaking budget we're talking about. I can certainly recommend the various Pro-DVCAM cameras I've been fortunate to employ, including Sony's DSR-500 used by DP (director of photography) Lloyd Francis for my production of *The 5th Wall*, and the old Sony DSR-200 Pro-DVCAM workhorse my cinematographer-son Morgan Schmidt-Feng used on many of our Feature Workshops productions (*Someone Like Me, Welcome to Serendipity, Loneliness Is Soul, Maisy's Garden, Chetzemoka's Curse* [Dogme No. 10], etc.). That $7,000 model (now found at around $5,000) was later modified and updated as Sony's DSR-200a.

Because of his job at LucasFilm, as George Lucas's documentarian, Morgan has recently become familiar with more high-end DV cameras, including Sony's Digi-Beta unit, and HD cameras. When I inquired about HD and the possibility of shooting something with that highest-end camera technology, Morgan warned me that the systems are very touchy. He said I would need a knowledgeable technician on the set because inferior images can easily result if great care isn't taken with image evaluation. Only when the technician can determine every nuance of what's being recorded, with the finest, highly calibrated video field monitor, can you maintain consistent quality.

Sounds pretty counterproductive to the new free-wheeling, freedom-inspiring qualities of DV—it's that very liberating ease of use that I'm so pleased to see the new medium offer. If you're ready to spend serious money on production equipment (my last warning—this stuff becomes quickly outdated or may just sit around while you edit, unless you rent it out), then you might want to look into the following units. I've added contact names and e-mails of my friends who own or use these cameras and who are willing to discuss the pros and cons with my readers (thanks, guys!):

> Digi-Beta/Sony HDW-750 high-definition camcorder (Morgan Schmidt-Feng, *morgan@filmsight.com*)
> Sony DSR-PDX10P (PAL) (Jon Jost, *clarandjon@msn. com*)
> JVC Gy-DV500U Pro-DVCAM (Larry Pado, *pado@fastrans.net*)
> Sony DSR-PD150 (William Farley, *farley@farleyfilm.com*)

Canon XL-1 (Yahn Soon, *withrom@aol.com*, or Galen Garwood, *ggarwood2001@yahoo.com*)

Sony DSR-PD100a (Chip Lord, *clord@earthlink.net*; Kirk Lohse, *klohse@cableone.net*; or Morgan Schmidt-Feng, *morgan@film sight.com*, who uses it as an off-the-hip documentarian backup tool)

Sony DSR-PD150/PD170

While supposedly a technical step down from the Pro-DVCAM line of cameras, the now-discontinued Sony PD150 ($2,500, but look for lower rates at discount houses) is nevertheless one of the great portable cameras, the outstanding quality of which has amazed videographers since the day it was released. If your coffers are full, consider this Sony a "best buy." When my writer/director friend William Farley was putting together a production team for his documentary on underground comedian Daryl Henriques, he hired San Francisco DP Adam Keker,

For a great DV camera in the $3,500 range, check out the Sony DSR-PD170 with 3-CCD broadcast quality, super low-light sensitivity, and dual-XLR outputs. (See *www.global-dvc.org/html/PD170.asp* before purchase.) (Courtesy of Sony Electronics, Inc.)

with his Sony PD150 DVCAM camera package. It didn't take more than one day of shooting for Bill to become an advocate of this fine camera and its extraordinary image and sound quality. Bill says Keker recommends using the European PAL version of the camera, Sony DSR-PD150P, if you plan to transfer your DV story to film at a later point. Of course, you would also need to acquire a PAL deck for transferring your PAL DV footage to the computer (Apple's Final Cut Pro/Express has a setting for PAL). At any rate, PAL would ensure that you achieved the highest resolution on a relatively low equipment budget (under $10,000).

Here are the items in the Keker-Farley Sony PD150 camera package, along with their description and relative cost. The best prices can be achieved by contacting mass retailers like B&H in New York City (*www.bhphotovideo.com*) or searching the Internet. But be aware: If the cost is *too* low, it might indicate an inferior/flawed model. Bill told me that some PD150s have problems with audio. I found an instructive Web site that talked about a hiss that occurs on the tracks when using an extra mike (see *www.urbanfox.tv/workbooks/sonypd150/hiss. htm*). Sony initially denied the problem existed but later offered an upgrade kit (Manual Audio-SIN Upgrade Kit) costing $150, which supplies manual audio mode signal-to-noise improvement. If you bid for a PD150 online, you need to inquire about the origin of the item, the status of manual audio upgrade, the warranty, and the return policy.

SONY PD150 CAMERA PACKAGE

Sony DSR-PD150 (3-CCD Mini-DV digital camcorder)	$ 3,365
Sony WRT822B66/68 (UHF body pack transmitter, with Sony ECM77BC (Omni lavilier mike with Sony connectors)	980
Sony WRR810A66 (portable UHF synthesized receiver)	960

Sennheiser ME66/K6 (shotgun mike with power supply)	404
Sennheiser MZW66PRO (black velour windscreen)	60
Sony ACVQ850D (AC/DC adapter/charger)	100
2-Sony NPF960 (Infolithium L series batteries)	210
Sony VCLHG0758 (wide angle lens)	272
Bogen 3221/3433 (tripod and pro video head)	319
Sony MDR-V300 (headphones)	90
CVS XLRP-XLRJ-3EXF (3-foot XLR male-to-female cables)	10
Sony HVL 20DW2 (20-watt light for digital camera)	100
PORSPD150 (portabrace RS-PD150 rain slicker)	150
TA979B (Tamrac 979 pro camcorder bag)	116
Flexfill (48-inch silver/white reflector)	87
Total	**$ 7,223**

NOTE: It's worth considering the purchase of the PAL version of the Sony DSR-PD150, PD170, and other DV cameras, for added sharpness of image, especially if you intend to blow up the results to 35mm film. At 25 fps, PAL runs closer to the 24 fps of film. If you're short on funds, you could possibly use the camera as a VTR deck, but the best-case scenario is having an additional $2,000 or so to buy an accompanying PAL DVCAM deck, like Sony's DSR11, which also delivers NTSC. Fortunately Final Cut Pro and Final Cut Express support PAL in their preferences.

CAMERA INCIDENTALS

It's great to have a top camera, but without great mikes like the Sennheiser (described in the PD150 package), a good, lightweight tripod that has smooth pans, like the Bogen Road Runner or other extras, you will find yourself at a disadvantage when trying to perform professional work. However, there are ways around most shortcomings, if you can adapt and get creative.

Tripods

Any discussion about tripods must eventually take shooting style into account. Think about it. If everyone uses a tripod, usually posting it about shoulder high to attain shots at head level, is it such a surprise that most movies look like they were shot by the same cinematographer? If all you had to place your video camera on was a 3-foot-high support box (such as a suitcase), automatically your "style" would be different. When I think of the films of Ozu I think of seeing Japanese families framed at ground level, sitting on mats having tea, enacting the small dramas of daily life (that have the power of thunderbolts!). That ground-level POV makes the movie a much different experience. So don't just buy the most expensive tripod offered. That unthinking gesture will (1) kick a hole in your "used-car" moviemaking budget and (2) preempt some of the originality from your process.

That said, what are the alternatives? A tripod can be replaced with any surface that is the correct height of the subject you're shooting (kitchen counter, the top of the bread box), but the search for the suitably tall item with which to get your shot is tiresome, especially when you're under the gun of being on a set, at a location, with actors waiting for your next command.

Still, what if you decide that you'll just use a hand-held DV camera, no tripod, and start shooting, as I did in Figueira da Foz, Portugal (see Chapter 1)? Because I hadn't packed a cumbersome tripod but was determined to "shoot a movie, I started making up shots in which I could set the camera on a surface and still catch a person's face for several minutes in a "locked-down" shot. If I wanted a solid shot (no camera jiggle), I had to adjust each interaction with actors, sometimes having them sit on the floor to meet the lens of the camera that was held firmly to a chair seat. Suddenly I was forced to adjust my usual manner of shooting and frame shots from different angles and placements. Later on, I got my hands on a nice lightweight tripod, which came in very handy for a shot of Alfons Engelen standing on the beach at sunset, telling about his three-month-long trek across the Sahara desert with the nomadic Blue People when he was twenty-three years old.

So do you see how radical a control factor the tripod becomes? For *Morgan's Cake* I used a borrowed, top-of-the-line Miller Pro Fluid-head tripod (*www.miller.com.au/*) and introduced the idea of pans away from action as part of a recurring shooting motif. These pans had to be smooth, the kind that sort of float away from the subjects during the long takes I'd been shooting. For these pans, I wanted to use a delicate touch, starting each movement slowly, maintaining a constant speed as I swung away from the actors, and finally, at the end of the pan, slowing down gradually and halting at a predetermined, precise spot where the final composition was satisfying. That kind of a careful move required a sturdy tripod. The Miller Pro came with thick wooden legs, ensuring stability as I performed the left-or-right-sided pans. Using a modern, lightweight aluminum tripod advertised for DV cameras, it would take an extra bit of skill for some moves of this nature, mostly because there will be no heavy camera to naturally impede the action.

While you can make a movie without a tripod, it's nice to have one along, something that isn't too large or cumbersome. My artist/moviemaker friend Galen Garwood had a New York leatherworker build him a tubular black leather case for the Bogen tripod he took to Thailand for his *Phenom* movie, about the plight of the Asian elephant (see Chapter 11). The over-the-shoulder case, loaded with a modest-sized, lightweight tripod, gave him the control over his shooting environment, enabling him to grab shots in the field when the opportunity arose.

As you saw in the Farley/Keker Sony PD150 camera package budget, $319 was allotted for a Bogen tripod. That's certainly a reasonable price for a good DV tripod. Bogen's 3066 tripod has sold more than 100,000 units, so it is a favorite among shooters of video. Their 500 series offers a great array of lightweight tripod choices (visit their Web site at *www.bogenphoto.com*). Some of the attributes you want to have in a tripod are (1) fluid head, (2) leveling bubble, (3) separate pan and tilt locks, and (4) return to center springs. Also, if you are shopping on a showroom floor, open the tripod to its fullest height and see if it wobbles. The cost of lightweight tripods that meet all these requirements for use on DV production can easily reach over $1,000.

If you are operating on a used-car budget and don't necessarily need a tripod that makes smooth, fluid pans, look into still-camera tripods, new or used, on *www.ebay.com* or even in antique malls, where old camera equipment is often not thought of as particularly valuable and is priced accordingly. I purchased a high-quality miniature tripod with telescoping legs for $60 at an antique store. It was one of those tripods that compacts into a slim, 9-inch steel body and still can reach 4 feet in height (but is a bit wobbly at full extension). At any rate, it's convenient for use on high surfaces like a kitchen table or counters in restaurants, to get a little ten-inch lift for different compositions. Anyway, look around. You might luck out and find a top-quality tripod for under $50 that fits your needs and pocketbook.

Steadicams

If you have an extra $500–$1,000 to spend and are doing a lot of hand-held shooting, you may want to purchase a Steadicam for your video work. This piece of apparatus allows your camera to virtually float down a hallway, as you've seen many times on TV. Of course, a low-budget answer to making this kind of shot with DV is mimicking the movement of a floating camera with smooth hand-held shooting. Using a small camcorder like the Sony TRV10, I can produce surprisingly smooth walking and following-actor shots if I hold the camera body in my right hand (I wrap the over-the-shoulder strap around my wrist several times until the camera becomes an extension of my arm) and hold the fold-out screen with my left hand. This two-handed grip works well, even helping to get a level shot (see the photo of me using this technique while shooting *Bear Dance*, in Chapter 1).

For shooting steady shots from a hand-held position, give your arms time to adjust to the newly attached weight. That means the first few takes will probably not be acceptable. But after a few minutes of shooting you'll find your muscles firming up, helping to eradicate any jiggling. I try to add some spring to my arms, imagining and then implementing a bounciness that protects against sharp, sudden jerks that can wreck a good shot.

The Canon XL-1S, with its 3-CCD Pixel Shift Technology, three shooting modes
(Normal Movie, Digital Photo Mode, and the cinema-like Frame Movie Mode), 4-channel
digital audio, and interchangeable lens system, is often a first choice among DV feature
filmmakers. Check out their online owner's club *www.canondv.com/XL1owners/*
terms.htm for discounts on repairs, a hot line, and personal XL settings on file. (Courtesy
of Canon USA. The Canon logo is a trademark of Canon Inc. All rights reserved.)

Another hand-held shooting tactic is to move the camera as the actors move, becoming part of their impromptu dance. After a while you
can almost predict where they will walk next, when they will sit down,
and other moves they are considering. Of course, you can control their
movement with a direct voice command (removed later during editing). Tell them "Sit down" or "Go to the window and look out," or call
for whatever action is appropriate to the story you are telling. Just keep
the commands as brief as possible, so that the rhythm of the scene
isn't disturbed for more than a second or two.

Those who aren't confident about delivering suitable hand-held
shots will want to keep the camera on a sturdy tripod, and perhaps surf
the Web for the latest home-grown Steadicam-type appliances. I found
a site that helps DV moviemakers construct their own Steadicams,

cranes, and car mounts, at what seemed like affordable prices. Check out *www.dvcamerarigs.com* and see if one of their offerings can be of service to your feature-length DV project.

> **NOTE:** Any time you falter during hand-held shooting, make a lousy composition, or jerk the camera, you can call "Cut" and restart the camera from a new angle. This gives you the opportunity to design a hard cut for the edit. Just make sure that the actor repeats the last line of dialogue and the last action, to give you overlapping footage for your edit point. And make sure your exposures match for the shots you will assemble.

SOUND GEAR: MATCHING INPUTS TO YOUR DV CAMERA

When you're ready to buy a 3-CCD digital video camera (Mini-DV, DVD, or Pro-DVCAM), be sure to choose one with professional XLR outputs. Having these standard professional outlets ensures that you can record the highest fidelity (provided your microphones are equal in quality) through high-output cables, or over a wireless system connected to these outlets. If you are using a boom pole to record sound on location, with a sound person outfitted with a DAT mixer on the belt so that two channels of sound can be adjusted and recorded simultaneously, you'll want to shop for only those video cameras that offer XLR, like the Sony PD150, PD170, Canon's XL-1S, and the like.

Shooting Without the Pro XLR Outlets

On the cheaper side of the equation, even my 1-chip Sony TRV10 delivers CD-quality stereo sound from its Sony ECM-HS1 Electret Condenser microphone. Instead of depending on a full-time, on-location sound recordist, I can simply record video and sound myself, letting the fact that I'm on double-duty dictate on-the-set shooting limitations. Since I don't have a sound person to swing the mike between two people talking, I may instruct my actors to (1) not talk until they sense the camera pointed in their general direction, (2) wait for my

voice command before they speak, which means I have had time to angle the mike in their direction, or (3) repeat a line, so I can reshoot a
portion of the sequence. When I ask for a repeated line of dialogue, I
usually move my position and reframe the actor to set up a logical cut
in the sequence.

By going with the 1-chip Mini-DV camera for your first foray into
the life of making no-budget digital features, you can still expect CD-
quality sound to match your 500+-line-of-resolution images. It just
may take some time to understand the moviemaking process with regard to your DV camera. Here are some possible ways to control the
on-location shooting for the best sound:

1. Always wear earphones while shooting. You need to listen very carefully and at all times to the exact quality of sound and volume level being received by the camera. I recommend purchasing the kind of
earphones that lock over your ears and hang out behind your head,
over your hair. These earphones are less obtrusive than the over-the-
head variety and generally less conspicuous, which is often to your advantage when shooting in public places. You can purchase the kind of
Sony earphones I use (Sony MDR-G52) for under $20 at most record
stores (look carefully and you can see them covering my ears in the
photo of me shooting a tableful of Portuguese actors, page 37). If the
set is controlled and you have an extra $100 to spend, the Sony Profes-
sional MDR-7506 Dynamic Stereo headphones are a good buy for
editing use as well (the Sony specialty "digital video" headphones will
cost about double).

2. Set up your shot so that your microphone favors one actor's dialogue. If two people are speaking, set up your shot so that the camera
and mike are aimed at both parties at once (move them unnaturally
closer together if necessary; the camera usually makes people look far-
ther away from each other than they actually are). Test the level of
sound you are receiving by having actors talk together while you keep
the camera in standby/record mode. If both voices are clear, without
one dropping too far down in volume, you're set to go.

3. When shooting totally improvisational shots, simply stop the action when the sound becomes less than acceptable (the volume too low, etc.). Call a halt to the action midstream and reposition yourself for a cut that you can make later when you assemble the footage.

Think cuts. If an actor is talking to someone in the scene and suddenly turns his head away from you, you'll immediately hear a drop in volume over the earphones. The sound level is unacceptable. You need to halt the proceedings, so call out the word you like to use, like *Cut!* or *Stop!* The command *Freeze!* also works well, since the cut you're trying to design into the sequence can be perfectly matched to exactly where the actors were standing, their exact positions (even hand and head angles) frozen for restart after *Action!* You need to explain that "freeze" means exactly what it says: that they remain completely frozen in place while you set up. And don't feel rushed (but don't dawdle either!) as you temporarily subject actors to this physically demanding limbo. Make sure your camera is set to record, that you have your focus and exposure set and locked down, that you have the desired framing and a good, steady, hand-held grip or tripod mount before shooting recommences. Once you're recording, instruct the actors to repeat the head-turning motion (as in the previous take) when you call *Action!* In the editing room, you will find a well-planned edit awaits. By continuing to halt actors or nonactors midstream and build in cuts as you shoot (at least every time the sound volume falters or the image is unacceptable), you'll be adding a nice dynamic to your particular method and style of shooting.

Also recheck exposure as you go. Does it look and feel similar to what you saw before the cut? If the flesh tones are the same, the cut should work, even if the background values have shifted somewhat because of new camera placement. Of course, if you go from shooting against a darkened part of a room to a back-lit window, the difference will be too great, so spend however long it takes to create a usable jump cut for that situation. You may be able to patch an exposure mistake later with Final

Cut Pro or Express color correction filters or bring up volume during an NLE mix. (*Caution*: If the sound is much too low, a hiss of background ambiance will accompany increased levels.) Ultimately, it's best not to rely on anything but getting it right while shooting on the set.

Like any other part of the moviemaking process, if you pay close attention to consistency (in this case delivering good picture and sound quality on every shot), you'll find you can, in a sense, match what's delivered by high-end cameras. I'm not suggesting that mere technique will increase your 1-chip Mini-DV camera's resolution to the 700 or even 900 lines that the higher-end $4,000–$15,000 cameras supply. But you can definitely deliver great images and top-quality sound—certainly sufficient quality to make a presentable feature. By mastering your DV feature later to Digi-Beta, you can hold the highest digital quality you attained, then dub it to VHS/DVD. Or just strike individual DVD copies right off your Mac's Super Drive. If the story you are

The breakthrough Hi-Def JVC GR-HD1 Mini-DV camcorder (priced under $4,000) converts 720/30p digital HD and 480p progressive wide images into the 1080i high-definition standard for viewing on the latest HD wide-screen televisions. (Courtesy of JVC Americas Corp.)

telling is captivating, and the supporting shots and sounds have a consistent quality and style that's appropriate to the subject matter, you can produce a feature that has a chance for success with even the most basic and inexpensive DV camera.

LIGHTING FOR DV

I hope I'm not being too extreme when I say that *any* light will work for DV, but that's basically the case. Since you can see exactly what you are recording, you can either accept the results or decide to add an extra light source as you shoot. Have you tested your DV camera by shooting without lights to see the amazing amount of low light it picks up? My Sony TRV10 has surprising capabilities in this regard, including a Night Shot and slow shutter setting for shooting in the dark. Recall that we used this surveillance camera look (greenish, glowing images) for critical scenes in our UCSC Feature Workshop movie, *It's Not About the Shawerma*. By experimenting with my DV camera in low-light situations, I've found I can combine the Night Shot green and B&W mode settings to create a great new look of high-contrast, charcoal-like images. Even shooting in a darkened hotel room (creating scenes for the FW production of *Release the Head*), I could almost flare the light by turning up the exposure meter. In a sense, "lights" have become gratuitous with digital cameras (see more about the Dogme 95 style in a later section and in Chapter 6). Unless you want to replicate the exact feel of Hollywood-style set-based movies (as opposed to the gritty, sense-of-the-street/European-*Open-City*-style realism), shooting with available light will serve most indie concepts just fine.

A word about creative lighting. Since the effect of any lights used while shooting DV can be evaluated on the viewer or LCD fold-out monitor, why not experiment? Try using just a flashlight for night scenes (give an actor a good reason to be holding one). Or buy a cheap droplight at the hardware store, the kind you'd use to work under your car. How does that $15 single-bulb lighting work? Is that enough illumination for you? Does the minimal lighting improve your video image? Before answering that question for yourself, you need to be certain you are actively adjusting your onboard DV camera exposure settings (*don't* purchase a DV camera without this manual exposure adjustment), finding the best setting for the look you want from your footage. What other strange and effective lighting combinations can you imagine? (If you acquire Red Giant's Magic Bullet software [*www.toolfarm.com*, discussed in Chapter 7], you can apply more than a dozen different lighting presets during postproduction, either those meticulously matched to the chemical processing that labs use on Hollywood blockbusters or unique combinations you design yourself). The more unusual lights you choose (that precisely fit your characters and what they do in your story), the more special and original your movie will become.

If you find yourself shooting subjects in a darkened, low-light setting (as when videotaping a rock band in a club), first examine the shot's exposure while on automatic setting. Next switch to manual and play with the dial. If you can't get a satisfactory exposure, try adding one of the effects settings (like Night Shot, B&W, even Art if your camera offers that image-abstracting option). Then use autofocus to make sure you're capturing your subjects as sharply as intended, locking down with the manual setting after you've got your subjects properly framed. When you get the urge to frame from a different angle, click to autofocus again, move the camera, refocus on the subject from this new location, and reset to manual (keeping your exposure setting locked down as you change camera position). Repeating this procedure, you'll be sure the image won't be jerking subtly in and out of focus as the camera searches for the correct setting. In such low-light situations you'll need to trust the camera's automated functions to focus on what your eyes can't.

Minimal DV Lighting Package

If you absolutely feel that you need lighting equipment, start by purchasing a professional fold-up reflector (about $100), something you can use mostly outdoors to add more light on actors' faces in darkened situations (in shade, under a tree, in a cave). Just don't overdo it—your actor's face could end up with a newscaster glow, unnaturally hot and golden beyond reason.

Portable Lights for DV: The Arri 150/4 Light Kit

In the 2000 edition of *Feature Filmmaking at Used-Car Prices*, I sang the praises of the Arri 150/4 Fresnel lighting kit with handy shipping case (*www.arri.com*), which my son Morgan owned and used for several Feature Workshop productions—and I haven't changed my opinion. With its three lights (a 650 and two 300s), we covered every lighting need from Morgan's point of view. He even lugged them up to Port Townsend for our Dogme 95 shoot of *Chetzemoka's Curse*, just in case we changed our minds about going it without lights. (As it turned out, Morgan could have saved himself the trouble; the Arri shipping case stayed shut.)

For those of you who want the full lighting package for your production, filling the set with what appears to be the full professional array, here's a $400, six-day rental package that your cinematographer

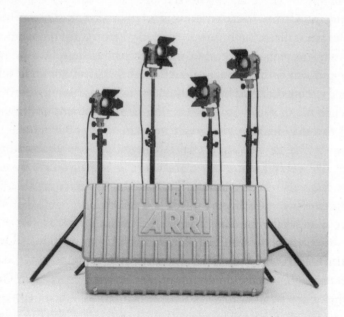

The Arri 150/4 Fresnel lighting kit (*www.arri.com*, priced at about $1,000) offers portability and dependability, and comes with a rugged shipping case. (Courtesy of Arriflex Corporation)

friends will enjoy using (what we rented for our Feature Workshop production entitled *Maisy's Garden*):

C-stands (five)
Flags (four solids, 24 by 24 by 36 inches)
Doorway dolly (with skateboard wheels)
Dolly track (three 8-foot sections, one 4-foot section, and a curved 6-foot section)
2K (mole Rochardson) Fresnel
Shiny boards (two 4-by-4-foot gold and silver sides, plus two stands)
Junior stands (two)
Nets (assortment of stop reducers)
Assortment of gels

Unless you've convinced your investors that Dogme 95 (no lights) is the way to go, your cinematographer may get the confirmation to reserve and have delivered to the location (by union driver) a moving van–sized truck filled to the brim with lighting equipment. But, really, doesn't it seem redundant to use lights with DV, given its low-light capabilities? Even my cheap Sony Mini-DV camera can pull light out of a dark corner of the room, and its Night Vision mode, especially when coupled with the B&W setting, can shoot clear, bright pictures in a nightclub setting.

THE SHOOTING SCHEDULE

So you have your equipment ready. Now it's time to get prepared for the shoot. Once you've told your actors and production helpers the exact day, time, and location at which you'll start shooting your feature, the Shooting Schedule comes into existence. Because you can't afford to jerk people around with changes to this schedule, you must be absolutely certain that you will stick to the first shooting date before you spread the word. You must honor this commitment above all else. It doesn't get much more serious (as far as artistic work goes) than this. So be extremely careful to take any and every consideration before planting the start date in other people's minds and on their calendars.

Of course, without any real funds for production or promise of high salaries that will keep people attached, you may find that the schedule has to change midstream. Perhaps you have to accommodate a main character's suddenly altered job schedule, or a change in location access might require a quick reshuffling. But for the time being, treat your schedule as if it's written in stone. The movie will begin principal photography on such and such a date.

In my experience, anything shorter than a week of sustained shooting for a feature will probably not deliver enough scenes and shots to your editing bay. The week-long commitment of moviemaking focus is important in ways that are not so readily apparent. That duration of at least seven working days helps you to completely shut out your normal real-life activities, as you stretch to create something new. You're going to be transforming yourself with this activity, turning everything around you into possible material for a movie. Even if you have a script that is completely rendered and unchangeable (in your mind, anyway), you will find that the energy of the shoot will make the normal priorities of life shift in ways you can't possibly anticipate. You need that week of unhindered effort to allow this inner mental and emotional activity to percolate. You need to give yourself this gift of artistic creation, so that the work can benefit from the *new* you.

The most precious gift your movie can give to others is the newness of ideas, insights, and observations that the audience can't receive any other way. The very best indie movies will supply new information vital to our becoming better, more fully functional human beings. You can't create shots, sounds, or story lines that deliver this amazing experience unless you are open to the magic on the movie set.

As the first day of the shoot looms, you have to have a production board or notepad on which you have written down all the needs, met and unmet, so you can see them at a glance. If you want to use the suggestion I've made in my earlier filmmaking books, tape 4-by-6-inch index cards together for a wall calendar, seven across and five down; this gives you more than enough space for listing all the production needs that arise during the last month of preproduction. On the large cards, one for each day, you can write down notes with pertinent names, places, phone numbers you need to remember, highlighting in red, yellow, and blue certain important items you particularly want to keep in mind as the countdown continues. Somewhere on your "production board" you should have the following items in order to keep your upcoming shoot properly organized:

1. *Contracts and Releases.* Have you made out a profit-sharing contract (see Appendix B for my Feature Workshops gross collaborative contracts)? It takes time to determine the standards of fairness in this regard. If you're paying people nothing or very little, you'd better protect your friendships by giving good shares away to those who help you realize your dream. At my Feature Workshops, I've continued to design contracts with gross profit point sharing, so that, if any sales occur, everyone will see money at the same time. Shared revenue is distributed to fellow writers, directors, and actors after the loans I've made to the production are paid back. My expenses usually include a final sound mix, mastering the movie to Digi-Beta to obtain the full digital quality of sound and picture.

My cinematographer/coproducer (my son Morgan on many of the FW-produced features) and I receive the same cut as any of the participants paying a fee to join us. I have to respect someone's committing time and funds to be a collaborator, and, regardless of their actual creative contribution, they have at least provided an investment toward our goal of making the best feature we can in the allotted time of ten days. So, for example, when ten people join up, as they did for *Someone Like Me,** Morgan, myself, and collaborators each receive about 7 points of the 85 percent writer/director's share. (The remaining 15 percent is comprised of the 5 percent share for operating costs for my Feature Workshops and the 10 percent held for getting the movie blown up to 35mm film.)

---

*A 56-minute documentary, *Cinovation,* by Alan Richter and Kate Taylor, covered the shoot, including interviews with myself, collaborators, cast, and crew.

When it is all your money, your equipment, your script, and your editing bay, you can be more protective of your lion's share, perhaps retaining half of the money (a traditional producer's share), while giving helpers and actors a respectable payment if something big happens (the Sundance Grand prize, a New York run, a Miramax roll-out to selected theaters).

Think about the contract in real money terms. If your movie earns a million dollars, are you ready to give half of that away if you've allotted 50 percent of your movie to cast and crew? Then you'll pay tax on the windfall earnings (another 25 percent or more carved away), in addition to lawyer's fees and related expenses. Suddenly your millionaire status shrivels to a few hundred thousand dollars. So protect yourself as well as your moviemaking compatriots. If one of my workshop features hits a million-dollar payday, I'll collect my $70,000—one-tenth share of 85 percent minus tax, etc., and be happy to clear up some personal debt and get a new computer!

2. Actors. Are your performers ready? Do they have the information they need to show up at the selected location? Do you have their cell phone numbers and e-mail addresses? Are you sure that they have the latest rendition of your script and have memorized the material? Or are they ready to jump into the unknown world of high-speed improvisation, where they will help you create a movie with their own dialogue and ideas, everything happening on the spur of the moment? Are they giving off excited, positive energy about the shoot? Call them a few times in the last week to keep them informed about the final schedule and in touch with your own positive energy.

I haven't mentioned rehearsals, but certainly you can include them in the preproduction schedule leading up to the shoot. You'll want to maintain a fine balance between having actors and nonactors ready with memorized dialogue and keeping the performances fresh. While I personally tend toward few or no rehearsals, you might like everything a lot more tied down. It will take a few feature shoots to determine what's best for your particular vision of moviemaking.

And get your Actor's Releases signed (see Appendix D). If actors or nonactors don't fill out release forms, signing and dating them, you can't put those individuals in your movie. If you do, no one will ever distribute the work, and you could be sued to remove that portion of the movie. Your profit points and everybody else's will be completely worthless.

3. *Equipment: Camera, Sound, Lights.* Regardless of whether you purchase a DV camera, rent one, or hire a cinematographer who owns one, you need to keep up with the costs, pickup times, and parameters of how the camera operates. Don't use a camera unless it offers *fully manual controls* for focus, exposure and white balance settings, CD-quality sound recording ability, and FireWire connection to a computer for editing. Be fully informed about the camera you intend to use.

If you are spending extra money for a boom pole sound recording rig or hiring a sound operator with this equipment, make sure the sound is under control. Will you need additional rental items such as wireless mikes, cables, or a mixer? When and where do you pick them up? Write the details down on a card at your wall calendar.

Set up a time with the lighting and grip company for pickup and delivery of your lighting package. Do you have enough transportation capabilities for all the equipment you've reserved? You will need cars with large enough overhead racks to handle C-stands and perhaps dolly tracks (on our *Maisy's Garden* shoot it took one car's roof for just the dolly tracks). Write all this information down on your thirty-five–day 4-by-6-inch note card wall calendar, and cross off completed tasks. I realize that many of you will use the modern equivalent of my note card wall (a Palm Pilot or other electronic notepad), and this is certainly an OK way to go. It's just that the large size of the note card calendar helps to show that the moviemaking process is *top priority* and that you're allowing it to totally take over your life. Only with your complete commitment and focus can your movie be the excellent final product you are working so hard to create. If you fail to shoot a connecting shot (a cutaway of, say, a person grabbing a water glass), then your scene may not cut together properly. Without suitable organizational skills you may miss a vital stitch of the complex moviemaking quilt you are constructing. (Were they holding the glass in the same hand, as in the previous master shot?)

Every moviemaking detail—from the believability of actors and nonactors to the framing of shots, from the cohesiveness of the story to the quality of sound—will need to be scrutinized before the shoot, and well-managed when you direct. While you may entrust some of these details to others, most likely you'll carry the full burden as you shoot and pay for any transgressions later in the editing room. If you find that your hand is shaking as you tweak the entries on a Palm Pilot, then go for the big note card calendar and enjoy marking a big X through the items you accomplish—you'll really feel in control!

4. *Stock: Mini-DV/DVCAM Cassettes or DVD-R/RW Disks.* Have you ordered enough DV cassettes or DVD disks? Are ten 60-minute Mini-DV cassettes (ten hours) enough tape stock? Is there a nearby store where you can buy more if you run out—or get DVD-R one-time disks or a rewritable DVD-RW, which won't supply a backup of scenes shot, but certainly can deliver images for capture each time you record over it? Should you get a few 80-minute Mini-DV cassettes (useful for scenes with exceptionally long action sequences with no break for changing cassettes midstream)? Write "GET 80-MIN. DV CASSETTES" (or "GET DVD-RW") in large, black, bold Sharpie-type letters, and later cross out the reminder on your wall calendar when the goods are on hand (use a thin line when you cross out something, so you can still read the message). This should help you gain confidence when, with a glance at the board, you can see which items have been taken care of.

5. *Locations.* Have you talked with the legal owners or guardians of property on which you plan to shoot and obtained their signatures on a Location Release (see Appendix E)? This release is a good tool for your peace of mind, since it states in clear language that you're going to be taking up space on a particular day (or run of days) and that you have the legal right to do so. Pay a small fee of $50 to make the owner happy so that you have a locked-down location. You will absolutely need to get this firmed up if your entire movie or script is centered on a key location where all the action takes place. You certainly don't want to feel insecure about your right to be in a place when you shoot (all that angst in your head), so get this one thing under control as soon as possible. If you get turned down by a landlord who refuses to give you the right to shoot on his or her premises, then just figure that's meant to be and find yourself a better spot to make some great shots. Use every "bad" response as an opportunity to make your movie better.

I must admit that I have gone to locations after a shoot, to solidify the legal aspect of a movie that I thought might be good enough to see distribution or TV sales. Believe me, it's not fun to be that vulnerable, especially when you think you need all the main locations signed off. Fortunately, on our *Chetzemoka's Curse* (Dogme No. 10) hometown shoot (where I live, Port Townsend, Washington), I was able to get Location Releases from everybody (three in this case) after the fact. Right up to the first day of principal photography I was just not emotionally prepared to risk losing the hotel room ambiance that I felt was vital to the characters and scenes I had in mind. So we just went ahead, shot for four days, edited the next six, and got our movie entirely completed in a week-and-a-half (the standard crash course production schedule for my Feature Workshops movies, *www.lightvideo.com/workshop.aspx*). It worked out; people were nice enough to sign the legal forms after the fact. But it's definitely to your advantage to be tougher and more vigilant than I was that time.

6. Props. If you aren't shooting by Dogme 95 rules, which forbid the importing of props to the location (see "The Dogme 95 Vow of Chastity," Chapter 6), consider what items will add flair to your central concept or ideas. Sometimes I've found that a special prop can unlock new ideas, even save a production from getting bogged down. In the improvisational style in which I usually work, especially at workshops, I'll often have a few special props available in a bag somewhere on the set. A classic example of letting a prop propagate scenes was during the 1998 production of the Feature Workshops DV feature *Loneliness Is Soul*. The story of the prop actually begins with my standing around at a garage sale with my filmmaking friend Bill Farley (*www.farleyfilm.com*). His feature *Of Men and Angels* screened at the Sundance Film Festival's Dramatic Competition, the same year as my *Morgan's Cake*. As I stared at a huge dragon head mask lying in the driveway of the sale, Bill approached me and said emphatically, "You have to buy that! You're making a movie!" The price tag was $25, which seemed like a lot of money for that pile of greenish rubber, large enough to enclose someone's head and then some. I was hesitant, but Bill wouldn't hear of it. "I'll give you the money!" he proclaimed shoving bills in my direction. Bill's advice had served me well in the past, so I reached down and grabbed the mask (it was a heavy, well-made piece of professional costuming), got out my own money, paid, and threw it in the back of Bill's car as we drove off to other sales. "Good," said Bill. "You're going to need it."

About three days into the Feature Workshops shoot, ten to twelve people were milling around lead actor Yahn Soon's apartment. Cables lay all over the place, Morgan's camera sat on its tripod, and the idea well ran dry. Maybe I was the only one who realized things were stalled, but it was nerve-wracking. "What to shoot next" is always the mantra on the set of a movie based on improvisations, created from nothing. We had been doing well—incredibly well, in fact—but what now?

Staring at the messy floor, I suddenly noticed the dragon mask and pulled it out from under a grocery bag of pretzels and chips. It still didn't look like much, but it was all I had and I clung to it like to a life preserver at sea. I handed it to one of our writer/director/actor participants, Alexander Marchand, and he immediately placed it over his head. Speaking from inside he sounded far off, as if in a cave. He growled and I laughed. Something worked there! Ideas flowed again. In the story, Alexander's character was a kook who left little gifts on the doorstep of the woman character's home. We now shot Alexander wearing the mask while sitting on the stairs leading up to the apartment. We figured out that the landlord (played by another Feature

Workshops writer/director, Hal Croasman) should appear and accost the dragon-headed stranger, first mistaking him for the Yahn character, then confronting him and finally ordering him off the property.

Later, we shot Alexander, masked, on Telegraph Avenue in Berkeley, playing a hand organ (a nice musical prop!) while holding a sign that said, "Looking for Tracy" (a tie-in from his real-life story, which we'd shot earlier). Integrating our dragon-headed character with the other Berkeley street people resulted in pretty funny footage (several engaged Alexander in conversations, which we caught on DV). To connect the street scene to our ever evolving story, we designed a conversation between Yahn and "the dragon" on Telegraph. Yahn played it so sweetly and realistically; he asked a few questions, such as "Who's Tracy?" and the answers echoed out from inside the rubber headpiece. Somehow Alexander's character even succeeded at bringing pathos to the mask, its persona of grisly rubber teeth and off-putting, greenish sheen eventually becoming an essential element in our patchwork plot. (Thank you, Bill!) So before you shoot, hit a few garage sales and buy some of those interesting items you think you have no use for. One of them may provide just the charm you need if the moviemaking gets stuck.

7. _Food, Provisions, and Accommodations._ There's no getting around the fact that, if you can't feed your cast and crew members, you're not going to have a very happy set. And if these people are giving their precious time to help you make a movie, then you should provide the meals. To be specific, when you meet with your lead actor or cinematographer for breakfast, it's your credit card, cash, or check that pays the $10–$20 for both your eggs, coffee, orange juice, and whatever they order. If you arrange to have some of your vital people meet you at 7:30 A.M. at a certain restaurant, the reward you need to give them for their getting up early and driving there (perhaps even supplying transportation for you and additional people to the set) is a good hot meal. And if they order the most expensive thing on the breakfast menu, you need to realize that if they're working on your project for deferred salary or a very small per diem ($20–$50 a day), you're still getting the deal of a lifetime. Your old friends and the new pals you'll make during the shoot are helping bring your dream to life. So enjoy the breakfast! You'll be paying for lunch and a few $100 dinners too while the credit card(s) holds up. Great Chinese food for eleven people should come in around $110. Japanese would be—well, more! If you've spent only $700 on food by the end of an eight-day shoot with, say, five to seven key personnel (yourself, a cinematographer and assistant/gaffer, the location sound person, the actors), then I'd say you're doing very well.

Craft services and catering also need to be attended to because any shoot, no matter how tiny, will need a selection of munchies and drinks on hand. At least have the basics—sandwich-making materials (bread, peanut butter, jelly, cold cuts, cheese), chips, cookies, water, soft drinks, coffee, tea, juices—foodstuffs that will keep your people's blood sugar up, especially during those boring breaks between setups or just in off moments. People need sustenance during a shoot, and you need to provide it. If you have a Costco card this is when the yearly fee can be earned back and more. Fill up that cart with the goodies that will keep the human element of your shoot adequately fueled.

If you're going the professional catering route or, more affordably, hiring a friend who likes to prepare satisfying vegetarian and/or meat dishes, then you'll have a first-class shoot on your hands. I spent more than $4,000 to cater my *American Orpheus* shoot (a lot of money, but fortunately I had a few investors helping out), supplying breakfast, lunch, and dinner to twelve or more people for ten days. That's more than 360 servings for around $10 per person per plate. And it was the best investment I ever made. Imagine how it felt when the caterers suddenly arrived at the set (my house) with trays of delicious offerings. It was like having an unseen, mother-like provider, who kept serving up this lovely food just when we all needed it. The dependable arrival of prepared meals seemed to signal that this moviemaking enterprise was correct, that I was doing something right. Just for the emotional payoff, I'd say that catering is the way to go. And in the end, if you are working off a substantial budget for a complex DV feature, you'll ultimately save money on your food budget by going this route. Most of us can't usually afford to have our own chef to serve an assortment of fresh meat and vegetarian fare (local produce, non-hormone chicken, line-caught fish, etc.), so why not give yourself, your cast, and your crew this wonderful high of being provided for in style while you have the excuse of feeding your dream.

Regarding the cost of lodging, supplying shelter for cast and crew on a moviemaking expedition can quickly skyrocket your budget if you're anywhere other than the most remote areas where the cost of a room is still $40 per night. Paying a total of $480 for three rooms (with bath) to stay and shoot somewhere special for four days seems like a reasonable trade-off. That's about what we paid when we shot on two separate occasions at Marta Becket's ghost town of Death Valley Junction, lodging at her old Amargosa Hotel while we shot *Welcome to Serendipity* in 1998 and *My Bounty Hunter* in 2001. In my town of Port Townsend, we shot *Release the Head* with collaborator John Barnum, who stayed at the Waterfront Hotel for ten days for around $400. So perhaps one of your limitations for doing a location shoot should be locating a picturesque setting that is off the grid enough to charge pre-2000 prices.

NOTE: When I was planning my eight-day desert production of *Emerald Cities* in 1979, my friend and fellow moviemaker Bill Kimberlin told me I needed to supply hotel or motel rooms for cast and crew or I'd endanger the shoot. He felt that people who were giving everything they had—their heart and soul—to the moviemaking process needed at least a roof over their heads and a hot shower. I knew they had showers at the local campgrounds, but I had to agree with Bill. And if a soon-to-be lead actor you've chosen to head up the cast makes $200 a week (after taxes) at a minimum wage job, it's up to you to be savvy enough to offer a $250 salary for the week of shooting. Don't be too cheap to treat people better than they expect when they are helping you on your moviemaking quest.

8. *Transportation.* Even when you make a movie around your home town, you can figure on filling up a few gas tanks (maybe spending less than $100) as part of your budget. If your friend offers to pick up actors and other crew members, hand him a $20, even if he only uses half a tank. If it's your movie, where you're playing producer as well as writer/director, you'll need to take care of the bare essentials, or you'll be inviting hurt feelings, an erosion of positive energy, and perhaps even the total collapse of your production.

On a grander scale, for an outing to an exotic location such as Death Valley (one of my favorite haunts for moviemaking), you'll need plane tickets into Las Vegas (get a special gambling junket ticket if you can) and probably a night at one of the cheap hotels on the strip for under $50. For the maximum discount if you're booking a block of rooms, call several months ahead and ask for the corporate rate or AAA discount. (I hope I don't have to tell you to keep those production funds away from the slot machines or at least to set a maximum amount you'll let yourself lose.) Of course, you can just head out to the desert or some remote place in a rental car ($200–$400 for a week, including insurance), with another $100 for gas. You can either make a motel reservation or take your chances finding a cheap place along the road where some desert stories and desert rats await to help you form your free-flowing DV desert narrative adventure! While not trying to push my desert shooting preference down anybody's throat, I will add that jumping into remote areas for a DV moviemaking adventure can be affordable, especially when using Las Vegas as a travel hub. Moviemakers Barry Green and Karen Gloyd of Fiercely Independent Films (*http://softscreen.us*), have relied on the amenities of that fast growing city to start an independent movie studio (check with them for soundstage and DV gear rates), as well as launching the Independent Cinema Expo (ICE) there in 2003.

Of course, if you have your moviemaking van up and running (see Chapter 10), you can forget the motel/hotel expenses, take your time pursuing the various locations of your movie, while your actors sit at the table behind the driver playing cribbage. If not behind the wheel yourself, you're on your G4/5 laptop writing new scenes from what the actors have been talking about for the last half-hour (or editing yesterday's footage). At any rate, however you pull off the on-location shoot, make sure to budget for at least the gas in your buddy's car.

9. Incidentals. Incidentals are what you buy when you stop in a minimart while you're filling up your gas tank. And incidentals aren't cheap. Suddenly you have to part with another $50 bill for miscellaneous necessities: water bottles for everybody, candy, a few sandwiches, a couple of donuts, soft drinks. (Now we're up to $75!) You know you've become victim of trivial incidentals when you suddenly have dropped a couple hundred dollars and don't know how those fifties disappeared. You're probably better off hitting a Payless or, better yet, a Costco, where an entire twenty-four-bottle box of water bottles will cost under $10.

With a little extra planning (Costco) you can save more than a hundred dollars. That money could be applied later to getting a new filter pack from Joe (*www.joesfilters.com*) that will artistically elevate the final cut (see Chapter 7). If you're trying to make your DV movie on a shoestring, you need to be just as creative about incidentals as you'll be with your concept, script, casting, shooting, and final assembly.

While I'm not going to lump the purchase of Mini-DV, DVD, or DVCAM stock into the incidentals budget, there will undoubtedly be other unavoidable related costs: batteries for the radio mikes, the extra cell phone fee for having a free roaming ability when you're in remote places, rentals (a better microphone, lights, or light stands), or "practical" lightbulbs (that screw into normal lights but supply extra illumination). And you may want to have a 4-by-4-foot piece of solid black felt, plus black gaffer's tape, which can be used to blacken or null out a piece of furniture or reflective area when you shoot. If you push-pin it against a wall you'll have an ample backdrop to isolate a talking head for narrating or whatever (just a thought). You never know when a nice, dense, black piece of cloth will come in handy on a shoot.

In the old days of shooting film (and if that's what you're still doing, good luck!), there was a good long list of incidentals for 16mm.

Now, with the immediacy and portability of the DV camera, and no need for orange sticks to clean out the film gate or a pressurized air canister to blow out the film dust debris, the costs of incidentals for DV is almost nil (especially when shooting the no-lights Dogme 95 style; see Chapter 6). All you need is a lens cloth (the kind you can often get for free in professional camera stores), your battery charger, and the pile of Mini-DV/DVCAM tapes or DVD disks you bought in bulk at one of the many discount houses on the Internet.

10. *Last-Minute Agenda: Credit Card Preparation, Disabling E-Mail, Putting Your Real Life on Hold.* While this point is somewhat self-explanatory, let's just add that you don't want to be dealing with the everyday burden of answering all those e-mails (deleting all the junk mail) while you're shooting. But you might want to hear from an actor who decided to communicate with you in this way. What I recommend is that you open a new e-mail account just for your shoot.

At any rate, if you feel ready, it's time now to prep the actors as you head into production!

4
DIRECTING ACTORS

For the DV features I've been creating (see Chapter 1), as should be very apparent, I rely tremendously on my actors. In fact, with my guidance, the actors make up a great deal of the dialogue, alter and create the story lines, and interact with people and places to generate drama through new ideas (which I pick up on to extend the narrative of the movie-in-progress). In short, my actors are everything. So I love them, treat them as well as I possibly can, feed them well, and share major chunks of profit points, especially since I'm pretty much going to take over their lives for the week and a half of solid moviemaking it often takes to create a feature-length work. Just thinking about using other humans to make one's art brings up a lot of questions. While I may not have all the answers you need, I'll try to address some of the obvious concerns.

How do you get actors to say their lines truthfully and stay in the character you wrote or imagined for your story? Well, the first thing you do is cast the part correctly. If you go the traditional route, you actually send out an audition call for actors by placing an ad in *Backstage* magazine (*www.backstage.com*), and then evaluate the ever growing pile of headshots that flood into your P.O. box or e-mail (looking them over with your coproducer/camera person/significant other). You'll quickly understand that no matter how many people might question your decision to make your movie, a whole lot of people out there are glad you're doing it. Maybe your ego will even take a big leap from there. You might begin to think that your project is pretty awesome, simply because all these actors are begging for a part based only on what you wrote in the short ad ("indie production wants . . ."). Well, maybe that's true. But how does it really feel to have all that human resource at your disposal? And what will you become, as a person, at the end of the selection process, having rejected two hundred hopefuls for every one you accept? Is playing god good for the soul? Perhaps I'm too sensitive to auditions because I made a movie about one (see *1988— The Remake*). I'll add that almost everyone who tried out got the part, since the auditions *were* the movie, which was about the struggle to get noticed by moviemakers, the desperation to become something other than "undiscovered."

At any rate, I'll throw a challenge out there. I believe I could make an amazing feature with any ten people you reject. In fact, pick the "worst" ten actors you interview, e-mail me at *lightvideo@aol.com*, and together we'll make the most amazing movie you, I, or anyone else has ever seen. Yes, perhaps I'm straying from my point, which is that good acting is a state of mind. Only the very, very best actors can deliver a performance that is completely real and honest—completely down to earth—while reciting scripted dialogue. I tend to select fascinating people to act in my movies, people who are usually part of the local pool of talent (a few back fences away, friends of friends, acquaintances) and let the movie flow in their direction. If they're willing to jump into my movie without a script (or even premise, see Chapter 1), then the final result is a celebration of their innate intelligence paired with my moviemaking inventiveness.

What you're after is a cast of humans who are ready to give their all, heart and soul, to tell your story. Or, in the case of my DV improv moviemaking, they must be ready to explore, jumping into an adventure with no (as yet) known boundaries or final destination. You may need to coach and rehearse your actors, supplying them with brilliant dialogue, while I will need to listen carefully to what mine have to say and encourage them to help me create characters akin to themselves, who can express their most deep-seated truths. In both instances, we need to "control" our actors. Let's call that control "direction."

DIRECTING ACTORS WITH A HAND-HELD CAMERA

If you go the most spontaneous DV route and shoot the movie yourself with a Mini-DV, DVCAM, or DVD camera gripped in your hand (performing the role of on-location sound person as well, either by hooking them up with lavalier mikes or by recording sound using an onboard mike), the scene making will boil down to just you and your actors. There will be basically no crew—only you. Imagine how this process compares to big Hollywood shoots where the actors perform their intimate alone-in-a-room scenes in front of a crew that can number more than a hundred. In my case, they will actually be alone in a room with just me and the unimposing little DV camera. So, from the start, their performance will be different. They won't be manipulated by the energy of so many onlookers. Maybe J-Lo's ego can handle (even feed on) that sized crew, but I think that most other earthlings, or at least shy people, would be thrown off by that kind of public yet private experience.

As I've explained previously, the way you dance around actors while shooting with a DV camera will affect their performance. If you've ever watched documentaries on Hollywood movies being shot, you'll see that those directors often monitor takes by wearing earphones. You'll also want to be wearing earphones so that you can clearly hear the dialogue being recorded and determine if a shot is correctly acted or not. The small nuances that separate truthful dialogue from false words must be detected by the director, and earphones can help you evaluate each performance. If you hear a false note, call a cut or pause and have the actor or nonactor repeat the lines. Of course, you'll take that reshoot opportunity to check focus and reexamine the exposure, making sure it matches the previous shots (i.e., not too light or too dark). And if you have arrived at a new idea of what they should say or a new direction that the action should take, you can explain that now. Since the process of shooting a free-flowing feature on DV is building ideas upon ideas, you'll regard this temporary halting of the scene as a *good* thing, something positive, a chance to regroup and move the ever evolving concepts further along.

If you shoot with a tripod, with some distance between the camera and actors, you'll need either an on-location sound recordist (with boom pole and mike) or a radio mike/lavalier microphone attached to the lapel of one actor (with the sender unit hidden under the shirt). If you have only one sound input, you'll need to direct your actors to stand close enough together that you can successfully record two or more people at the same time off the one actor's lavalier microphone. This is the kind of making-do you'll need as you delve deeper into your moviemaking process. Either that, or head out and purchase a more expensive camera, something that can handle two XLR cables (two lavaliers, or a lavalier and a second sound source). Making movies (doing art) is problem solving. If you want #2 actor's dialogue to be picked up as clearly as #1 actor's, then move them together as close as possible to the hidden microphone (they don't have to be hugging!); you'll know when they're close enough by what you hear in your earphones.

So the technical needs of shooting with inexpensive DV equipment makes moviemakers adapt their direction of the actors to sometimes solve a sound problem. Your direction, in this case, is to tell the actors to "please stand closer together, so you both can be recorded on one mike." Perhaps the entire movie you make will require such intermingling between the actors, just for the sake of sound recording methodology. Hand-held shooting may be a factor in creating a special intimacy of close-up shots, since you need to be fairly close to the actors to record their dialogue correctly with a standard, top-mounted microphone. You'll be in their faces, and that will add a distinct dimension to your storytelling.

STANDARD DIRECTING TECHNIQUES

Making actors deliver a great performance, especially when they aren't trained actors to begin with, may be too high a mountain to climb for DV moviemakers who are already doing everything themselves. But if you can keep them on course, you can get your story told. Am I saying bad acting is OK? No, I'm just saying that you need to work effectively with what you have. If your friend Dickie isn't delivering the kind of believable performance you think you need, then reduce his part, maybe halt his dialogue, and present his character in some other fashion. ("He likes to take notes," another character might have said about him in a previous scene. So, we get to read what Dickie is thinking by peering over his shoulder as he writes, and the story moves forward without being damaged by his marginal acting.) I know I'm still dealing with "directing" as if it were simply a technical issue to navigate around, something that you need to protect yourself from, but frankly, when you're shooting DV (even film on an indie set), this may be the best advice I can give.

David Mamet, in his fine book *On Directing Film*, talks about direction with regard to moving a story along with juxtaposed cuts, while the actors follow orders from purely an action standpoint (go there, touch the door knob, open the door). In his book he deals with what

Rick Schmidt, center, directs a scene from his 1992 feature, *American Orpheus*, explaining the intended flow of improvisational dialogue between actors Jan Burr and lead Jody Esther. (Photo by Julie Schachter)

keeps a movie interesting and watchable: If you don't know where it's leading you'll be curious to find out! Mamet is a proponent of the belief that the more you leave out, the better the movie becomes. The less you follow the actors around (with a DV camera) and the more you concentrate on the cuts and juxtapositions, the better the end result. So less is more. He recommends stripping everything ornamental from the movie—removing the narration and the descriptive—and what remains is story. Mamet says, "The story is the essential progression of incidents that occur to the hero in pursuit of his one goal." In Mamet's world everything centers around a hero, what he or she wants, the obstacles in his or her path, and what happens if the hero doesn't achieve the goal. To immerse yourself in Mamet's book, including the transcript of his lecture at Columbia University, is to absorb some tough-minded thinking on a variety of moviemaking issues, not least of which is that actors need to do more than act.

Another excellent book to check out is Judith Weston's *Directing Actors*, which focuses on communication between actors and their directors. Sometimes it comes down to using the wrong words when trying to nudge a performance that needs improving. If you ask your actors to try harder (add drama, get sadder, etc.), they may just tighten up and become even more artificial. So what are the proper commands to correct a faltering performance? Go back to Mamet's core advice: Have actors simply *do* the action and forget acting. Weston builds on this and has some well selected quotes from actors to elucidate. It is reported that Marlon Brando once said, "Just because they say 'action' doesn't mean we have to do anything." Weston cites an example of Dennis Hopper worrying about Robert Duvall's performance when he directed *Colors*. Even as experienced an actor as Hopper couldn't detect that Duvall was doing anything to act his part. Duvall's performance seemed too minimal and even boring while it took place on the set. But once in the editing room, Hopper realized that the performance was there—and solid! This story seems to make a good case for separating the jobs of directing and shooting a movie. Not everyone can handle the complexities of controlling performances while also framing shots (anticipating needed cut points) and controlling the quality of images and sound. But if you want the ultimate control over your DV, you'll have to give this shooting-while-directing effort a try.

Weston also cites "not listening" as another epidemic-sized problem that often occurs between actors. This is not a problem in the realm of improvisation, where actors must listen because they have no idea what will be said next. Weston says that when actors don't listen to each other, aren't interacting in a natural way, they affect the flow of dialogue, destroy believability, wreck the pace, and ultimately render the shots unusable. Weston helps you, as a prospective director, become more sensitized to detecting your actors' level of concentration, though she notes just how difficult it is to spot this kind of lag in focus during a shoot. Weston recommends remaining as relaxed as possible while directing, so that you can sense any tiny blip on the radar.

One of the many revelations Weston offers in her book is that the director who only watches a video monitor probably won't be able to detect whether the actors are listening to each other. She recommends that the director stand right next to the camera and watch their "naked faces." I found this advice very interesting. How can Weston's advice be applied to a videographer who is shooting a feature on DV? Will a DV moviemaker be able to spot bad acting if he or she shoots and directs at the same time? The solution may be shooting an hour of DV cassette at a time, then watching it on a monitor or onboard LED screen of the camera, to determine if what is recorded will be of sufficient quality with regard to both acting and cinematography. If not, you'll of course need to reshoot.

Both these books (*On Directing Film* and *Directing Actors*) offer a great deal more instruction and inspiration than I can impart here, and they should be at the top of your must-have book list. Go immediately to *www.amazon.com* and place your order!

FULL-PARTNER ACTORS

Ultimately, I feel it's the DV moviemaker who must *think* the story down the tracks, with the actors hanging on, trying to keep up with the new twists and turns. If the moviemaker detects a major flaw in an actor's solidity of purpose and commitment to the project, then the actor should be gently told he or she is being replaced. In this regard, both you (the writer/director) and the actors must serve the story and the storytelling process and make room for its success. If you are shooting a full-out improvisational feature, it's a given that the actors *are* listening—that they're totally focused, turned on, and fully in the moment—because they're using their own intelligence to create dialogue, as well as offering plot and story concepts. If you have actors of this caliber, then for heaven's sake write them into your contract as full partners earning a solid chunk of the gross profit points, representing hoped-for profits from the indie venture.

SHOOTING FOR CUTS AND CONTINUITY

As director, it is critical that you pay tremendous attention to planning cuts, so that the separate pieces of DV you record will fit together when editing commences. If you are shooting one-to-one (i.e., shooting a shot or scene and moving on), then *everything* you shoot must connect later when you assemble your story. If there isn't a viable cut from one shot to another, you will have to work doubly hard to make the movie flow through that botched transition. Correctly designing cuts as you shoot is an art that takes practice and experience, but, if you are a cautious sort of person, you can at least wonder after each shot if you are covering yourself (see "Remembering to Shoot Cutaways" in this chapter).

Either as an "all-seeing" director or with the help of a continuity person, you must be aware of what people are wearing or not wearing as the scenes are shot and the story progresses. That way you aren't faced with the impossibility of cutting from a man wearing a hat to the same person hatless in a continuing sequence. (Where did that derby go?) This is another good reason to leave the laptop at home (let the production manager carry one around instead). Your senses must be finely tuned at all times while shooting a feature, alert to all those seemingly insignificant details that, if overlooked, can cause you great trouble later in the editing room.

DIRECTING WITH THE FREEZE TECHNIQUE

When you are directing an actor, part of your control will come from how you frame the camera and keep it focused, with the exposure properly set and good sound levels maintained. Actors' performances will also be affected when you call "freeze." They must hold their positions while you reframe your shot from another angle and recite back to them some of the dialogue they've just spoken (for the overlap so you can make that built-in cut). You'll find you quickly become involved in a moviemaking dance that taxes your memory. Either you'll know exactly where the actors will move (i.e., have the shot blocked out) and exactly what dialogue will be spoken (i.e., scripted), or you'll know nothing, neither what they'll say or where they'll move. You may give them the gist of the improvised scene, let them know the parameters of what they need to accomplish, but when you start rolling they might end up doing cartwheels through the hotel's lobby of their own volition, bringing strange and unexpected expressions of their own to bear on the open-ended process. So you, as the moviemaker, must continually be adjusting to the action, sometimes playing catch-up. (Walk around to the front and have them take that spin again!) You are controlling the movie and the performances—"directing"—by how you shoot and how thoroughly you overlap the actions for cut point protection.

Whether you call out the word "cut" or just pause midshot, lowering your DV camera to readjust your microphone or allowing the boom person to get an improved audio recording angle with the mike, you are the final arbiter of quality. If you control actors, telling them exactly what to do (giving voice commands from behind the camera if you're shooting) and stopping recording every time you spot a false moment, then that's "direction." Or if you stop after bad shots (clumsy camera moves, bad focus, low-light conditions, poor sound), then that is also part of being a director. If you continue to impose a high level of quality on a shoot, the end result should equal the best job you could possibly do at this stage in your moviemaking career.

Some people will argue that shooting the camera (being your own director of photography), thinking and planning the cuts as you create complete sequences, and monitoring the actors' performances are too much for any one person to do. They'll suggest you delegate the various jobs (hire a cinematographer, continuity expert, etc.) and devote yourself to that one aspect of moviemaking where your "true talent" lies. Well, in the so-called real world of Hollywood moviemaking, that might be an option. But in the smaller scope of DV moviemaking you really need to try operating that camera yourself, finding your own way of seeing. And as you frame reality for your shots, the exercise of "thinking cuts" will help tighten the entire moviemaking process. Out of this mix will come your unique style. When you finally create a solid work, people will call you a "good director," little realizing that you had to be a great shooter, clever sound recordist, great editor, and a creative writer/improviser, not to mention an adequate director of the actors (great casting) to pull off your directorial debut.

REMEMBERING TO SHOOT CUTAWAYS

Without wasting much DV stock, you can take the opportunity after each recorded sequence to protect your master cuts with *cutaways*, those little pieces of footage that are tightly framed on the movements of hands (a hand opening a door), feet walking, eyes, little gestures (a close-up of a cigarette put out in an ashtray or a wine glass being brought to the lips), and other actions. Certainly a full-faced reaction shot of an actor who is listening while someone else is talking off camera falls into the cutaway category. In *Morgan's Cake* a series of cutaway shots of people chewing their food during the picnic table scene became a sequence in itself, all the mouths munching together in an extremely close-up assembly showing a first glimpse of Morgan's girlfriend Rachel's parents. So sometimes shooting cutaways can pay off beyond just protecting what came before.

And don't drop your movie director's quality control guard. Even short takes need to have an honest and realistic presence (same lighting, focus, and careful framing) equal to the master takes. The actors still have to be in the correct mindset to pull off these bits and pieces correctly. If any clothing changes have been made, it won't hurt to reshoot the actual changing of a shirt or jacket, or the removal of sunglasses (and reverse action—the sunglasses go back on). In the end, it will be these extra shots that ensure the cut; so by all means take the necessary time to get them done in good style.

WORKING WITH A CREW

Like it or not, when you make a movie you are assuming a leadership role in the ongoing activity. You are, by definition, the big boss, and everyone will be looking to you for motivation—a clear vision of what needs to be done next. Sometimes you won't have an answer: You'll be temporarily stumped. Yet you shouldn't feel humiliated because of this lapse: *You* must protect *your* concentration on the set. How?

I recommend a stalling technique. At one point while preparing to shoot an important scene for *Morgan's Cake* in soundman/actor Nick Bertoni's basement (he was our on-location sound recordist, monitoring a hidden mike on his workbench while also performing), the cinematographer, Kathleen Beeler, asked me to explain the content of the upcoming scene. I had no idea, so I told her I'd explain after we got the lights set up. I was stalling for time. As I helped to prepare the area for the shot, it finally came to me: Nick could tell Morgan about his father's untimely death at age fifty, something he had told me about ten years earlier. Nick felt his father, unfairly used by the company, had died of a heart attack due to corporate stress, and he swore it wouldn't happen to him. Sometimes old friendships can supply golden opportunities like this one, so by all means involve your personal friends in the moviemaking process as actors, crew members, editing consultants, and ultimately publicists.

MAINTAINING THE PACE OF THE SHOOT AND A SENSE OF PURPOSE

Having the opportunity to arrive on the set everyday or at a predetermined location will be the payoff for all your fortitude, hard work, risk taking, whatever got the pipe dream of a movie this far along. You toiled long months with purpose, and now you attack each day's problems with the same determination. Your job is to rack up enough good scenes and footage to have a feature's worth of DV when you finally reach the edit suite (i.e., wherever your computer is located). Inside your head is a kind of metronome clicking away, like a pianist uses to keep the beat. You're on a roll. Every hour you are getting new ideas/shots, either moving the ever-evolving story ahead with your role-playing improvisational approach, or nailing scripted dialogue with actors proficient at their craft (who are listening to each other, even if they already know each other's lines and cues).

Determining the pace of the overall movie *while you're still shooting*—guessing how it will play on the screen, though the months of editing are still ahead—is very difficult. On the other hand, maintaining the pace of the shoot is something you *can* do just by showing up promptly each day, working hard without overextending your helpers or yourself, and inserting well-placed coffee breaks for the cast and crew.

NOTE: Carefully schedule meals so that they occur dependably every day. Make lunch sometime between 12:00 noon and 1:30 P.M., when blood sugar levels lag for most people. Dinner should occur between 6:00 and 7:30 P.M. Missed meals will not help your DV cause, but there are exceptions. You don't want to pull the plug on an elaborate setup before you get it shot. Keep your craft services table supplied with enough sandwiches and hot and cold drinks to get you, your cast, and your crew through the production.

CHANGING DIRECTIONS:
LETTING THE MOVIE "MAKE YOU"!

Does George Lucas know the scenario of his next *Star Wars* movie? Probably. That's what he does: Puts out action-packed, sci-fi potboilers for the Saturday afternoon matinee crowd. Oh, did I hit a nerve? Should I give him more credit, as Joseph Campbell did, for being the "Homer of our time"? Well, even if he is, there is a predictability to his product, and he can most likely keep the productions coming ad infinitum (he owns, Industrial Light and Magic [ILM], the special effects house all the big professionals use). You and I, on the other hand, are probably experimenting in different directions, pushing the indie envelope. We're trying to look deep into the quiet moments of existence, creating more home-grown dramas that can gain their power only through the level of truth telling we achieve. And since we may have no idea where the DV moviemaking adventure will take us, we have unlimited possibilities. So, it seems we're luckier than George!

While exploring these various tributaries of thought, we'll be making profound changes in our regular lives as well. The moviemaking process will make us more careful (given our attention to details during the shoot), more responsible (we take care of our people), and, dare I say, more adult (only an adult would have contracts available). Contrary to some family members' opinions, making movies has actually brought us closer to being good citizens. That certainly doesn't mean we have to always agree with the current presidential incumbent, but it signals a maturity that has suddenly grown fuller, as it will in anyone who tackles the complex DV process.

Doing art helps us learn how to tell the truth. So if you're a parent, buckle up your seat belt and prepare to hear some reality check information from those who really know. Get yourself turned on to painting, sculpture, dance, music, graphic art, and DV (which uses all the art forms packed into one). And if you're a kid, just tell it like it is and let the chips fall where they may. (Isn't it time that the grown-ups learned something?) If you are an effects wizard, you may set the movie world on its ear with your unique vision. I very much look forward to seeing earthshaking flicks come out of the Commotion, Art-Matic/VTrack, After Effects software applications (see Chapters 7 and 11).

DAY ONE ON THE SET OF A DV FEATURE

When the day on which your shoot will commence rolls around, you can be relatively sure that you'll see moviemaking action. That's the magic of commitment. In my used-car filmmaking book, I offered a way of defeating inertia by suggesting that if a filmmaker purchased fourteen rolls of film stock (at a current cost of around $2,000 for more than 2 hours of shooting in 16mm) and placed that precious material in the refrigerator with a note on the door explaining that on such and such a day it would become outdated, then something definitely would get shot. Sometimes putting the cart before the horse works to get the creative juices flowing.

For DV moviemaking there are a few other ways to shock the system into action. One is purchasing a DV camera: You've made the sizable investment; now *use* it! Another is buying a powerful Mac or PC computer (see Chapter 5), along with a box of expensive NLE software. (Load the CD, follow instructions for installation, and edit—what?) In any event, you should experience the sensation of knowing that, when you wake up the following day, you'll be meeting friends and associates who have agreed to help you create a feature-length DV, based either on your finely rendered script or on your courage to follow an intuitive, role-playing flow. Here's a moment-by-moment rendition of what it will feel like on the set that first day.

Leaving Your House

If you have done your preproduction paperwork, you'll leave the house with a carryall bag containing:

1. Actors' releases (Appendix D).

2. Location releases (Appendix E).

3. Several copies of the profit-sharing contract (Appendix B).

4. A script or outline for what must be shot.

5. A water bottle (sometimes you will need that drink and should always have this instant fulfillment at hand).

6. A master phone or e-mail list of all major people involved.

7. A cell phone (yours or borrowed) to use as the "walkie-talkie" to control where everyone is at all moments of the day, whether stuck in traffic, etc. (*All cells must be turned off when shooting!*)

8. Possibly a laptop or Palm Pilot, as long as it doesn't become a distraction. Even if you're trying to bring it along as (a) your security blanket, (b) an organizational tool for checking storyboards, reviewing scripted dialogue, making new notes/ideas, writing e-mails, or (c) an electronic schedule board to keep track of what's shot—I'd still say forget it. Why? Your focus needs to be on more essential things, like tuning into each actor's subtle vibe, getting into the nuances of selecting camera placement, carefully designing cuts, and so on. Settle for an old-fashioned, superslim, 2-inch-wide paper notebook that fits easily into your shirt pocket.

9. Cash in your wallet—a couple hundred dollars for unforeseen events (batteries going dead, a highway toll, a subway fare), along with $20 bills for paying an actor's fee to surprise walk-ons.

10. Credit cards for covering meals. Try using a debit card, as I do, that's connected to a DV moviemaking account, so that you can add up all the expenditures on the movie and know your exact bottom line of production cost.

11. A second pair of shoes stored in the car. You're on your feet a good part of ten or more hours, and might need a change.

12. A sweater, second-layer shirt, or light jacket, in case it gets either too hot or too cold on the set (you may need to adjust immediately, as you stand next to the DV camera or hold it).

13. A funky prop you brought along because a good friend insisted that you might need it when you run out of good ideas.

Have we left anything out? Check your index card bulletin board. Is everything crossed off? How does it feel to be so well prepared? I didn't list a parachute, but all this other stuff is essential. No laptop? You left it home? Good. Your real focus needs to be on the magic of getting your DV movie off on the right track.

5
MAC OR PC COMPUTER EDITING PLATFORM?

Because a computer platform could cost more than half of our $3,000 used-car budget, let's examine what equipment will undoubtedly be at the center of your digital editing activity. Ideally, the computer you select will have a fast operating speed, offer many gigabytes for media storage, and be paired to a monitor or laptop screen at least 15 inches wide.

While the computer must be affordable, it must also be enough of a pleasure to operate that you don't have to become more of a computer technician than a moviemaker. And it always takes a while to familiarize yourself with the working style of a computer, learning about its quirks and those of the software programs upon which you will depend. The ease of editing depends on the compatibility of the computer and the NLE software you load onto the hard drive. If the computer is lightning fast but the editing software is confusing and time-intensive, that will ultimately undercut your ability to complete your feature. You'll want enough computer speed (probably the minimum is 800 MHz for Mac, 2 GHz for PC) to be assured that the images can play smoothly at 29.97 frames per second without a jerky delivery. Faster computers save on the rendering time it takes to realize effects beyond the usual 1- to 4-second fade-in, fade-out, and dissolves. For instance, a water ripple effect, set to run 8 seconds on Final Cut Pro 3 software, might take 15 seconds to fully render on a Mac OSX 933-MHz computer like mine before I can watch it play at high resolution on my monitor.

If you're trying to decide between purchasing a Macintosh and a PC, just comparing price or comparable speed will not give you the full picture. You'll never really know the difference between computer platforms until you first try out a PC (Dell, Sony, etc.) and then drop into an Apple store to test drive a Mac. Unless you're thorough in your approach to selecting a computer—which means reading magazines on the subject (*PC World, MacAddict, MacWorld, DV, Videomaker, MovieMaker, Filmmaker*, etc.), surfing the Internet for discussion groups and further information, and having some hands-on experience—you might find yourself stuck with a bothersome system that is too costly to correct quickly.

The Web is a hotbed of information about the war that rages between Mac and PC users. If you type "Mac vs. PC" into the *www.google.com* search engine, you'll get page after page of sites devoted to this squabble. Try *www.digitalvideoediting.com* or *www. wired.com/news/mac/*, and see what is offered in the way of the pro-Mac debate. At *www.digitalvideoediting.com/2002/07_jul/features/cw_ macvspc2.htm*, you'll find a face-off between the Dual 1 GHz Mac OS X with 512 MB ram, the Dell Precision Workstation with 2.53-GHz chip, and the Dual Athlon 2000 MP by Boxx, what they call "Round Two" in the ongoing argument.

You'll certainly find staunch support on both sides, as well as a few fanatics. At *www.Ihateapple.com*, a then thirteen-year-old Todd Arneson made known his dislike for Apple computers in general. If you surf the Web long enough I'm sure you will come up with his counterpart, who raves that Macs are the only correct choice for digital moviemaking. Without a blush, I admit that I fall into this category. Editing DV features with Final Cut Pro 3 software on the Mac OS X computer, even with my less than dual 933-MHz chip, 60 gigs, and 768-MB memory, has been an experience of sheer delight and productivity (Final Cut Pro 4 offers even more editing pleasure!). But don't let me sway you unduly in the Mac direction; by all means, do your homework and decide for yourself.

Dual 2-GHz Power Mac G5, exceptionally fast and quiet. (Courtesy of Apple)

MAC

I have personally stuck with Mac computers since 1998, when Apple (*www.apple.com*) offered the G3 with an option to install the then new FireWire IEEE 1394 card. (Within a few months they came out with the G4 with a preinstalled FireWire option.) My early G3 (300 MHz, 64-MB RAM doubled to 128-MB RAM, with only 8 gigs of storage) had input for RCA and S-VHS, making it media-friendly. While this early model put me through some painful learning curves, you can mostly forgo the traumatic moments I experienced at the dawn of DV by just writing a check for the current systems. It's all there to get you started. Mac computers supply moviemakers with a fully compatible digital moviemaking workstation, complete with free iMovie NLE editing software and CD/DVD burning capability.

Because of my personal satisfaction editing on the Mac OS X G4 computer installed with Final Cut Pro, it is very difficult to wholeheartedly recommend any computer platform and NLE software other than the latest and fastest that Mac has currently available within your used-car budget. With the advent of the new OS X operating system, Mac has pretty much eliminated the problem of computer crashes. My OS X didn't crash once during the many months I spent editing two features at once—3 hours of raw footage from *Bear Dance*, my Figueira da Foz movie, and 13 hours from *Release the Head*, a Feature Workshops production—going back and forth between two separate LaCie external hard drives of 80 gigs and 120 gigs respectively.

Some PC-equivalent computers are much cheaper at $1,000, as compared to the $1,500 base price of most G4/G5 Macs and iMacs. Please keep in mind that the G4 I use (nondual 933-MHz speed, 768-MB RAM, 60 gigs, and OS X) is now much discounted, as are all computers a year old or more, and can be purchased for under $1,000. If I can edit two features on Final Cut Pro 3 simultaneously with this G4, then you can certainly cut your feature on a less-than-showroom-floor-priced Mac. Go to *www.apple.com* and other discount sites (*www.maczone.com*, *www.macwarehouse.com*, or even *www.ebay.com*) and see what's available in the new or used/discounted computer section.

PC

If you feel more comfortable with a non-Mac computer, you can look forward to a smaller initial outlay of cash for the platform (under $1,000), and you may save some money buying PC-based NLE software as well. You'll also have the option of putting together your own unique computer system piece by piece, designing everything from memory to SDRAM, as well as a processor, to your own specifications.

Look into how efficiently a PC computer uses its memory tied to media files in particular and how readily it reacts to editing changes and rendering effects. But don't be fooled by the advertisements of PCs being faster than Macs just because they advertise Pentium processors with 3+-GHz "hyperthreading technology" compared to Mac's 2.5-GHz offering. The real test of speed will come during your editing procedures.

Moviemaker Bill Kimberlin's Dell 650 workstation offers an array of choices for selecting the various components: Intel Xeon processor with hyperthreading technology, Intel motherboard, and Matrox graphics card. (Courtesy of Dell)

If I'm editing in Final Cut Pro/Express, I can move (drag) scenes around without stalling the computer memory, then hit the play bar to view the cut at 29.97 frames per second and to hear clear CD-quality sound emitting from my speakers. If an old 933-MHz Mac computer like mine can run smoothly with almost 4 hours of edited and tweaked scenes (with transitions from fade-out and -in, dissolves and more exotic water ripple effects in place) without crashing or dropping frames, how much faster do you need a computer to be?

Unfortunately, until Steve Jobs of Apple Computer, Inc. decides to share Final Cut Pro/Express with the PC world (at present Final Cut Pro and Final Cut Express are available only for Mac computers), you won't experience the delights of which I speak.

Still, for some producers, like Bill Kimberlin, a former special effects editor at Industrial Light and Magic (ILM), the PC offers a freedom to modify his platform as time and cost permit. Bill recently shared his PC platform plan with me by e-mail. He said he'd settled on a Dell 650 workstation (go to *www1.us.dell.com/content* and click on "workstations") driven by the Intel 2.40 Xeon processor with hyperthreading technology, bringing the total base cost up to approximately $1,700. To that he decided to add an Intel E7505 chip motherboard (*www.intel. com/design/chipsets/e7505/animate.htm*), 1-GB DDR266 ECC SDRAM, and a $400 Matrox Parhelia graphics card (*www.matrox.com/mga/ products/parhelia/home.cfm*). For an extra $50 to the Dell PC total price (or $2 more per month if using the $40- to $50-per-month extended payment plan), he'd also acquired the ATA 80-gig hard drive, bringing the total platform price to more than $2,000.

To supply the Dell PC system with a means of digitizing digital video images and sound (as well as analog), Bill included the Datavideo DAC 2 transcoder (around $500), so that he could input either DV or older video formats (e.g., Hi-8, ¾-inch), along with Betacam SP, for editing and mastering. We're approaching $2,500 by now, not counting tax. To give the platform the option to burn DVDs, Bill says he'll probably purchase the Sony DRU-500A (*www.sony.com*), since it was designed to play every format, adding that he'll install it himself for further savings. From Bill's e-mails I could discern the careful research behind these choices of hardware for his ideal moviemaking workstation. When you are a hands-on computer person, there's got to be a sense of great accomplishment when you compile a unique system such as this one (for a cost of about $3,000 plus tax).

On the digital editing front, Avid's Xpress DV ($649 at *www. macmall.com*) is Bill's low-cost NLE of choice. His familiarity with Avid over his more than twenty years as an editor for George Lucas makes this a natural. He says he'll add a specialty Avid keyboard (*www.bella-USA.com*, $109) for easy access to keystroke shortcuts. Adding this $758 (plus tax) software and keyboard total to the $3,000 for a PC platform, he's looking at approximately $3800 for his fully loaded DV workstation.

A fully loaded Mac G5 (around $3,000 plus tax), which includes all the components (graphics card, FireWire, and CD/DVD burner), coupled with Final Cut Pro 4 ($1,000), comes to $4,000. (With Final Cut

Express for $299, the total would be only $3,300.) The $3,000 total price this book celebrates on the cover relates to purchasing a less powerful computer than a fully loaded one (plus monitor, DV camera, and editing software), while still creating a viable feature-length moviemaking workstation. The price of a Mac G4 933-GHz (nondual) like the one I use (I'm able to edit 4 hours of fine-cut footage on the Final Cut Pro Timeline, using two La Cie 120-gig external hard drives, for capture storage) can now be purchased for less than $1,000. Is PC really cheaper than Mac for making quality DV movies?

Bill presented his logic for going the PC route as follows: "The reason I went with the PC Desktop is so I can get the latest gear at the best prices. The Mac just sells you a box with little choice. You cannot get the latest Intel processor or the best prices. You cannot get Hyper-Threading chips. You can't upgrade at will. It all has to be Mac products at Mac prices." And you can be sure he's upgraded since supplying me with these 2003 product specs!

So there's your choice. For more information on future PC options, in both the hardware and the software departments, please give Bill Kimberlin an e-mail hello (*bill@wiredbay.com*). But keep it short: He's currently remastering his hit documentary on American drag racing, *American Nitro*, for the international DVD market and launching several new DV projects. Thanks again, Bill, for sharing all this carefully researched information.

COMPUTER AND SOFTWARE COMPATIBILITY

To round out this discussion of platforms, let's reexamine the compatibility issue. Apple has designed Mac to work specifically with Final Cut Pro/Final Cut Express digital editing software. The drag-and-drop technology makes moving image and audio files a flawless procedure. There just aren't any compatibility issues when selecting a Mac platform. It all works the first time out. If you go the PC route, you have to be extremely careful to purchase the precise components that fulfill all the needed jobs for NLE of DV material, without overloading any portion of the program, which could result in faulty capture, unfulfilled transitions, stuttery playback, and the like. I realize that PC has a much larger portion of the market of home computing, but that doesn't mean it's better. It just sells to a wider audience that is generally uninformed about DV media editing needs.

Yes, earlier Macs were somewhat unstable and prone to crashes. Not so any more with Mac OS X. Keep in mind that even those earlier "iffy" 9600 Mac platforms supported numerous Avid editing suites and ran dependably without crashes. I never suffered a crash or glitch during the more than ten Feature Workshops DV features I produced with Mac/Avid editing. Any money you think you're saving by going the PC route can be quickly eaten up by compatibility problems—getting the right video card, monitor, and other components. Mac has its DV editing tuned to perfect compatibility, and for that it's worth spending an extra $500—if that is even the cost! As you'll learn in Chapter 7, feature-length editing requires a lot of concentration, so why not go with the system that's most apt to deliver a successful, intuitive flow, leaving technical hassles behind?

It might sound as though I'm on a crusade, still promoting Mac over PC—and in the middle of the PC section! But to be a trusted DV moviemaking guide, I'm pretty much bound to the facts of my own

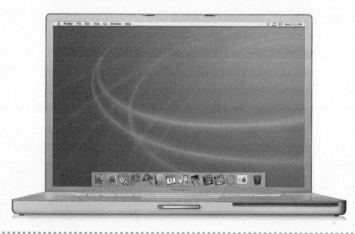

Few with deep pockets will be able to resist Mac's G4 Power Book, with its giant 17-inch screen, up to 2-GB RAM, 1.33-GHz chip, Bluetooth, 80-GB hard drive, SuperDrive, and resolution up to 1440-by-900 (*www.apple.com*). (Courtesy of Apple)

artistic experience, offering thoughts on the equipment and editing methods that I've personally employed or thoroughly field-tested while producing my own no-budget features. Since I have no stake in the Apple company or any of its competitors (not even a single share of stock, unfortunately), I'll let the experts at Apple wage their own case for switching from PC to Mac (*www.apple.com/switch/whyswitch/*).

AFFORDABLE EDITING SOFTWARE

To go with a good computer you'll need an easy-to-understand professional NLE software program with the ability to render a completed, broadcast-quality DV feature for export to tape cassette or DVD. What you need to determine is which NLE software program works best for you. Follow your intuition. If an editing program is just too hard to master over the months of intensive editing (a year of your life can easily be spent on this activity), you'll want to switch to another software product. It's difficult enough to make sure your movie is as tight as possible, delivering the narrative flow and emotional flavor of your material, without adding a struggle to learn your software. Editing is alchemy. You need to make editing changes without diverting your thoughts from the intuitive process. If you have to stop either to accommodate new foibles of a program or to relearn its procedures, you can't reach that deep place in your psyche where the real editing must occur.

Final Cut Pro

With the unveiling in 1999 at NAB convention in Las Vegas of Final Cut Pro ($994, *www.apple.com*, *www.maczone.com*), the digital moviemaking world was changed forever. Suddenly anyone could edit movies professionally at an affordable cost. At NAB we watched in awe as the FCP beta testers showed off their bold, lightning-fast editing moves on the large projection screens. (Final Cut Pro 4 testers gave an equally mesmerizing performance in 2003.) We learned that, for the $1,000 cost, you came away with a full drag-and-drop editing program, with built-in special effects to rival Adobe After Effects. The effects, from motion altering to titling, were all there in the same dynamic editing

For $349, any Final Cut owner can upgrade a previous version to the fabulous Final Cut Pro 4, which features full sliding sound mix controls, LiveType for animated credits, and real-time special effects. (Courtesy of Apple)

package from Apple, fully configured to operate smoothly on a Mac. For those of us who were already Mac moviemakers, it was a no-brainer. We'd been given the greatest gift imaginable. Apple was offering us a previously unattainable studio-level $50,000 editing package (think Avid) for only $1,000.

With its drag and drop technology, Mac editing (on iMovie, Final Cut Pro, or Final Cut Express) couldn't be simpler. Imagine this: Just a mouse click on a scene in the Timeline (which displays perhaps two stereo soundtracks and a single picture track) highlights it as "active." You can then hold down the mouse on that cluster and drag it right over other scenes to a new location. In seconds you've changed the order of assembly! To shorten a scene, mouse-click the razor tool at the desired cut point. After highlighting the isolated extra footage, hit Delete. Your movie is shorter! Maybe you changed your mind? Either type "Apple-Z" for undoing (and the original sound and picture lengths are immediately restored), or simply position the cursor at the end

Apple's widescreen iMac (20") sports a G4 processor running at 1.25 GHz, with pixel resolution up to 1680-by-1050, a good low-cost alternative for editing with Final Cut Express/Pro. (Courtesy of Apple)

points, click on the mouse, and drag the sound and picture sections right back to their original lengths. It's so simple it's magical!

Final Cut Express

Final Cut Express ($299, available at *www.apple.com* and at various discount houses) is the final, liberating NLE software offering for no-budgeters, since it basically supplies every editing process and tool of the more expensive Final Cut Pro system, only without some of the highest-end special effects. You still get drag-and-drop; a 4-hour Timeline; color balance; sound mix and EQ capabilities; two hundred transitions, filters, and effects (fades, dissolves, wipes, page turns, etc.); offline/online cutting (saving storage with low-resolution images); edit decision lists (EDLs); 24-fps editing (for the new Panasonic AG-DVX100a cameras, etc.); 16:9 wide screen; ninety-nine tracks of video and audio compositing; motion graphics and animation; ninety-nine levels of undo; and the ability to import Photoshop files (and various other graphic files). You also have the choice to export to Mini-DV (and DVCAM) or to QuickTime (and MPEG4), as well as DVD mastering with Mac's iDVD (included in most Mac computers) or DVD Studio Pro. Thanks to Apple's competitive spirit, this fabulous yet discounted editing software cuts loose the $700 needed for your first 500+-lines-of-resolution CCD Mini-DV (or DVD) camera.

Avid Xpress DV

Of course, Avid has now met the Final Cut Pro challenge with its own low-cost NLE software, Xpress DV ($649, *www.avid.com/xpressDV*, available for both Mac and PC), which fully integrates with its great high-end versions. This new cross-platform NLE follows the same function lines of the once pricey, original Avid NLE technology ($50,000–$80,000 and more), which led the way for modern, Hollywood-level NLE editing as we know it.

Avid Xpress DV and companion PC laptop. (Courtesy of Avid Technology, Inc.)

For those already proficient with Avid, this software offers a new and affordable DV editing experience, away from expensive Avid suites to, perhaps, your home office (a good business deduction, not to mention the convenience). Xpress DV features eight video tracks (with the capability of nesting to an unlimited number of tracks), more than one hundred transitions and effects (resizing, peels, wipes and pushes, fades, dissolves) and Pro Tools audio mixing capabilities. This Avid software has the same well-organized filing systems as its more expensive versions, ensuring that, when you rename a file in the bins (where your media files are itemized), you will find it automatically renamed in the Timeline as well.

If you're an Avid fan and have a DV editing budget around $2,800, you should be able to get a turnkey deal at ProMax (*www.promax. com*), a ProMax Pentium 4 that includes computer installed with Avid Xpress DV and monitor. For a Final Cut Pro 4 turnkey system (dual Mac G5, FCP 4 software, computer screen, and professional studio monitor), Promax prices start at around $6,000. But since our full digital video workstation budget of $3,000 must also include a DV camera, we have to work a bit harder to get the affordable deals and cut corners wherever possible.

Adobe Premiere Pro

Perhaps you'll end up with the standard Adobe Premiere Pro ($599), which offers a well-designed demo tutorial to get you started. Premiere has been around for a long time and certainly helped usher in the DV revolution. It has been said that Final Cut Pro was envisioned by a group of Adobe expatriot software designers who broke off to make a new NLE product with every editing tool they could imagine thrown into one program. Well, they did it! But for some DV moviemakers— those comfortable with the program with which they started—Adobe delivers dependable editing for PC with a reasonable price tag (see *www.nextag.com* for costs as low as $350).

NOTE: Be certain your computer comes equipped with the appropriate hardware for burning DVD and CD copies. Mac's G4, G5, and

Adobe offers the entire Digital Video Collection: Adobe Premiere Pro, After Effects (required for Magic Bullet plug-in), Illustrator, and Photoshop for just $999. For those PC-based DV indies who want to push the envelope in media manipulation, this is essential wish list software. (© Adobe Systems Inc.)

iMacs with Super Drive come preloaded with their iDVD program for burning movies to DVD and selling your completed works over the Web and by mail order.

MONITORS

When selecting a monitor, keep in mind that the screen should be at least 15 inches to allow you to properly view your images, look for flaws from the shoot (boom poles in the frame, etc.), and access the overall proficiency of your running cut. If you can screen your final cut on a larger flat screen or projection screen, so much the better because a large format screening (before an impartial audience) will give you the best chance of evaluating your cut for theatrical potential. You've certainly seen the ads for iMacs, with the included 15-, 17-, and 20-inch flat screens suspended above the small, half-round base. When those products hit the market, it meant that any college student who could afford it could start making movies at a crowded dorm desk, with a monitor that could be easily pushed out of the way for other schoolwork. (How do they compress all the computer's components into that small space?) And with Apple's announcement that they would offer a 20-inch screen for iMacs as well as the standard 15- and 17-inch, the most compact desktop digital moviemaking workstation had fully evolved.

If you have a small 12-inch Mac laptop, it is still possible to hook up a larger second monitor for two-screen editing using a cheap Apple-to-VGA connector cable (available at *www.apple.com* for about $30). This is important for inspecting your images in closer detail. More expensive Mac laptops, especially those with the 17-inch displays, are awesome but unfortunately beyond our immediate $3,000 used-car budget (which must also include a DV camera). While we can't afford to spend $1,299 for the 20-inch flat screen cinema display monitor from Apple, a 15-inch monitor from Sylvania (TF722), like the one I bought for $140 at Costco to make up my two-monitor workstation, does the job just fine.

So compiling our hardware and software items within the $3,000 total takes some arduous number-crunching and penny-pinching strategies. Subtracting roughly $1,500 from our full budget either for the DVD/CD-burning iMac, Mac G4 or G5 or for the Pentium PC and monitor, $299 for editing software, and $200 more for an inexpensive monitor, we are left with only about $1,000 for a Mini-DV camera with a FireWire connection (and the problem of being $200 over our budget for taxes, unless you purchase in a no-sales-tax state). That doesn't take into account money for lights, sound (mike, boom, and/or radio mikes), and other incidentals. If you elect to purchase an older computer (perhaps still new but discounted because it isn't this year's model), you'll be able to count more dollars into your camera equipment fund.

NONLINEAR EDITING OVERVIEW

The final question you need to ask yourself is how labor-intensive will it be to master Avid's Xpress DV, as opposed to either Final Cut Pro/Final Cut Express or Adobe Premiere? In Chapter 7, I take you on a walk-through of the most basic Final Cut Express/Final Cut Pro editing steps (almost identical for both Final Cut products), from capture to cutting and reassembly within an hour of sitting down at your Mac. Avid Xpress DV may be more difficult to learn, unless Avid has been your NLE of choice and its editing commands have become second nature. In any case, first use what's available (Mom's computer, school iMacs, etc.), and put aside "camera" money while testing various software products firsthand. I'm sure that with some hands-on experience you'll discover the computer system and editing software that's just right for you.

6
GOING DOGME 95

I n January of 2000, as I started to gear up for a new Feature Workshops production in Port Townsend, the subject of shooting according to Dogme 95 rules came up in a phone conversation with my son Morgan. He was talking about all the luggage he was planning to check at the airport for the flight to Seattle, including a large, three-light Arri kit (lights and stands), a tripod tube about 4 feet long, and another bulky, 2-foot-high square box filled with all the assorted cables, extension cords, sound gear, sandbags (small ones mostly used with the light stands), and perhaps a few changes of underwear. Well, I'd seen him navigate this rolling caravan of equipment through an airport and helped him negotiate the aisles and thoroughfares with that heavy load. Suddenly the idea came that we could avoid all that hassle if he would just consider going Dogme 95 for the shoot. While he heard me out and considered the proposition, he played his devil's advocate role by weighing the pluses and minuses.

"I just don't want a movie I shoot to look unprofessional," he said.

My best retort was, "Have you seen *The Celebration*?"

"We saw it together!"

"Well . . . ?" I continued.

"Well?" returned Morgan. Sparring with a son is different from sparring with other collaborators, mostly because family members can talk back more easily and are able to push emotional buttons without much effort. Fortunately, Morgan and I had worked out most of our kinks over a series of coproductions, getting to know each other very well through the making of six previous DV features and a couple of 16mm film shoots. Between two shoots at remote locations in Death Valley and making *Morgan's Cake* together, we had survived some pretty intense situations. By now we had learned to listen carefully to each another.

"Well?" I repeated. "What do you think? As per Dogme rules, no lights, no tripod, no heavy airport routine. Wouldn't that be nice for once?"

"OK. I'll think about it . . . but Dave [Dave Nold, our soundman and cowriter/codirector collaborator who would fly in from Berkeley with Morgan] and I will still bring all the stuff, just in case you're wrong about this, change your mind. That way, we'll still have all the lights in Port Townsend."

It was clear I couldn't stop him from terrorizing the airport personnel with all his gear (and it would cost me $80 beyond the airline tickets for the extra checked items), but the topic of no lights was at least open to discussion. Of course, I admired Morgan's thoroughness and expertise in all matters related to DV cinematography. Once he arrived in Port Townsend and had reread the Dogme rules, he began to acquiesce, agreeing that it might be a good bet for shooting the movie. I'm happy to report that the equipment boxes of lights and tripod remained on my living room floor, unopened for the duration of the shoot.

THE DOGME 95 VOW OF CHASTITY

If you haven't yet visited the Dogme 95 Web site (*www.dogme95.dk*), you may want to check it out. You'll find their manifesto posted there, along with a list of moviemaking rules (The Vow of Chastity) you need to follow to make an official Dogme 95 feature. I know what you're thinking. Rules are dumb. Rules are for other people. Of course, I agree. We're individual and original artists, so what possible use could we have for rules of any kind? I personally have lived almost my entire life bucking rules. But I still decided to take on the challenge of the Dogme 95 Vow. Why? I thought it might be fun to have some limitations on my artistic process for once, to use the parameters of the Dogme 95 approach to intensify my focus.

The youngest Dogme 95 signer on *Chetzemoka's Curse,* Marlon Schmidt, then age 14, directs the "Cups" scene, while his fellow collaborator (and brother) Morgan Schmidt-Feng shoots hand-held, per rule 3 of the Dogme 95 Vow of Chastity. A third collaborator, Dave Nold, records sound. (Photo by Julie Schachter)

A former art professor of mine at the California College of the Arts, Marie Murelius, once said that the hardest thing for an artist to do is to create limits. She said the best work is done when artists impose some restrictions on their activity. Instead of painting (sculpting, photographing, videotaping, drawing, etching) any flower in the world, the artist could easily spend three or more years painting just one type of flower, a daffodil, say, focusing closer and closer on the shapes, colors, complexity—the miracle of just that one small creation. Look at Georgia O'Keeffe's abstract oils of flowers and skyscrapers. Her work certainly demonstrates the power of a limiting process (and the resulting professional and commercial success possible). So my decision to follow the Dogme 95 rules, while a surprising change from my usual process, offered our collaborative team (Morgan, Dave Nold, Lawrence E. Pado, Maya Berthoud, my younger teenage son Marlon Schmidt, Bay Area editor Chris Tow, and myself) the power of intense focus, and the possibility of earning official Dogme 95 certification from Denmark.

The Vow of Chastity follows. I shared and discussed this list of rules with our collaborators on location in Port Townsend, on January 16, 2000, the evening before our ten-day production was to begin. After you review the list, read on to learn the impact that each rule had on producing, writing, directing, shooting, and editing our 81-minute feature *Chetzemoka's Curse* (Dogme No. 10).

THE VOW OF CHASTITY

I swear to submit to the following set of rules drawn up and confirmed by DOGME 95:

1. Shooting must be done on location. Props and sets must not be brought in (if a particular prop is necessary for the story, a location must be chosen where this prop is to be found).

2. The sound must never be produced apart from the images or vice versa. (Music must not be used unless it occurs where the scene is being shot.)

3. The camera must be hand-held. Any movement or immobility attainable in the hand is permitted. (The film must not take place where the camera is standing; shooting must take place where the film takes place.)

4. The film must be in colour. Special lighting is not acceptable. (If there is too little light for exposure, the scene must be cut or a single lamp be attached to the camera.)

5. Optical work and filters are forbidden.

6. The film must not contain superficial action (murders, weapons, etc., must not occur).

7. Temporal and geographical alienation are forbidden. (That is to say that the film takes place here and now.)

8. Genre movies are not acceptable.

9. The film format must be Academy 35mm.

10. The director must not be credited.

Furthermore I swear as a director to refrain from personal taste! I am no longer an artist. I swear to refrain from creating a "work," as I regard the instant as more important than the whole. My supreme goal is to force the truth out of my characters and settings. I swear to do so by all the means available and at the cost of any good taste and any aesthetic considerations.

Thus I make my VOW OF CHASTITY.

_____

_____ _____
NAME   DATE

Following Dogme 95 Rules During Preproduction

Before I go into the details of how the Dogme 95 rules influenced our shoot and edit, I'd like to describe the preproduction atmosphere leading up to the arrival of the collaborators, Morgan (camera), Dave (sound), and St. Louis engineer Larry. Those who have visited my Web site (*www.lightvideo.com*) already know that my Feature Workshops are ten-day affairs. This supertight production schedule includes an introductory evening (usually a Sunday night) when we all sign contracts, then a four- to five-day shoot, followed by five days of editing, to arrive at a final cut by Day Ten.

You could say that the pressure is so intense that there is no pressure. In fact, things are actually more relaxed than on a twenty-day shoot. One-to-one takes suddenly seem expected. Sticking to a central location feels comfortable and sensible. And having a small cast and crew sharing workload together (beyond any "union" distinctions), the norm. Even though I've coproduced, with Morgan, more than ten feature-length movies this way, it will still feel impossible when we hit a hundred. Why? Everyone knows that you can't make a movie in that short a period of time! You see, mere mortals can't possibly control the universe enough to force this outcome. It's up to the moviemaking gods to let you and your work succeed. Though I'm not religious in any traditional sense, I still find myself imagining the Greek gods on Mount Olympus, standing around an all-seeing crystal ball, looking down at our activities and laughing. Perhaps it's just for their amusement that they don't quash our productions, let us fall on our faces right out of the gate. I think the gods are curious enough to grant puny mortals impunity, just to watch and enjoy what transpires. We feature workshop moviemakers can only stay focused on the immediate work, with no time to worry about difficulties around the bend or the sheer lunacy of it all. I think that's what ten-day start-to-finish production schedules have going for them.

As executive producer of impossible ventures, I do feel some real pressure leading up to the arrival of the participants, and that forces me to have *something* in place beforehand. Going into the January 2000 Port Townsend shoot, it certainly seemed up to me to secure (1) a locked-in central location (i.e., have a location agreement form signed by the owner) and (2) some actors/nonactors ready to perform. Oh, and wouldn't it be nice to have (3) a story line. I say "nice" because I've learned over the years that knowing the story beforehand is not essential to making a good movie. Sometimes just starting to shoot real-life dialogue with good, intelligent people can get your feature rolling.

Thinking back to early January 2000, it's hard to believe that I had none of these ingredients ready with just ten days to go. Talk about pressure—and the gods laughing! I knew Morgan and Dave were flying in; I'd paid for their tickets. Morgan would bunk at my house, and Dave would stay at the Palace Hotel, a Victorian-era Port Townsend landmark that charged very reasonable rates. Larry Pado e-mailed me with his itinerary, assuring me that he would arrive in time for our introductory Sunday night dinner and contract signing. And I had helped book him into the Palace Hotel as well. But who were the actors? And at what locations would we tell our as yet unknown story? And would everyone want to go Dogme 95 or not? Since the world hadn't ended with Y2K, I couldn't use that as an excuse for being a lousy producer. I had very few days to figure something out.

Finding Maya Berthoud

Checking my Feature Workshops answering machine one morning, I heard the voice of a young woman inquiring about becoming a PA (production assistant) for the upcoming production. She immediately made it clear that she couldn't afford the $3,500 fee but still hoped to get involved, working for free if necessary. I phoned her back and discovered that she had learned about the workshop from one of the few fliers I'd placed around town. I agreed to meet her but said she would still have to fill out an application form, giving me her basic information (age, education), along with the required half-page real-life story from her family history. She agreed, and I mailed her the necessary form (the same that I currently e-mail to prospective workshop participants).

When I checked my Feature Workshops mailbox (P.O. Box 1914, Port Townsend, WA 98368) the next day, I found Maya's application, and it was a winner. Her real-life story was deeply personal, articulately told, intelligent, and gripping—all the qualities I hope for in my indie productions! My eyes must have widened as I read on, because I suddenly realized that this twenty-three-year-old woman, Maya Berthoud, could be the central focus of the movie. Meeting her the following morning at a local cafe, just six days before the shoot, confirmed my hunch that she was attractive, personable, mysterious, and— most importantly—fully committed to joining our ragtag production team.

After breakfast I asked Maya to accompany me as I checked out the accommodations for Dave and Larry at the Palace Hotel. By then I was interested in using the hotel as the central location. I had been granted permission by the owners to shoot in the rooms occupied by our people but had not yet risked asking them to sign an official location release, partly because I was worried that it might feel too "Hollywood" and I didn't want to change my low-key, hometown status in their eyes. And with the production being so tenuous, I felt I couldn't emotionally afford even a small setback, such as being turned down for that location; so I broke my own rule and waited until after the shoot to request and get the release.

As Maya and I wandered through the 1880s hallways, opening up the various rooms, it became apparent that something exciting could be shot there. I found myself mentally situating this young woman (someone whom I'd known for less than an hour) into the plush, red velvet wallpapered Victorian settings. What part could she play in the hotel? I wondered. A maid? A hostess in the lobby? A tourist? What would keep her in one of the rooms? Maybe being a prostitute? In the end, her performance covered all of the above, with the prostitute part lightly implied in a few scenes, adding some dramatic tension. In *Chetzemoka's Curse* Maya would ultimately become a woman who inhabited the whole of the hotel.

Back outside by the car, getting ready to part after our morning location scouting, I asked Maya once more if she was absolutely sure she could commit to working on the production for the four days of shooting, doing some acting, writing, and directing—that is, internally directing her own performance, making up improvisational dialogue, telling her real-life story. Before she could answer, I offered to cover any lost wages from her waitressing job and promised to make her a full cowriter/codirector collaborator—a signer of our profit-sharing Feature Workshops contract (she, myself, Morgan, Dave, Larry, and editor Chris would all receive equal gross profit points if and when the movie sold). "Yes, I absolutely *do want* to be in the production!" she said emphatically, making direct eye contact so I would have no doubt about her sincerity. All right! We shook hands on it.

Finally I had something on which I could hang the upcoming production.

What I Had . . . and Didn't Have

In the final days before the shoot would begin, I counted up the knowns on my fingers. We had (1) a camera, sound gear and boom, and mixer; (2) a cinematographer (Morgan) and sound recordist (Dave); (3) a lead actress (Maya); and (4) a central location (the Palace Hotel).

We didn't have a script or story line, but after watching the dynamics of the workshop shoots in the past (*Chetzemoka's Curse* would be our eighth feature since 1997), that didn't panic me particularly. I had learned from the production of our 1997 feature *Someone Like Me* how a movie with a fairly solid, preconceived story and ten big scenes blocked out had its own inherent difficulties. When you attempt to shoot a feature in just four days, having a somewhat tight story line and scenes simply means that you are relentlessly run by your own story's demands. You're playing catch-up the whole time, trying to fulfill the goals you've set in place. But on those productions where we had less than a nailed-down script or plan, a more natural moviemaking flow came into being, the collaborative team enjoying the input of new ideas and information instead of dreading changes. We didn't have to jump through hoops. So, although I felt anything but secure going into a shoot without a story line, my experiences told me that I could survive and that something good might develop as a final result. I reminded myself that our past DV feature, *Loneliness Is Soul,* won a top prize at the Figueira da Foz International film festival in Portugal. A panel of ten international film festival judges had decided to award it Best Script in the Main Feature Competition (selecting our work over thirty other features from around the world) when, in fact, there was no script!

I decided not to be nervous and instead just concentrated on having all the tangible things in place as the days counted down to Morgan's arrival. The hotel reservations were solid, and Maya knew to meet us for dinner that upcoming Sunday evening. Morgan would buy the DV tape, and I'd reimburse him. I would pick up him and Dave, along with the equipment, at Seattle's Sea-Tac Airport and drive them the fifty miles (including a ferry ride) back to Port Townsend. With agreement from both Dave and Larry, we had two rooms at the Palace Hotel in which to shoot scenes, and the management of the Palace Hotel said they had no problem with us shooting in the lobby as well.

Regarding getting other actors and performers into the mix, I was happy to hear back from my friend, lawyer and author Steve Gillard, that he would love to participate. I immediately thought of Steve telling a real-life story, either something I hadn't heard (always an exciting proposition) or the one I knew about, how he and his wife, Sue, had visited Port Townsend years ago and made a decision right then and there to quit their jobs and move to our little coastal town. That would be a nice offering for a movie: how to trust your instincts and enact your dream. And Sue also offered to tell a story to the camera. By the time the shoot ended, their daughter Jessica had also told a true story, while son Joe graced us with on-camera conga music, as per the Dogme 95 rule 2: Sound must never be produced apart from the images, and music must not be used unless it occurs where the scene is being shot. My teenage son Marlon, playing his customized Hohner mouth piano, joined Joe to produce on-location music for some of the scenes we shot at Chetzemoka Park. So, thanks to the Gillard family, I suddenly had a larger cast to depend on with just days to go. No story yet, but a cast!

If you've ever attempted to make a feature, you've probably found that virtually your entire being is affected by the countdown to production day. You go to sleep with four, three, two days to go and each morning wake up with ideas. That's what the process of being an indie moviemaker is all about. Nothing is set in stone until *you* say it is. Your mind is always scanning for new ideas and solutions to problems you continue to identify. Your subconscious mind is a problem solver. So during your waking hours you follow leads you've imagined in your sleep. Something urges you to call this or that person, ask certain friends for help (possibly a future coproducer among them), or drive to some abandoned building where you meet a person who just happens to own the property and gives you permission to shoot. The point is to let the concepts flow and listen to the almost silent whispers in your mind. The forces of the universe are on your side, helping you to survive your artistic pursuit. May these forces always be with you!

ENACTING THE DOGME 95 RULES: SIGNING THE VOW OF CHASTITY

It felt pretty strange to sign something with the word "chastity" in it, but that's what our small group did at our first meeting. After everybody read the list of rules, there was almost instant agreement that this seemed a good way to go. Morgan had toted the lights and tripod up the coast from Berkeley for nothing, but he still felt it had been a wise precaution, and I concurred. So it was agreed that no lights would be used on the set, that we'd shoot and edit only with sync sound (aside from adding music, this is how most of our movies were made anyway), and that images would be recorded by hand-held camera. None of us could have fathomed that, when newcomer Maya Berthoud signed The Vow, she would be on her way to becoming the first woman Dogme 95 director in history. (*The New York Times* January 27, 2002, Sunday edition, Arts and Entertainment "Corrections," would substantiate that Ms. Lone Scherfig of Denmark made Dogme No. 12, *Italian for Beginners, after* our Dogme No. 10, *Chetzemoka's Curse.*)

So there we were, ready to embark on a movie according to rules initiated by a group of Danish mainstream movie directors who decided to reject the clichés of commercial filmmaking and seek a deeper truth for the moving image. Here, in detail, is how our moviemaking process was affected by the ten rules of Dogme 95:

Rule 1: Shoot on Location

Shooting must be done on location. Props and sets must not be brought in (if a prop is necessary for the story, a location must be chosen where this prop is to be found).

To begin with, all my movies have been shot on location, so there was absolutely no problem working within this parameter. The Palace Hotel had agreed to grant us access for our video shoot. To the hotel owners, video meant noncommercial and thus no big deal; they said they had previously allowed another video production to shoot there, so we weren't intimidating them with a new situation.

The lovely Victorian-era rooms, complete with antiques and 1880s color schemes, prompted me to consider outfitting Maya in Victorian garb, and I wondered if I could find some kind of adequate costume for her on the premises of the hotel. I was trying to stay within the requirements of the Dogme rules and still fulfill the needs of the production. Is a dress a prop? Well, perhaps it is, though actors, unless they're nudists, must wear something. In any case, when I found a Victorian costume shop right across the street, literally 70 feet away from the room that Larry would occupy, I felt I had no choice but to rent a blue, late nineteenth-century period dress for Maya. It turned out to be a perfect fit! I suppose I took the risk of violating Dogme 95 certification rules when I acquired the dress and moved it across the street to the hotel for use in our movie, but the addition of the costume so perfectly fit the surroundings, locking Maya into her role as part of the tourist trappings of the town, that I felt I had no choice. And, as it turned out, the Dogme 95 Secretariat accepted my costuming decision after I explained the circumstances, still granting us official certification.

NOTE: A moviemaker can present the Dogme Secretariat with a list of "production sins" when applying for the certification, to be "forgiven" as some of the founders themselves have been. See *www. tvropa.com/tvropa1.2/film/dogme95/news/index.htm*. This lively interview by Peter Rundle with writer/director/Dogme founder Kristian Levring, maker of Dogme No. 4, *The King Is Alive*, about the process of shooting a Dogme movie, also covers rules he broke during the production. So list your Dogme transgressions as you shoot (presumably a very short list) and save it for later. If the Dogme 95 collective continues their current moratorium on issuing official certification, at least your movie will be certifiable when the opportunity next arises.

Rule 2: No Separate Sound

The sound must never be produced apart from the images or vice versa. (Music must not be used unless it occurs where the scene is being shot.)

Since we were shooting digital video and recording sound directly to the camera via a boomed exterior microphone connected to a Shure audio mixer, it was clear we never would be producing sound apart from the images. Anyone who shoots with video need not worry about this problem, since all sound is sync sound. And if you find you need to use narrations but don't want images competing with the words, you could conceivably shoot in a pitch black location (a closed closet or a basement with no windows), or cap the lens so that the image is solid black. That would give you the traditional look that filmmakers know as "running a narration over black leader." Look at the indie movie *Stranger Than Paradise* by Jim Jarmusch. Notice how all the long fade-outs (blackouts really) affect the values of the movie. Movies operate on a principle of contrasting elements. If the movie screen is dark for 20 seconds, the images that pop on the screen after that black section seem brighter, crisper, than the previous shot. The moviemaker could use that style of narration over a black screen for their Dogme 95 movie. Just remember that making a movie for potential certification is not about tricking the Dogme 95 Secretariat or being deceitful in any way. It's about using the specific limitations to get more creative in your search for truth in cinema.

'Regarding the use of music in a Dogme 95 feature, the only way to include music is to actually have musicians or singers performing, either live or on a recording being played while a scene unfolds. Here's the *rule*'s wording again: Music must not be used unless it occurs where the scene is being shot. Have you seen the first *Godfather* movie by Francis Coppola? Remember how the Lake Tahoe wedding band music infiltrates all the scenes, even those of Marlon Brando tucked away in his dark office; we hear music playing at a lower volume somewhere far off. That's all acceptable for a Dogme movie, as long as the band is actually playing while the scene proceeds. Of course, if there were pauses in the shooting, between takes, while the one song was playing live outside, each jump cut performed in the editing room would make the music jump ahead as well. For *Godfather*, the office scene was completely edited and then the background music laid in on a separate track, running through all the tiny cuts, thus breaking Dogme 95 rule 2 by virtue of its being produced separately from the images.

In *Chetzemoka's Curse* the first opportunity we had for including music occurred in the Palace Hotel hallway, where actor and musician John Sanders played his bass just outside Maya's room (the room with the plaque reading "Marie's Suite," where collaborator Larry Pado actually slept during the shoot). You can hear the music coming through the closed door as Marie says goodbye to one customer (played by Larry) and invites the musician in for his session. We don't know exactly what it is she conducts in there, but the scenes were set up to be provocative. When she asks the young male customer, "So what do you want to do today?" he answers, "Just talk," which indicates that the menu included other possibilities.

We also included music played in the distance during a park scene between Maya and her boyfriend Adam Karagas, a conga drum and a wind piano played respectively by Joe Gillard and my son Marlon Schmidt. You never see the players, but they are there, performing live as the action continues. Joe played the conga again for us in a dramatic scene in which Maya pleads with Adam to take her along on his upcoming trip.

Another nice musical moment occurs when Maya is walking down the main street in Port Townsend and happens to pass a street musician, Robert Rutledge, who (unstaged by us) was playing a steel guitar. After the shot was completed (the camera walks by Rutledge and the volume of his music naturally recedes), we asked if he wouldn't mind playing the song again on camera and telling a real-life story to the camera as well. He agreed, pouring out the rest of his bluesy song as he sat on a picnic table at the downtown beach, then telling a tale from his heart about inadvertently wronging a woman he loved. Including Robert in our movie was one of those lucky serendipitous events.

The movie ends with a few strong musical moments. In the scene after Maya has just returned from a trip away, we see her in her old hotel room, now wearing street clothes instead of her frilly blue dress. She inserts an audio tape into a boom box and walks slowly about the room, closing the blinds at all the windows while musician Paul Baker's song "Your Name Has a Story" emits from the speakers. Given that Paul (*www.epiphanyfunhouse.com*) had just made up the song on the spot a week earlier as he sat at my dining room table (I grabbed a cheap Sony recorder to catch it on tape), I was happy that the Dogme 95 people passed a positive judgment about including music from that kind of source. And for the rear title sequence we had saxophonist Quincy Griffin playing his horn just off to the left of the TV monitor, where we were shooting the changing credits right off the screen. Quincy's silhouette can just barely be seen at the end of the movie, when the camera pans over to where he was sitting. Quincy (*bquincygriffin@yahoo.com*) cocreated the music for *Daughter from Danang*, codirected by Gail Dolgin and Vicente Franco, which won the Sundance Film Festival's 2002 documentary Grand Jury Prize for Best Documentary and was nominated for an Academy Award as Best Documentary in 2003.

One thing the Dogme 95 rules help to do is to push moviemakers away from Hollywood-style soundtracks, those wall-to-wall musical scores that aim to manipulate each and every emotion in the viewer. Do we really want to be told exactly how to feel as a plot develops? Music recorded on location, derived from obvious visual sources, seems to foster more cinematic truth because of its juxtaposition to what is actually happening. And while you could include a scene coupled with the audio from a real music source on location and not even show the musicians in question, it's probably worth video-recording the actual performance as proof that the music indeed emanated from an on-site source, in compliance with rule 2.

Rule 3: Only Hand-Held Cameras

The camera must be hand-held. Any movement or immobility attainable in the hand is permitted. (The film must not take place where the camera is standing; shooting must take place where the film takes place.)

This next rule is not so easy to implement, since it takes a certain skill and strength to operate a hand-held camera to good effect. Fortunately for our *Chetzemoka's Curse* production we had Morgan Schmidt-Feng on board as cinematographer because, after years of shooting, he had not only developed a great eye for framing, but he could also hand-hold the camera seemingly forever, without shaking it anymore than what you'd expect when it was locked down to a tripod.

When you envision hand-held camera work, please don't think that it will be used exclusively for long static shots. One thing the small DV cameras offer with their light weight is a fluidity of shooting, giving the operator the opportunity to swoop past various objects in a way that only a Steadicam could have done in films. Imagine a shot that runs along the surface of a kitchen table, moving through a gap between the pepper and salt shakers (everything staying in focus thanks to the autofocus), gliding with ease past the shiny silverware and then along a checkered landscape (a flannel shirt), and ending with the image of an actor's eyes. Anyone can make that shot with the new lightweight DV cameras and their large fold-out screens. So get creative and experiment with your DV camera. You may discover a brand new way of seeing and invent new camera moves and images that we will all want to emulate.

The second part of this rule is confusing: "The film must not take place where the camera is standing; shooting must take place where the film takes place." This means, I guess, that the camera is mobile in all respects, that the camera must follow the action in a truthful manner, and that it must be an active participant of the story. Instead of bringing in the players to a camera mounted on a tripod (tripods are forbidden if you shoot Dogme 95), you'll use the camera more like a

With a good solid grip on his Sony DSR 200 camera, Dogme collaborator and cinematographer Morgan Schmidt-Feng shoots lead actress and collaborator Maya Berthoud for *Chetzemoka's Curse* (Dogme No. 10). (Photo by Julie Schachter)

microscope for investigating human emotion close up, seeking out the hidden moments of real-life drama. See *The Celebration* (Dogme No. 1) by Thomas Vinterberg. The camera is a deadly accurate tool in that movie, a hypocrisy detector flipping over every rock to reveal the (sometimes ugly) truth beneath. That's what you want to achieve with your Dogme 95 movie.

NOTE: Perhaps the Dogme rule 3 demands that the moviemaker or DP put quality time into an exercise program for the hands and arms, using the period of preproduction to build up added mid-torso strength to accommodate the extreme physical challenges of shooting hand-held. With practice you can greatly improve your hand-held camera skills.

Rule 4: Color Only and No Lights

The film must be in colour. Special lighting is not acceptable. (If there is too little light for exposure, the scene must be cut or a single lamp be attached to the camera.)

For some B&W purists this rule will offer several stumbling blocks. Certainly, I would have opted against going Dogme 95 for my low-budget feature *Morgan's Cake*, which relied on an interplay of black-and-white 16mm imagery and several color video sequences and artifically illuminated setups. I would not have been willing to sacrifice such important visual elements just to get a certificate. So if you have conceived your movie in black and white, or lusciously lit, I wouldn't recommend violating that aesthetic. Save the Dogme 95 adventure for the next one!

Regarding shooting in color, the first thing you'll notice about most DV cameras these days is how bright and colorful the images appear on the viewing screen, in almost any low- or normal-light situation. So shooting strictly in color without lights doesn't look like much of a problem from that perspective. What the Dogme founders seem to be after is a sense of present-day realism, which is mandated by their rule 7 (that the film "must exist in the here and now"). Since black and white tends to date the images, carrying the viewer back to an earlier time period, it is forbidden. But shooting in color is a worthy challenge, and color video can offer the moviemaker a broad palette with which to paint by natural light.

And since it's video, you can instantaneously see what the final image will look like. If things are too blue on the viewing LED screen of your DV camera (or on-site true color field monitor), they will be too blue later when you edit. So you'll need to analyze whether the colors that exist where you shoot affect your emotions appropriately for the story that's developing. If you're video taping your scenes almost as a documentarian, you need to frame your shots carefully (blue room, blue people) and incorporate that aesthetic into your cinematic statements. Maybe it's worth seeing the *Three Colors* trilogy (*Red, White,* and *Blue*) by filmmaker Krzysztof Kieslowski to observe how he incorporated the color-based themes into his stories. And if you stick to the letter of the law of Dogme rule 4, you won't tamper with the color setting during editing, although there will most likely be shifts in values as you proceed through the 35mm transfer (rule 9) and VHS/DVD mastering for video copies.

As rule 4 states, you can either shoot until the darkness overtakes you or attach a single light to the camera. Somehow, the single-light idea sounds like you'd be illuminating your actors and locations with something akin to a mini-searchlight beam. If you know your story will take you into low-light situations, using one light is certainly a good alternative to not shooting at all. Keep in mind that some of the most powerful movies ever produced vacillated between low and highly lit scenes. A lot of the teeth of Orson Welles's *Citizen Kane* comes from such dramatic lighting, offering vast areas of darkness on the screen contrasted by small, illuminated patches of the frame where an actor is located. As with all other rules, make sure that the limitations you impose on your production only help to make the movie better. That's the only way to play the Dogme game.

And with regard to rule 4's other wording ("If there is too little light for exposure, the scene must be cut"), it is up to the moviemaker to interpret what "exposure" means. Since you'll be shooting in DV, most likely with a camera that can see shades right down to a single candlepower, you'll get some kind of exposure in almost any situation. In *Chetzemoka's Curse* we show Quincy playing his sax after the end credits in a shot that requires you to look very closely to make out his image (the sax's metal mouthpiece glistens out of the dark background). We didn't stop shooting just because it was difficult to make out the full figure of a human being in the frame.

In any case, once free of the headache of lighting every scene, your production can move ahead much more swiftly. You're suddenly on a rollercoaster of a ride where you can make quick decisions, following whichever story threads seem appealing at the moment. No longer are you victimized by the usual drag between time-consuming lighting setups. With camera in hand, you can freely go about your intuitive cinematic dance, letting natural and available artificial light illuminate your subject.

NOTE: After a day of shooting in color, check the rushes on your video monitor and decide if the trade-off of no lights is making your script and movie-in-progress a more powerful work. With luck, it's a good aesthetic marriage; if not, forgo shooting by Dogme 95 guidelines, maybe even setting your DV camera to B&W mode for sharper video recordings!

Rule 5: No Optical Work or Filters
Optical work and filters are forbidden.

As with the other Dogme 95 rules about adding artificial elements to your moviemaking process, The Vow of Chastity forbids the image manipulations that most movies you see in theaters utilize from the very start. You can forget having a James Bond–style montage opener: no naked women twirling around in antigravity rooms, bouncing off diving boards into primary color pools. But you can come up with real-time effects if you are creative. Knowing that your blue tones exist mostly in the early morning sunrise portion of the day, while your golden yellows (occasional reds, blues, oranges) are delivered at sunset, you can create strong color statements if you plan in advance and get a few good breaks from Mother Nature.

Without the possibility of doing manipulative optical work, you must be all the more inventive to create a unique opening title sequence. What are the ways you can imagine for presenting your credits, hand-printed or typeset, before the opening scene? I devised simple opening titles for *Morgan's Cake* shooting press-on letters on clear acetate sheets stuck across a doorway, while the scene commenced behind. Aside from use of lights to control the illumination, all my hand-held shooting from a wheelchair (poor man's dolly) would have fallen neatly within the Dogme 95 guidelines for that rolling sequence. Of course, the freeze frame enacted during editing to hold the main title to perfect centering would not have been acceptable, since it was accomplished optically at the lab.

Rule 6: No Superficial Action
The film must not contain superficial action. (Murders, weapons, etc., must not occur.)

Ideologically, this rule is the most important because it directs the moviemaker away from the insane preponderance of violent action movies that have clogged the cineplexes in recent years. Do we really need more movies about gangsters in the streets, macho turf wars, or vigilante action heroes? I hope not too many of you shout "Sir, yes sir!" Haven't we imbibed enough murder and rape on screen, far too often been the voyeurs of a villain's depravities? Did *The Silence of the Lamb*s really deserve an Academy Award? Was that the *best* signal to send to other mainstream moviemakers (ready with the knockoffs and sequels)? It was a good, gripping, suspense-filled ride, but there were other good movies that year that offered much more. That year, 1991, saw Mike Leigh's second feature, *Life Is Sweet,* a very warm-hearted tale told through intimate human moments. And *Boyz N the Hood* by John Singleton, though violent, at least offered a cautionary note, a bid for improving a life under the most difficult and dangerous of situations. Apply this test: *Can I learn something useful about my real life from watching this movie?* You'll see that many of the so-called "best films of the year" fall short. The Dogme 95 founders set The Vow of Chastity in place to oppose just this kind of superficial story-telling. Why should we celebrate—or create—movies that make us more paranoid and frightened of each other? The mindless overuse of violence in many mass entertainment–based Hollywood movies is not something to aspire to. Forget the guns, the gangsters, the war zones, and aim the camera back on the small moments that make up our lives.

Rule 7: Here and Now Only

Temporal and geographical alienation are forbidden. (That is to say that the film takes place here and now.)

Again the Dogme 95 founders are trying to keep us grounded in the reality of the moment by not allowing a work to use the traditional "movie magic" of pretending the action takes place in another time (such as Sherlock Holmes's London) or a false location (like the Hollywood back lot illusion of a Hong Kong street). In my mind, rule 7 ensures that a movie answers to today's problems, somehow includes the most current issues, real people's pain (and happiness), helps create the most modern cinematic discussions on the state of our world for any given year.

But is this enough of a reason to strip moviemaking of one of its most effective illusions? Must we forgo the use of a flashback? Ruling out this device actually helps the Dogme 95 moviemaker maintain a strong driving momentum, which, coupled with the hand-held/no-lights dictum, makes for something approaching a nonfiction, documentary approach to fictional storytelling. If the DV moviemaker applies this rule and the previous ones we've discussed to trying to produce a scenario rife with cliché, such as a story revolving around a group of rich people visiting a castle and the working class help that serves them (as in Robert Altman's *Gosford Park*), it's a good bet that the results will be totally different from what anyone expects—especially if you use real servants and real rich people for your actors! Your Dogme 95 movie will have originality of style and unusual gumption. That's the gift of going Dogme 95.

Rule 8: No Genres
Genre movies are not acceptable.

A genre movie is something that falls neatly into a clearly defined category of picture, usually identified in a word or two:

> Gangster flicks: Everything from *Little Caesar, Public Enemy,* and *White Heat* to *Some Like it Hot, Bonnie and Clyde, The Untouchables, The Godfather.*
> Westerns: *The Squaw Man, Destry Rides Again, Stagecoach, High Noon, The Wild Bunch, How the West Was Won, Silverado, Unforgiven.*
> Love stories: *Love Story, Jules and Jim, Sundays and Cybelle* (Serge Bourguigon's great 1962 Oscar winner about the bittersweet friendship between an abandoned twelve-year-old

[Patricia Gozzi] and a pilot [Hardy Krüger] suffering from amnesia), Vigo's *L'Atalante, Moulin Rouge*.

Detective/psychological thrillers, film noir, crime dramas: *The Maltese Falcon, The Third Man, Taxi Driver, Serpico, Deep Cover, The Conformist, Twelve Monkeys, Unbreakable, Murder on the Nile,* Alfred Hitchcock's *Vertigo* and *The Birds, Citizen Kane*.

Romantic comedies: *The Seven Year Itch, Annie Hall, Pretty Woman, The Muse, Maid in Manhattan* (or almost anything with Goldie Hawn in it).

Sci-fi: *Close Encounters of the Third Kind, Star Wars, Blade Runner, Tron, Terminator, Total Recall, The Matrix*.

Horror/slasher: *Halloween, Psycho, Night of the Living Dead, The Butterfly Effect*.

Comedies: *Big Fish, Clerks, Ferris Bueller's Day Off, There's Something About Mary*.

Action/adventure: *Pirates of the Caribbean, The Lord of the Rings, Cold Mountain*.

Teen flicks: *American Pie, American Pie 2*.

What all these movies have in common is they meet certain standards of their genre.

With a Dogme 95 movie—or any original movie—you don't really want to meet anyone's requirements. I know that sounds strange—following Dogme 95's strict rule 8 that says don't follow any strict rules—but there you have it! Maybe some of your favorite, just plain weird movies (*The Sacrifice* and *Solaris* by Andrei Tarkovsky, *Frame-up* by Jon Jost, or *Adaptation* by Spike Jonze) don't fit anywhere except in someone's top twenty favorite films list. That's what you want to focus on as models for your own no-budget creations. Make something that can't be categorized.

Rule 9: Academy 35mm Only
The film format must be Academy 35mm.

This is a very tough rule to abide by if you have no money and are shooting on low-cost DV. I'm really not going to be very good at defending this one, because it has caused me some financial hardship. The distinction between video and film is so meaningless at this point, with great video projection systems (InFocus projectors, *www.infocus.com*, make a wall-sized digital image look just like your computer monitor's fine-grain rendition, for under $1,000) and 24-fps video cameras. I can't see the logic in this one, other than to make sure that there aren't too many Dogme 95 movies in existence.

Of course, there are VHS/DVD copies of Dogme 95 movies at video stores and for sale online, so that must mean it is acceptable to

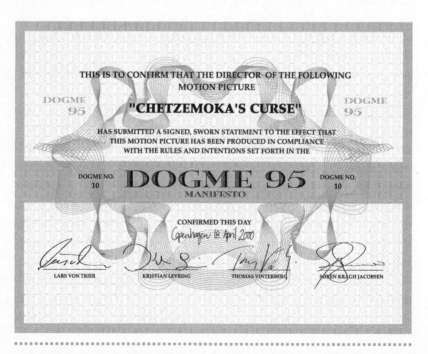

Our *Chetzemoka's Curse* (Dogme No. 10) is one of only thirty-five movies to date that have received official certification by the Dogme 95 Secretariat in Denmark.

distribute a Dogme 95 movie on various video formats. In any case, I hope this rather severe rule will be eliminated, or at least amended, to encourage a more rapid outpouring of Dogme truth-telling features.

Rule 10: No Director Credit
The director must not be credited.

This is another tough rule, but I stand by it 100 percent. Remember my statement, as an art student applying to graduate school, that I wanted to "make enough elegant works of art to become a living legend before I graduate"?

With my cocky proposal I wanted to explore my subconscious drive, wondering if I was doing art just in the hope of becoming rich and famous. Did I consider all the hard work to be just a prelude to celebrity, or did I derive pleasure from the process of discovery and the subsequent accomplishment of an arduous task? Do we really know our innermost secrets with regard to our drives and intentions? Maybe part of our ability to work extra hard comes from trying to prove our worth to others. If you have parents who have invalidated you in some way (nothing you do ever seems to please them), you can easily find yourself caught up in a process of trying to prove yourself worthy of their respect. Unfortunately, it's often the case that the closer you get to success, the more these negative forces try to squelch your hard-won positive energy and achievements. That's because your risk taking and out-of-the-box thinking may be an affront, contradicting the priorities by which they've lived their lives. So your father or mother may never hand down the self-esteem you seek. But you can use that angst as fuel for withstanding the difficult path of producing independent feature-length movies. You can either prove them right about their good-for-nothing, misguided son or daughter by giving up, or you can show them what success looks like.

If it's the actual artistic work that pleases your soul deep down, shooting and editing your footage into a multilayered embodiment of glorious truths, then do you really need the accompanying on-screen credit as "director"? And, of course, everyone will eventually discover who made the movie anyway!

■　　■　　■

At some point you'll arrive at the end of your shoot in one fashion or another, whether taking the Dogme 95 route or going down the Hollywood-style road, with script to blocked-out scenes, multiple takes, and coverage, all now affordable with inexpensive DV tape and disk stock. Or maybe your method has evolved into something between the two, where your intuition has room to stretch, and you've developed a flow that delivers. What counts is that you've made the attempt to put down your unique vision on digital media, where none of the quality will be diminished as you assemble the pieces. No matter how unusual the results achieved, the one thing we all have in common at the end of a shoot is that a new adventure awaits: editing.

7

ELECTRONIC EDITING:
FINAL CUT EXPRESS, FINAL CUT PRO,
AND MORE

No matter which DV camera you use to record your high-quality digital images and regardless of how well you directed your movie on location, there comes a point when the entire project's fate rests on editing all the pieces together. Suddenly you will need to select the best takes and determine the correct pace and flow of a feature. Even if you hire an editor to sort out your movie, someone who can log and capture footage into a computer and start assembling shots, it will ultimately be your job to direct the effort, be the driving force behind getting the movie completed to the highest standard possible.

EDITING OVERVIEW

What is editing? Well, it's an act of creation. You will take all those hundreds (or thousands) of tiny elements of sound and image and somehow align all that information in a way that tells a singular story or explains a singular experience. The quality of editing will determine the success or failure of your project. The final compilation of your various scenes and shared moments of human (or animated) reality will ultimately determine whether your movie will be embraced, first by the programmers of the festivals who must fill their schedules with work they believe is exceptional, and later by the audiences to whom it is presented. Acceptance somewhere automatically brings a feature to the attention of other programmers, who can help launch it at Sundance, Berlin International, New Directors/New Films, and other important festivals and showcases whose scouts and "consultants" are always looking for discoveries.

At some point after your feature is selected by the gatekeepers (we're thinking positively here), you'll find yourself sitting in the dark with a roomful of strangers watching the movie you spent many months editing and finalizing. Will your movie hold up? Will it offer something new? Will audience members, watching your projected DV feature (the digital light projectors are awaiting), be so moved as to tell all their friends "See this movie!"? If they do give your movie good word of mouth, it will be clear that you have successfully found the emotional center of what you shot, and you will have let that core tell you how to cut the entire movie into a cohesive whole. No matter what you've shot, you can raise your footage (pictures and sounds) to this highest level of consciousness if you just keep editing and exploring your body of footage with an open mind. You can take it further than anyone could possibly imagine, as long as you don't stop short of eliciting the fullest potential of your footage.

With investors and friends becoming impatient for the release, you may need to exercise extra diligence and determination to persevere for years beyond the shoot toward refining a cut. At worst, the multitude of scenes you recorded (as a first-timer or even as a seasoned writer/director who pushed the storytelling envelope) is a muddled mess with little cohesiveness and some stretches seemingly impossible to connect. And strangely enough, it is often just from playing with footage that's in utter disarray—a failed shoot, basically—that a kind of higher-level, "new" movie can emerge. Why? Moviemakers have to work harder, go further, get more creative than usual to make a functional movie out of the bunch of ill-fitting, hodgepodge shots created in the course of their nonlinear storytelling. Yes, I'm saying that it can actually be better that you shot something less than cohesive, with little in common with the typical Hollywood product. I know this surprises you because you thought you were making a movie to become successful. Well, that's still true. Success can still happen. It's just that the route to that goal may take much longer than you think.

The depression you'll feel, the worry when the edit doesn't fall right into place, must be supplanted by the understanding that you've begun a fantastic new adventure, in which editing will call into play your highest level of perceptiveness. To cut your movie together, you must understand yourself and your world on a much advanced level. Because of this problem you've created for yourself—all those hours of footage to edit—you must become more enlightened before the solution to your cut is apparent. This dilemma could actually be compared to the *Lord of the Rings* saga. You are now on an adventure, off to new lands where, instead of delivering a ring to a fiery pit, you must deliver your DV feature to the marketplace. That stretch of time between starting out (shooting) and completing your journey as editor of a DV feature is fraught with problems no less challenging and disorienting than Frodo's journey.

Editing is almost always more than just assembling scenes into some order or cutting actions together (wide shot: *he reaches for the TV remote control*; closeup: *his hand grips the plastic*; super-closeup: *his fingers press the channel changer*). Through continual immersion in your material, you must somehow create a living and breathing entity. By being supremely sensitive to what you see and hear while reviewing your footage, carefully analyzing what the scenes and the complete whole are trying to say, you can make an enduring work that people will watch years from now. And you don't need two towers to affect people deeply. You just need to get truthful with yourself.

Editing *A Man, a Woman, and a Killer*

Here's an example of the difficulties I faced editing my first feature-length movie, *A Man, a Woman, and a Killer*. I had hired my then twenty-year-old friend and roommate Wayne Wang (*The Joy Luck Club, Smoke, Chinese Box*, etc.) to direct on location, while I planned to do the camerawork in 16mm. Neelon Crawford and Lee Serrie were brought in as the on-location sound recordists and paid a total of $1,500 for two weeks' work. I was spending $5,900 to produce the shoot in Mendocino, California, and purchased a box of forty-five 11-minute rolls of Kodak #7276 B&W 16mm filmstock (about 8 hours of footage, equal to 8 Mini-DV standard cassettes) to cover eleven days of shooting. None of us had ever shot a feature-length movie before, though Wayne and I had created a short film together, *1944*, which had won a 1st Place prize at the Ann Arbor Film Festival the previous year. Anyway, we believed we could pull off a feature.

While ostensibly the movie was about a gangster (played by Dick Richardson) and his girlfriend (played by Carolyn Zaremba) waiting in a farmhouse for a hit man (played by Ed Nylund) to come and kill him, the rolls of footage, soundtrack, and image work print that I found myself surrounded by back in the editing room just weren't capable of yielding this simple story line result. The parts, connections, and transitions just weren't there. I knew that Wayne felt he'd failed in his direction, but, hey, I was game to keep trying to edit the footage into something. Months went by. I shuffled the assembly around, fine-cut scenes over and over, but to no avail. There were many who thought I was battling a lost cause. Even after a year—twelve months of 8- to 10-hour days, five days each week of editing—I still couldn't "find the movie." Yet there were some really great scenes, beautiful shots, and strong dramatic moments in the footage, and I refused to give up either on the material or on my substantial financial investment (I spent all $11,000 of an inheritance). I was latched onto that footage and was going to ride it forever, if that's how long it took to get a final cut.

Sometime during that difficult year it became painfully apparent that I just wasn't smart enough to figure it out. And I accepted that, humbled in a way by the task and the vastness of it. "How do I get smarter?" I wondered. Well, to begin with I gave myself longer breaks, taking myself away from the edit room for a few days at a stretch for rest and relaxation in soothing locations, like the old 1880s Mendocino Hotel (still a reasonable getaway deal at the current rate of $100 a night for a room, with bathroom down the hall). There on the fog-swept California coast, mere blocks away from the red house on Kelly Street where we'd shot the movie, I recouped energy. By the second day I felt alive again and ready for more in-the-trenches editing warfare ahead. Over time I came to realize that, while there might not be tangible editing progress, just my staying on the job (fending off creditors, borrowing more money while surviving the weekend caretaking of my little kids, Heather, Morgan, and Bowbay, from my first marriage) was a kind of achievement.

At home in Oakland, across the bay from my San Francisco editing room at W. A. Palmer Lab, I took more breaks, saw movies when I could, and decided to read books to get smarter. (I had to get smarter!) One book that fell my way at a garage sale was the memoir of playwright Tennessee Williams. I started reading and suddenly got incredibly charged up. It showed me how an author could jump all around in a time frame. The book had me in 1940 one second, 1974 the next, just with a paragraph heading, and yet all the thoughts and words flowed cohesively together as a quality experience. I wondered if I could exercise that same kind of freedom, take those kind of liberties with our *MWK* movie.

Back in the editing room, fired up by the new input, I started shifting things around, making the first third of the movie Part I, about how Dick saw the world (his "gangsterism"), using flashbacks and flash-forwards to structure the material. Part II became actor Ed

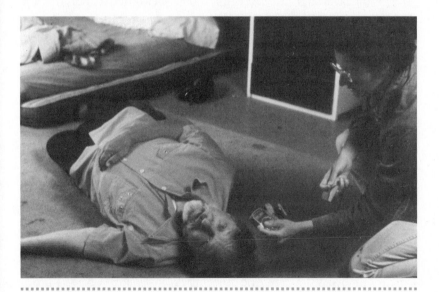

Actor Ed Nylund, as Uncle Jim, plays dead for Lee Serie's light meter reading on the set of *A Man, a Woman, and a Killer*. (©1975 L.L. Productions)

Nylund's section (Uncle Jim mistaken for a hit man) and took on the story from his vantage point. That left Part III for the finalé, in which female lead Carolyn Zaremba's unstable character Z shoots Uncle Jim and we witness his death and ultimately Dick's demise as well. I then brought the main three characters into the sound recording studio of the lab and had them each tell their real-life stories, what their lives were like growing up, how they felt about their costars (Carolyn and Dick had begun an affair during the shoot), and so on. I encouraged Ed to angrily denounce a certain scene he felt "didn't represent me." In the outs I found preclapboard, unstaged moments and put them back into the cut, basically using documentary footage from both sides of the actual takes. As soon as I pieced the narrations into the movie and added a color slides section I designed as a "credits drop," the movie miraculously came to life. Yes, I got all that creative energy (new ideas!) thanks just to reading part of a book. The movie, by virtue of the new editing decisions, suddenly became a film about the making of a film.

This breakthrough cut had come about when I understood that the main character, Dick, actually saw reality as if it were a foreign film being made about his life. With that realization I was prompted to add English subtitles to the movie, subtitling not only words Dick spoke, but also what other characters said, as if his mind was creating their reality. In a few places I used silent subtitles when Dick wrote feverishly at his writing desk. Early on in my film history education I realized that I *read* my favorite movies, including those by Ingmar Bergman (*Waiting Women, The Seventh Seal, Wild Strawberries, Persona, The Hour of the Wolf, Cries and Whispers*); Jean-Luc Godard (*Breathless, Alphaville, Two or Three Things I Know About Her*); Jean Renoir (*The Grand Illusion, Rules of the Game*); Francois Truffaut (*The 400 Blows, Jules and Jim*); Pier Paolo Pasolini (*Teorema*); and many other subtitled movies that had left indelible marks on my psyche. "Why not read our movie too?" I thought. The subtitles I created added a foreign film–like flair to our B&W footage And since it was in English (viewers heard the English words as they watched them appear on screen), I could play with the realities of subtitling. Some I'd hold like a freeze frame, letting an idea hang on the screen as uncaptioned dialogue continued.

Fortunately I enjoyed the subtitling process, because it took me more than two months of work to type dialogue into a subtitle text and then have the more than five hundred two-line titles typeset, kodalithed to negatives, and taped down as separate cells ready for the lab to shoot. This time-consuming act of "unnecessary" subtitling ultimately gave our movie an original style that prompted the Rotterdam Film Festival to hail *A Man, a Woman, and a Killer* as "a discovery" and fly me over to The Netherlands for the film's European Premiere.

The moral is to trust your instincts as you edit your feature. Don't become impatient, and don't be dissuaded from completing the task on your own terms. Remember, you have the final cut, so maintain the control to cut it to your complete satisfaction. This is your special time to invent new forms.

Because I was experimenting with the mix of real-life stories and fictional elements while trying to save *A Man, a Woman, and a Killer*, I was forced to develop a unique "editing vocabulary" that could build on itself. Years later, when collaborator Wayne Wang asked me to help him cut his future indie hit *Chan Is Missing,* I was able to exercise all the editing skills I had developed over eight years of cutting my own complicated features. And it was enjoyable to edit someone else's movie for a change, to sit there shaving off unneeded footage and effectively placing narrations (written for Wayne by the uncredited author Isaac Cronin) to help the film flow.

Here's an example of how some editing decisions can firm up the overall concept of a movie like *Chan Is Missing*. To help design a credit sequence at the beginning that spoke "Asian-American," I convinced Wayne to reposition a Chinese version of Bill Haley's "Rock Around the Clock" song that sat in the middle of the rough cut. I wanted to bring it to the front to combine it with a Chinese cab driver's slow drive through Chinatown. This cab driver footage wasn't as yet included in the cut, but since I had synced up the workprint and mag track for Wayne months earlier, I knew all the material, and this particular shot suddenly came to mind for opening the movie. I thought we could set up some white main titles to play off the dark, reflective windshield while shapes of Chinatown buildings passed by, then shift to black titles as the reflection turned lighter from the clouds drifting above. That combination of music and titles worked to kick off the feature in an elegant style that was intrinsically connected to the inner core of the material. That's what you are after when designing a credits drop to begin your movie.

If you enjoy the process of discovery, uncovering the strengths and weaknesses of scenes, inventing solutions to correct what is lacking, remaining steadfast in your belief that the footage has yet to reach its full potential, then you'll find a new kind of satisfaction and happiness when you get into a regular daily routine in the editing room (wherever your computer is located). Every day of work on a movie offers exciting challenges, a chance to make choices and exert artistic control to create something worth sharing.

And there's no real difference between film editing (Hollywood or indie style) and the electronic cutting you'll do. The DV moviemaker/editor must make it all work, designing a flow of images and sounds that make up a viewable movie right from the main titles through to the end credits. Accomplishing this may take a great deal more time than you bargained for. To be a good parent to your footage, to honor all those humans, both on the screen and off, who helped your project move forward against all odds, you need to muster the determination never to stop editing until the feature is completed. After a few months of editing, you'll start to get a second sense of just what abstract pieces are required to build a foundation that includes some kind of beginning, middle, and end. Remember, as editor/producer, you can demand that the writer/director (you) go out and shoot more footage, record additional narrations, take still pictures as a form of visual narration, even create special effects and transitions if needed. An abandoned project will haunt your career. You don't want that. Everything good—all the tools for having a successful moviemaking career—will come out of your hard-won solutions to your first feature's editorial problems. Without question, you must have the fortitude to complete that first feature, no matter how many years it takes.

I couldn't possibly have been successful producing the ten-day features with my Feature Workshops without having first experienced earlier editing trials by fire, solving the jigsaw puzzle–like juxtapositions of scenes in my first five features. It's taken all the skills I've accumulated, as well as an ever growing supply of new ones, to survive the editing of a DV feature in six days, even with the help of world-class Avid and Final Cut Pro editors on board. So good luck on cracking the personal codes of your own special editing techniques, developing that special brand of vision that you'll stamp on all your good works. But before editing commences you'll want to ensure that you can work unhindered and unbothered in an artistic trance at times, safely sequestered from the demands of the real world. To do that you need a system for politely declaring your workstation off limits, giving family members and friends the chance to respect your need for privacy. I use a simple color-coded sign taped to my office door: *green*—Walk right in; *yellow*—Please knock first; *red*—Do not disturb. Just pin the appropriate colored card to your door and start cutting!

Basic Steps for a Computer Cut

When I approach editing a movie, I like to imagine the job in the most general terms:

> Get footage captured inside the memory of my computer.
> Get it trimmed and rearranged (with transitions and titles added, along with music and possibly narrations).
> Export it to a final master copy, either printed out of the computer to Mini-DV or DVCAM tape, or burned to DVD.
> Possibly transfer it to Betacam SP or Digi-Beta, as required for national and international screening.

I don't really want to have to become a professional computer programmer to get these jobs done. Here's a list of the basic editing steps you'll need to follow whether cutting film, Mini-DV, Pro-DVCAM, or HDTV digitally on a computer:

1. Capture footage at the highest quality, importing high-resolution images along with CD-quality sound.

2. Name the shots and compiled scenes so that they can be easily located in a vast computer filing system (send all of one feature's media files to a separate 80- to 500-gig external hard drive's "capture" file).

3. Assemble the shots into scenes, then change the sequence around, shortening and lengthening shots to find the powerful breakthrough cut.

4. Add and render basic transitions (fade-ins and -outs, dissolves) as well as other well-chosen special effect transitions (water ripple, wipes, page turns, etc.) that fit intrinsically with your material.

5. Add music and/or sound effects (unless editing a Dogme 95 movie; see Chapter 6) in support of the story you are telling.

6. Compose and add credit title sequences to introduce your movie and to end it 70 to 90 minutes later.

7. Mix sound (so that no off-tones or drastic volume changes break the spell of your movie) and balance color (keep flesh tones natural unless you have a different creative goal in mind).

8. Create the highest-quality, longest-lasting master copy possible, burned on DVD with backups on Betacam SP and Digi-Beta cassettes.

That's my simple list. How exactly to accomplish each task with your particular software program isn't so simple, though. Each step is complicated or clouded over by all the options each NLE offers.

FINAL CUT EXPRESS

Fortunately for all those moviemakers without deep pockets, Mac has generously offered a pared-down version of their cutting-edge Final Cut Pro editing program, called Final Cut Express, at a cost most of us can afford ($299, *www.apple.com/final/cutexpress*). For those DV artists who outgrow iMovie, feeling constricted by their editing procedures, this is the next logical step toward becoming a professional DV feature film-maker. Of course, if the money is available, I'd say put the $1,000 on the table and buy Final Cut Pro (occasionally found for as low as $500 on eBay), but you won't really be losing any time learning the Express version, since the interface, editing tools, Timeline, and import/export functions are all fairly identical (and I won't need to repeat the basic how-to editing steps beyond what I've supplied in the Final Cut Pro section later). The point is that, as you continue to shoot more movies, tackle new themes, and build up your personal vocabulary and style of moviemaking, your demands in the editing portion of the process will expand exponentially. You'll keep pushing the envelope, seeing deeper into the possibilities of juxtapositions, modification of textures, and even animation (see "Advanced Effects Editing and Animation Software and Techniques" section toward the end of the chapter). It is certainly possible that you might even conceive some new editing proposition that is, as yet, impossible to accomplish on any NLE software system. As one of the moviemakers of tomorrow, you owe it to yourself to start editing with these higher-end programs that will give your creative work new muscle. Here's how to get started with Final Cut Express.

Preinstallation Final Cut Express Overview

It should be with real excitement that you first open up the box of FCE, knowing that you are on the threshold of thrilling artistic work ahead. If while you were in the store buying the software you stopped and read from the fold-out box, you know you have purchased an editing system that offers the ability to edit several projects at the same time. You also learned that you have access to a Color Corrector for adjusting differently lit clips, transition effects in the hundreds (previewing cross-dissolves, and wipes in real time without rendering), multilayering of video clips or graphic files, Boris calligraphy for stunning 2D and 3D titles (rolls, crawls), picture cutting tools just like Final Cut Pro (razor blade, ripple, roll extend, and split), soundtrack tools for on-site voiceover recording directly into the Timeline, level meters, EQ and audio filters, and more. Most importantly, your Final Cut Express is compatible with Final Cut Pro, so that at some point when you upgrade to the more expensive program, you can bring your project along.

> **NOTE:** Before purchasing any NLE software, check that it is compatible with the Mini-DV or DVCAM camera that you already have or intend to buy. Go to *www.apple.com/finalcutexpress/qualification.html* and locate your particular camera model on their extensive manufacturer list.

Of course, before making your purchase, you've also read about the requirements for running the software. Always read this carefully to make sure your current computer has adequate speed and memory for what you're intending to run. With Express the list indicates that you can use it with a G3 or G4, 300 MHz or faster. That certainly opens up the door for purchasing a much cheaper Mac platform (perhaps on *www.ebay.com*) than the expensive new G5s. More savings within our $3,000 budget means a better DV camera. But if you want to have access to real-time effects, like seeing dissolves between shots, you'll want to acquire a 800 MHz or faster single- or dual-processor Power Mac, G4, or PowerBook G4. And you'll need Mac OS X or later. If you bought a Mac OS X you'll probably want to upgrade to the Jaguar or Panther program and beyond. And finally, with 256 MB of RAM (384 or higher for real-time effects) and at least 40 MB of disk space for the program, you're set to open the box and get started.

Loading Express

If you take it slow, reading all the various pieces of paper included inside the Final Cut Express box, you'll find that registering the product will win you a free Joe's Filters Final Cut plug-in, Color Glow, the same one that was used to increase the red content of Julia Roberts's dress in Steven Soderbergh's DV feature *Full Frontal*. And once you register, you get the free ninety days of telephone support. I'll provide more information about Joe's great and affordable pack of more than

30 plug-ins later in the chapter (tip 14 in "Eighteen Tips for Advanced Final Cut Pro Finish Editing").

The two CDs that are included in the box represent the actual Final Cut Express application plus a tutorial how-to from DigitalFilm Tree company. We'll load the tutorial into the CD slot in a second, but before we do, it's worth reading the all-important sheet with the heading "Installing the Software and Using the Documentation." It starts with a note that if you go to *www.apple.com/finalcutexpress*, there might be some recent (free) updates, which are posted by Apple as they iron out the bugs for new products. So check what's available.

While the instructions for actual installation are relatively simple and can be accomplished just by following on-screen instructions, the "Recommendations for Good Performance" on the installation sheet are vital to your editing process and should be adhered to before installation. So leave the CDs on the table for just a few more moments, and take in these important don'ts:

:: Don't use your computer as a server (doing so causes dropped frames, etc.).

:: Don't use Final Cut Express while connected to the Internet via a modem.

:: Limit the use of scheduled software updates. (They recommend stopping "scheduled software updates" while using FCE, since updating can unexpectedly limit computer memory and speed during capturing and rendering.)

OK. Load the Final Cut Express CD into the disk tray of your Mac, but hang onto the envelope, which has two copies of your software serial number. Peel one off and stick it somewhere safe. Now double-click on the "Final Cut Express 1.0 Read Me" file, which at first glance seems to restate the system requirements that you read off the box, but may also have some additional information. I learned that I needed to update my Mac OS X 10.2 to 10.2.2, so it's worth paying attention to all the details of installation; in other words, proceed slowly so that you don't make mistakes that will require a reinstallation!

Next, double-click on the Final Cut Express folder. It opens to reveal:

The application (Final Cut Express folder).

Extras (Boris Calligraphy Docs, which has its own BorisCalligraphy.pdf user guide, and FXScript DVE's by CGM, which has three folders available: Softwipe patterns, Workshops/ Tutorials, and a ReadMe guide).

Documentation (Late-Breaking News.pdf, Opening an iMovie Project.pdf, and Final Cut Express UM.pdf).

Here you learn the good news—you can open and edit an iMovie in Final Cut Express—and the bad news—you can't import a Final Cut Pro project. Still, this allows you to upgrade your editing for any iMovie projects you may have worked on earlier in your DV career.

A double-click on the Final Cut Express folder opens two files, one to install the application (click on it and follow instructions) and one to repeat the cautionary notes we've read already (no Internet while editing, etc.). Once the application is loaded into your hard drive, you can double-click on the CD's Documentation file and read the steps for importing your iMovie footage, repeated below as a handy guide.

Importing iMovie into Final Cut Express

To bring an iMovie project into Final Cut Express for further cutting, just follow these four simple steps:

1. Go to the Final Cut Express bar menu and select File/Open.

2. In the dialogue box select the iMovie project file.

3. Watch the iMovie project open in the browser, which contains the sequence and clips as they appeared in the iMovie clips shelf.

4. Double-click the sequence to open the iMovie project in the Timeline.

Configuring Final Cut Express and Getting Started

Finally, after all the patience you've exhibited during the installation, it's time to activate the Final Cut Express working screens and controls, and get to work. On the hard drive, double-click on Applications. There, at the bottom of all your files, sits the Final Cut Express program.

A double-click loads the Final Cut Express Serialization registration. Here you'll enter your name and the serial number to gain entrance. Hit the Caps key and type in the capital letters, dashes, and numbers of the serial code, along with your name and production company. Hit Enter. If you've inserted your serial code correctly, the

With Apple's Final Cut Express, you have the identical viewing screens and Timeline of its high-end partner Final Cut Pro, but with a browser that handles captured movie files separately, much like iMovie's checkerboard slide bin. (Courtesy of Apple)

program should quickly appear, then run until a window shows up on the screen.

There you will be offered a choice of Choosing Setup. If you are shooting NTSC, then leave it on the DV-NTSC slot above and allow your Mac OS X to stand as the destination for the Primary Scratch Disk. (You can change it later in Final Cut Express/Preferences/ Scratch Disk when you add an external hard drive to your DV moviemaking arsenal.) Click OK and then Continue if no DV device is connected by FireWire, or Check Again if you have hooked up your Mini-DV/DVCAM camera. Presto! The two viewing screens appear (Viewer and Canvas), as do the Timeline sporting two video tracks and four audio tracks (ninety-nine tracks are available for both audio and video if needed) and the Browser window. The first thing you probably want to do is go to Final Cut Express/Preferences and change the levels of undo to "99." That comes in very handy with complicated editing maneuvers that must be retried many times before they deliver the desired results.

Then, if you will be saving your capture media on an external hard drive, click on Scratch Disks and hit the Set key where your Mac OS X hard drive is indicated as a source for your media. You'll be offered the chance to Choose a Folder. As soon as you locate your external device and click Choose, you should see your newly selected Scratch Disk file information appear, indicating the amount of storage presently available in GB (gigabytes). If you've partitioned your hard drive (see Final Cut Pro section up ahead: "Partitioning Your Hard Drive for Video and Audio Storage on a Scratch Disk"), then you can locate that storage area and choose it. In any case, you've made the first big steps to identifying and controlling the location of your media movie files in a vast computer system, which is a vital housekeeping activity when handling the large quantities of video and audio files that make up a feature-length work.

Capturing and Cutting with Final Cut Express

Before you launch into the Express program by experimentation, using only your intuition to capture footage or fool around with the Timeline and editing tools without a help manual, I suggest inserting the Digi-talFilm Tree DVD that Apple included with your program. It can help you solve editing problems that arise. So place the DVD in your computer's disk slot and load it. The first thing you'll notice is that a control panel for operating DVD programs appears on the screen (if it doesn't, or if it disappears because you've clicked somewhere else on the screen, just click on the dock and the play-stop-fast forward-reverse controls will reappear).

Click on the Play triangle and watch the title appear and then the menu. To review how you get started, click on that heading. You'll soon be watching a movie of a woman enthusiastically explaining what you have to look forward to with editing, then a man's voice discussing how to interface your camcorder, computer, and TV. In very clear animated images and narration you will be told how to set your camcorder to VTR mode as you approach the moment of capturing footage on Final Cut Express. Click on the pause symbol in the controls whenever you want to take a break from the tutorial. At any rate, the information slides by, supplying tips on how to save your first project file and set the preferences for your particular camera.

The next section in DigitalFilm Tree's instructional DVD is Capturing Video, where things start to get fun. For us moviemakers it's definitely a thrill to see shots from a camera suddenly running in high resolution on the computer screen. The DigitalFilm Tree's tutorial goes on to explain how to set in and out points for more accurate capture, then offers a section Organizing Your Clips (in the Browser window), telling how to create bins for filing like-subject shots. After that, Basic Editing will introduce you to the fundamentals of drag-and-drop assembly in the Timeline, along with using the Tool Palette (razor, ripple tools, etc.) and shortcut keys (which I cover in depth in the Final Cut Pro section—the tools are identical for both programs, as are most of the shortcuts). In very clear steps, the tutorial also covers Titling and Effects, Composing and Animation (definitely worth the time—the section on Animation alone should inspire you with the possibilities), Color Enhancement, Audio (Express offers a handy voice-over setting to record directly to the Timeline from your DV camera's microphone), and Delivery (printing the cut to a DVD, tape master, or Web).

So either stay with the tutorial as it introduces you to all the features of Final Cut Express and in turn helps demystify Final Cut Pro, or read on to the final section of DigitalFilm Tree, which describes the Apple breakthrough Delivery, how to create a Web page that could conceivably present your movie to millions on the Internet. Go to *www.digitalfilmtree.com* for further information about the company's contributions to the digital revolution.

FINAL CUT PRO

Because the new, less expensive Final Cut Express is virtually identical to the high-end Final Cut Pro (FCP) in file managing, edit tools, and settings, I'll be discussing the use of both products simultaneously. Except for the large-file batch capture approach and Memory Management extra file removal, Final Cut Express is quite capable of edit-

The large full-monitor-width Final Cut Pro 4 screens await the first viewable images, playable as soon as the *Bear Dance* highlighted "untitled" media file in the Browser is named (just click on it and type) and dragged into the Timeline. (Courtesy of Apple)

ing your feature. The trick is to keep your shooting ratio down, so that you don't have to remove media files until a project is completed. With my Portugal-produced *Bear Dance* movie, on which I shot just three Mini-DV cassettes (for 200 minutes—one was an 80-minute tape, adding 20 extra minutes to the total), I could capture all the footage and handle the memory storage on an external 80-gig hard drive.

For most beginning DV feature-length moviemakers, both Final Cut Pro and Final Cut Express will supply the same basic NLE procedures and editing tools that George Lucas used to accomplish the rough cut of *Star Wars Episode II: Attack of the Clones* and editor Walter Murch used to cut *Cold Mountain*. Here's how it feels to "go professional," arriving home with a Final Cut Pro box and the promise of a completed feature.

> **NOTE:** Make sure your current DV camera is compatible with Final Cut Pro before buying this NLE software. Check the extensive list at *www.apple.com/finalcutpro/qualification.html.*

Preinstallation Final Cut Pro Overview

Once you've paid $1,000 (plus tax) for Final Cut Pro (or less on eBay), it's critical that you take your time to introduce the editing program to the Mac OS X system correctly. Some important ingredients of your overall editing features can be lost if you jump too fast into installing Final Cut without first reading the Installation Sheet included in the box of software. The first thing you'll notice is that you should begin by upgrading your QuickTime to the Pro status. QuickTime runs your viewing of the captured movies and edit-in-progress, so you want to have the latest upgrade available. (Go to *www.apple.com* and click on Upgrades to check current offerings.)

Partitioning Your Hard Drive for Video and Audio Storage on a Scratch Disk

But even before you begin installing the QuickTime upgrade, you'll want to seriously consider partitioning the hard disk of your computer into several separate sections, so that some of your video and audio files representing your captured DV footage can be stored separately from your OS X (or OS 9.2) volumes. This will keep your computer running faster than if it were bogged down with all the media files you will need to create a feature-length cut.

With older Macs that have maybe only 60+ gigabytes of hard drive volume, it is important to define the usage of the disk volume so that the operating system won't have to spend time searching for files over the entire expanse. By partitioning 20 gigs for OS X, and allotting a minimum of about 10 gigs for OS 9.2, I was left with 30 gigs on my 60-gig G4 for the storage of video, audio, and media files. When I reformatted my Mac 933-MHz/768-MB G4 to this partitioning just after getting the software (partitioning erases everything on the hard drive, so you want to conduct this procedure early on), I'd already used my computer enough to notice the resulting increase in speed of start-up and overall pep. So partitioning will not only help you separate out the DV footage to a scratch disk (the 30-gig disk area for media files), but it will improve your computer's performance as well. And creating scratch disk storage separate from your operating programs and applications will safeguard the hard drive from being adversely affected by any file fragmentation that often accompanies such a large bulk of video and audio files.

Of course, with fast Macs, like the G5 and their ample gigs, it may not be necessary to conduct this kind of storage juggling. What's important is to set a capture scratch destination reserved for just DV footage.

Installing Final Cut Pro 4

Once QuickTime is updated to the Pro status it's finally time to click on the Final Cut Pro installation icon on your desktop, located in the same folder that supplied the QuickTime updater icon. Again, go slowly, first reading "Before You Install Final Cut 4.rtf" before heading into the full installation. Double-click on the orange "open box" FCP4 icon. Click OK and Continue to get through Apple's Agreements.

Then pick the destination for installation (Mac HD), and click Install. Restart computer afterward.

Once Final Cut Pro is installed and you try to run it, you'll need to enter your serial number from the registration papers and also reinsert the original installation software CD (if you removed it) to get the complete program to load.

NOTE: When Final Cut Pro 4 is first installed, an information box will open, asking you to run installers of Live Type Data (2 CDs) and Apple Loops for soundtrack DVDs. Skip this until later in the editing process.

Loading FCP 4 on the Monitor

Go to the Final Cut Pro 4 icon in Applications (Mac HD folder) and double-click. On the way to the Final Cut Pro program successfully filling your computer screen, the program will search for your connected DV camera. If your camera is already connected by FireWire, turn it on, set it to VTR mode, and click the Check Again button, letting Final Cut establish a link to your unit. You'll find that the software not only detects your camera type, model, and make, but lists it (or a similar unit) by name in the Video Settings menu (Final Cut Pro/Audio/Visual Settings/Capture Presets/Summary). Click on Continue if no camera is indicated. Soon your screen will fill with the generous Final Cut Pro viewing screens, Timeline, and other components of your editing software system.

Log and Capture: Importing Footage

With your camera attached by FireWire to your computer, and its VTR on and Final Cut Pro fully loaded, you'll want to reassure yourself that your DV camera's footage can indeed play (and eventually be edited) on the Final Cut viewing screens. By clicking on File/Log and Capture in the control bar (Apple-8 shortcut keys), you should see color bars filling the viewer with the words at the center. ("VTR OK" in white letters below the control buttons indicates that the system reads your DV camera.) This "disabled" warning will disappear as soon as the movie starts playing. When you click on the tiny, triangle-shaped Play button at the middle of the control console below the Log and Capture screen, making it yellow-illuminated, your footage should fill the screen (hit the spacebar to stop or start playback).

> **NOTE:** If you shot in 16:9, you'll initially be disappointed to see your images squashed into the boxy 4:3 format. To change to the intended 1:85 aspect ratio for your images, go to the Final Cut Pro/Audio Visual Settings menu, click on Sequence Presets Edit button, select 16:9 by clicking a checkmark into the box beside the ratio number, then "OK." Now return to your Final Cut viewing screen and click the Play button at the center. You should see your DV movie play in wide screen as you intended it to be.

Capturing Footage

To actually capture the footage you are viewing on the Log and Capture screen into Final Cut Pro 4, all you have to do is roll your movie and press the Apple shortcut keys Shift-C at the same time, signaling Capture-All. Suddenly the Capture screen fills with your movie footage and seems to run with less electronic interference than before. By just hitting this shortcut key command, you can import your images and sound directly into the scratch disk area of your Mac's hard drive (or external hard drive), which you selected earlier in Final Cut Pro/System Settings/Scratch Disks.

If you don't hear audio through your computer's speaker during this capture procedure, don't be alarmed. You can be assured you're importing the DV sync soundtrack as well as picture as soon as you drag the captured sequence from the project window into the Timeline and hit the spacebar to play your footage.

The default setting in System Settings regarding the amount of footage you can capture in this Capture Now mode is factory set at 30 minutes. Maybe try that for the first few chunks of imported footage before making a change. But you'll probably want to change it to 64 minutes (Final Cut Pro/System Settings/Scratch Disks/ "Limit Capture Now To" slot) just so you can devour an entire Mini-DV cassette's worth of footage in one capture. It will be a good feeling to know that a full hour's worth of Mini-DV cassette shots is already loaded in the computer with just a couple of clicks of the mouse.

Yes, I've forgone the tedious process of setting in and out points for every single shot, deciding instead to import a big bite of my movie and to cut up and assemble it (see ahead for these Final Cut tools and methods). This lets me jump right into pure editing without making decisions about in and out points before I've actually lived with my footage and can understand the natural beginning and end points of what I've recorded.

NOTE: Thanks to Square Box Systems (*www.squarebox.co.uk* in Stratford-upon-Avon, England), you can now enjoy amazing log and capture software, CatDV, which automatically breaks up your DV footage at each shot end, listing it for a first look inspection before sending it on to your computer for Final Cut Pro/Express or Avid Xpress DV editing. What this does is save many tedious hours of setting in and out points on your footage as you review a movie for capture. This is a big head start for anyone with a feature's worth of footage to manage and ultimately pare down to a final cut. The CatDV Pro version is well worth it at $275, while the low-end $80 version handles iMovie and Adobe Premier.

Loading Timeline with DV Movie Footage

The next step, loading into the Timeline the DV sequence you just captured in the Final Cut Pro 4 Project window, is also very easily accomplished, again just by dragging each file directly onto the Timeline with the mouse and releasing. You'll notice that the Timeline gets highlighted when you move a new file over its surface. That lets you know that it's active. For each new length of DV footage you are manually importing to the Timeline, drag it past the end of the last file in the Timeline before releasing. In a few seconds you can see the addition of an hour's worth of shots, with images running as light blue bars along the top, and audio files represented by light green tracks below that. To check that this computer magic is real, position the Timeline cursor over some footage and click on the triangular Play button on the console below the right-side screen. You should instantly see your movie playing and (if your computer's volume control is set above zero) hear the soundtrack.

If you'd like to get a visual representation of what the large one-hour chunk looks like on the Timeline, you need to reduce the size of the clip viewer plane by moving the corrugated-looking band control knob located between the two outward-pointing arrows directly below the audio tracks. Click on the right-side end of this expandable and contractible band and slowly inch it along. As you do, you'll see the sequence in the Timeline contract toward the left side. At a point about three-quarters of the way to the full left position, your hour-long capture will be clearly visible, with thumbnail identifying image located at the head of the picture track. It's now time to take a well-deserved pause and enjoy this landmark moment in your DV moviemaking career. You have arrived at the brink of turning your carefully shot DV footage into a high-quality feature.

Viewing Rushes

The first stage in actual editing is always to begin reviewing your shots as rushes. If you've imported your footage in a big file, you can avoid the extra wear on your DV camera, caused when the Batch Capture command runs the Mini-DV (DVCAM) tape back and forth in search of in and out points. By clicking on Play (hit the spacebar) and letting the movie run, you can now see and hear your DV footage. Wait to take notes until after the first full screening of all the footage. Soon enough it will be time to begin making a lot of decisions—about shortening scenes, changing the order of assembly, preparing to add music and transitions (fades, dissolves, wipes, other exotic effects), titles, conducting a final sound mix (see tip 7 in "Eighteen Tips for Advanced Final Cut Pro Finish Editing" later in this chapter), and full color correction (available with Final Cut Pro 3 and beyond)—before finally exporting the finished results to QuickTime movie, Mini-DV/DVCAM tape, and DVD.

While watching your movie's raw, unedited shots, you can begin to use some of the Final Cut Pro shortcut key combinations, which will be essential for positioning your footage for precise editing and reviewing.

Shortcut Keys for Viewing Final Cut Pro Footage

1. If you strike the Home key, your cursor will immediately be repositioned back to the first frame in the Timeline.

2. Hit the spacebar and your footage will play at normal viewing speed. Then tap the L key and your footage will start moving faster (you will still hear the audio at fast-forward speed). Each consecutive time you hit L, the speed of reviewing your clips gets faster. The three-L limit means three times as fast.

3. Hit the spacebar again to stop and then tap the J button. Now your footage moves backwards. Hit three Js and you'll send the movie into a fast rewind.

4. The inching disk, which allows you to move your footage back or ahead a frame at a time, is located right above the yellow/red/blue-colored square buttons console. Click-and-drag right or left to adjust cuts to their most precise alignment.

THE REAL FCP EDITING BEGINS . . .

Now that you've watched your raw footage, seen usable shots as well as all the random moments you inadvertently captured, the good, the bad, and the ugly all rolling by, it's time to start using Final Cut's

By adding one extra video track and two extra audio trakcs, you make room for audio dissolves and title superimpositions in the Final Cut Pro 4 Timeline. (Courtesy of Apple)

array of efficient editing commands to cut the movie into a tight and cohesive final product. Here's the first important shortcut key for making a cut:

Making a Straight Cut

As soon as you have determined the exact frame where you want to cut your synced audio and video clip (you've positioned the Timeline Playhead cursor needle at that cut point), hold down the Control key on your computer keyboard, and at the same time hit the V key. As soon as you type Control-V you'll immediately see the cut appearing in the Timeline, slicing through both the video and audio tracks, with little, red bow-tie–like shapes across each track. (They remind me of suture clips for holding bandages together.)

Next, hit the spacebar and allow the movie to play on, up to the next edit point that will represent the last frame of the length of footage you are isolating. (The Option-E shortcut keys will get you back to the first cut point so that you can screen-test the soon-to-be-deleted footage, running it from beginning to end again.) When the second point of cut is determined (use the inching wheel to get it precise), hit Control-V again. You have successfully bracketed the footage with front and rear cut points. In case you want to just move the footage you've isolated with the cuts (instead of deleting), this is a good time to add extra blank video and audio tracks by going to Sequence/Insert Tracks in the top bar menu and typing in the number 1 for video tracks and 2 for audio (since we're working in stereo), then hitting OK. Now you can also drag tracks up and down, along these new empty track pathways.

To finish the straight cut, highlight the equal-length picture and soundtrack footage between the "sutured" cuts, holding down the Apple key when clicking the mouse to highlight each separate track. You can see how the highlighted tracks have turned darker than the rest of the footage, the picture track turning brown and the soundtrack purple (see Step 1 on the next page). At this point you have the option of either deleting the highlighted tracks (just hit Shift-Delete) or moving that portion of the footage to a new location in the assembly.

For practice, using our Final Cut drag-and-drop technology, let's say you want to save some soon-to-be-deleted footage. What you'll want to do is move the highlighted sync video footage upward to the empty track above with the drag of the clicked-down mouse; the two audio tracks will automatically move down at the same time, even though the mouse is clicked on just the video. By keeping the pressure on the mouse, we can then slide the one video and two audio tracks down the Timeline to the right, and finally deposit them somewhere past the end of the cut for use later. Or, if we like, we can bring the tracks back to the normal, centered position with a downward mouse movement.

If you want to close the gap in the Timeline left from the removal of footage, click on that now empty space to give it a light grey highlight

Step 1: After isolating a portion of footage (you've sliced tracks with Control-V or the Razor tool [see text]) click to highlight the section for repositioning.

Step 2: Relocate the mouse pointer on the highlighted picture track (top track) and, while holding the mouse down against the table, drag it up slowly. As the picture track moves up to the empty video track above, the two stereo audio tracks will move downward, magically keeping their sync positioning as if connected by an invisible tether.

and hit the delete key. The footage to the rear will jump forward to fill in the vacated area.

Congratulations! You've shortened your assembly edit by removing extra footage and even saved it for use later. You can repeat this operation until you've discarded all the unnecessary outs. By removing extraneous footage you'll start closing in on the final form of your DV feature. And you'll learn that by using Final Cut's Razor tool (described later in the chapter), you can click exactly the same kind of piercing

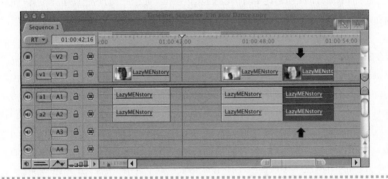

Step 3: Drag the repositioned footage to the right, down the Timeline, by the held-down mouse. Tracks being moved can either be stored outside the cut for inclusion later (just release the mouse and click anywhere on the Timeline to remove the highlight), or dropped back into the cut.

Step 4: By moving the mouse down the mouse pad with the pointer still clicked on the top track, you can move the video back onto V-1, with the two audio tracks moving up to A-1 and A-2, again part of the assembly.

cuts, but slice just one track at a time, for precision adding, subtracting, and repositioning. With a little experience you'll be able to repeat the highlight, delete, and drag-and-drop procedure as fast as your editing ideas come to mind.

Undo Your Edits: Ninety-nine Undos if Necessary

One great option that almost all nonlinear editing programs offer is "undo," the ability to reverse your editing and click your way back to an earlier configuration in the cut. Click on Edit in the top control bar, and then just click on Undo however many times it takes to get back to a stable starting place to begin editing again. The shortcut key for an undo is Apple-Z, which you can tap repeatedly to retrieve earlier assemblies.

The undo feature is essential when working on complicated programs like Final Cut Pro or Express, which offer up to ninety-nine chances to restore a cut. As I've mentioned previously, when you first start editing, you'll probably want to add to the amount of undos you can access by going to the top control bar, selecting Final Cut Pro/Express, then clicking on User Preferences, where you can set the Levels of Undos to 99.

Changing the Order of Assembly

With Apple drag-and-drop technology, all you have to do to shift scenes and shots around is to select a shot in the Timeline. This allows you to drag-and-drop it right, left, up, or down. And you can drag directly over other scenes if needed, finally releasing the mouse to drop a shot (video and audio tracks together) in a new location. Notice how the scenes in the Timeline open a space at cut points for a new shot to be dropped in. This ability to change an assembly with such ease is the greatest gift that Apple/Mac has bestowed on DV moviemakers. With their Final Cut NLE programs, hundreds of hours of tedious rearranging have been reduced to minutes.

To reposition just one piece of separate video or audio track, click on the tiny peanut-shape-in-rectangle located at the top right of the FCP4

Final Cut Pro 3
"chain" lock/unlock

Final Cut Pro 4
"peanut-shaped" lock/unlock

Timeline. Now each section you highlight (hold down Apple key to mouse-click on several lengths) can be moved or deleted.

DOWN AND DIRTY EDITING WITH FINAL CUT PRO 3: DERIVING A FEATURE FROM 200 MINUTES OF FOOTAGE

When I got some clear time in early October 2002 to cut the 3+ hours of raw footage I'd shot in Portugal, I decided to attack the problem with the most direct editorial approach Final Cut Pro offered. Here are the steps I took to (1) capture footage, (2) assemble a cut, (3) add basic transitions of fades and dissolves, (4) clean up sound mistakes and mix levels, and (5) add head and tail credits. Some of the Final Cut Pro editing steps listed here will repeat information from earlier in this chapter, but since it applies to using Final Cut Pro 3, it offers tips on using the dated-yet-still-powerful earlier software, which can be found on eBay, factory sealed, for around $300.

> **NOTE:** If you go the eBay route, bidding on and winning a Mac G4 933 MHz computer and monitor (say $1,000) plus FCP3 ($300), you'll have carved out a $1,700 budget for your 3CCD camera if staying within our $3,000 DV workstation budget.

Log and Capture (FCP3) with the Capture Now Button

Since I wanted to have a workable rough-to-fine-cut of *Bear Dance* completed in just a few weeks, I used some major shortcuts. I didn't want to use up extra time setting in and out points for each logged clip before I captured the video into my LaCie external 80-gig hard drive. So I decided to just capture directly from the source, identifying my saves by titling, using abbreviated names for scenes. With only a little over 3 hours of raw footage from which to cut a 70- to 90-minute feature, and with many scenes running long (each of the numerous real-life stories I shot was several minutes in duration), I figured this direct approach would work fine.

After clicking on File/Log and Capture in the top bar menu (or using shortcut keys Apple-8) and loading the color bar–filled screen, you'll notice that the tiny square in the button controls at the bottom of the Log and Capture screen (above VTR OK) is lit up yellow. By pressing the tiny triangle next to it, you'll see the yellow-colored center suddenly appear there and hear your camera start to play. After a few electronic hums you should then see your footage appear where the color bars used to be. From now on in the log and capture process you will control your camera (the external device) with the computer screen buttons, using your mouse-controlled cursor to click on Play (triangle), Stop (square), Rewind (far left button), and Fast Forward (far right button).

The next step, the big one of actually capturing video and audio tracks while viewing large chunks of footage, is to move your mouse and click on the Now button, which is positioned inside a slightly indented rectangle with the word "Capture" at the top (the Clip button is to one side, the Batch on the other). Immediately a large viewing screen will appear in the middle of your computer monitor, and after a few seconds of black screen your movie will play as it's being recorded to your selected hard drive. When you reach the desired end point of the scene (if it comes before your allotted capture limit), just hit the Esc (Escape) button on your keyboard, which is usually located at the upper left-hand corner. The large Capture screen will now disappear, with the final image of your capture filling a smaller screening window, along with the white lettering "Untitled 0000" at the top.

What I do at this point is click on the image in the window and drag it right into my Timeline. As the file enters the Timeline, a grey shadow appears, representing the size of the file (in relationship to other captures, some will appear larger than others). Releasing the mouse, I see that the shadowy representation of my captured file disappears (this is normal), while a new, large Save window appears on the desktop.

In the new Save window I'm asked to (1) title the clip as a Save As and (2) indicate where it should be saved (the Where slot). It is important, to my editorial thinking, that I give the clip name some careful thought so that it is easily identifiable. You might have something like my "pedrobrickannachocolate" and "rosaCustomer/knifepool," with people's names and subjects of captured scenes you've bunched together (to be later cut apart for rearranging in the assembly).

NOTE: Always make a separate list in pencil or pen of your scenes and shots as you capture them, jotting down the order of images and sounds for each original Mini-DV (DVCAM) cassette. Keep the scene list in an obvious location (on the computer table, in a well-marked folder with the name of the production and bold printing to indicate it is IMPORTANT), so that it doesn't get lost. It might be wise to make a backup photocopy to stash at home with your tax forms or other carefully filed papers. If you ever need to redigitize something months after the initial capture stage of editing (a horrible thought—running through all twenty original cassettes looking for that 10-second cutaway of cigarette-put-out-in-ashtray), these notes will save you a lot of grief.

As far as where to store clips in my LaCie 80-gig FireWire external drive, I first went to File menu in the Finder and created a new folder, Figueira2002 (later altering it to Figueira2002CURRENT). I entered the new name in the Where slot (Capture Scratch), and chose Save, thus creating a QuickTime movie folder. To test the validity of my saved clip, I can double-click on it in the file and watch the QuickTime viewing screen appear, with my saved clip in the window. Using the built-in QuickTime controls, I can play the little movie clip, see the high-resolution picture, and listen to the sound to know it is intact. Of course, there's no need to repeat this double-check process each time; I'm just pointing out that this test is possible.

The final step in getting my picture and sound clip into position for editing on Final Cut Pro is to drag it as the QuickTime movie right into my Timeline (I can see picture and sound separate into three sections, one image, two soundtracks) and release. It's just that simple on a Mac.

NOTE: Sometimes in Final Cut Pro 3 when clips are dragged into the Timeline, one of the soundtracks will drop down an extra track, disrupting the precision of your electronic worktable. To correct this (i.e., to keep the two tracks next to each other so as not to confuse them with other music tracks or sound effects you may import), I suggest you unlock the tracks and picture by clicking on the tiny chain icon (upper right of Timeline) until the link shows it's open. Then grab the lower soundtrack rectangle (it will change to a purple highlight when you grab it separate from the other matching track) and just slide the mouse up the mouse pad until the aberrant soundtrack clicks into place. If a small minus or plus boxed number appears, just lower the purple rectangular track back down (the Apple-Z shortcut command will pop it down after each failed attempt) and try again until it finally snaps in without a minus or plus frames amount showing out of sync. Finally, click the chain-link icon again, to return sync lock to the Timeline.

Timeline Editing with Capture Now Saved Footage: Moving the Assembly Around and Adding Effects

Once you've successfully inserted all the captured picture and sound files to the Timeline with drag-and-drop, you'll want to assemble the pieces in a logical order that makes sense to your story. There are several ways to accomplish this, the simplest being just to click on an entire shot (hold down the Apple key when clicking to highlight each separate part of the picture and soundtrack, with chain lock clicked open) and drag it either forward or backward in the Timeline. Of course, this drag-and-drop technique can also be used to reposition a particular section of a shot that is cordoned off with a razor cut (see the Razor Tool section ahead). If you are building the movie from the front, then I suggest that you clear some of the scenes out from that end of the Timeline, so there's room to add new ones. In this manner, you'll be able to build a rough assembly of your movie very quickly.

Another way to build your assembly is to click on each scene so that it appears on the Viewing Screen, then set the in and out points with the sliding blue markers on the bar below the images. These markers can be either manually dragged into position or snapped there by clicking on the two buttons with triangle icons that reset in and out placement. Drag your carefully selected portion of the shot to the Canvas window where the file can be dropped into the highlighted Insert or Fit-To-Fill panel; these effects panels are invisible until your mouse-clicked-on file is slid into the Canvas window. When you release the mouse, your tracks (the file that was released) will appear in the Timeline, wherever your Playhead cursor is located. In this way, you can start jockeying around the different scenes, reshuffling your assembly to find the best order through experimentation.

Cutting and Deleting: Tighten Cut with FCP3/FCP4 Tools

As soon as you feel that your assembly is in the correct order, but in need of editorial refinements, you'll want to take advantage of a few basic editing tools offered by Final Cut Pro. In the Window bar menu select Tool Bench/Palette.

The Razor Tool   In the Tools column, one of the most essential items you'll find is the Razor, a parallelogram razor blade–shaped icon. If you click on this icon and move your cursor down to a track in the Timeline, wherever you click you'll see tiny red "butterfly clips" appear along the line where the image and/or soundtracks have suddenly been split. If you then highlight one side or the other from where the split has been marked, and hit the Delete button, that portion will disappear.

Use the double blade to cut through all the tracks from the top to the bottom of the Timeline or click the chain icon (peanut-shaped icon in FCP4) at the top right of the Timeline, and then use the single blade to select single tracks. This procedure of unlocking sync (clicking on the chain/peanut icon) and clicking razor-cut sections for removal or repositioning is the key to working on separate tracks, lengthening and elongating narrations matched to images, reordering footage, and making sound corrections such as extracting voice command words and refilling those gaps with copy-and-paste clean room tone (see tip 6 in "Eighteen Tips for Advanced Final Cut Pro Finish Editing"). But, again, don't forget to return to the open broken link chain/peanut and click it closed again, reconnecting all the separate tracks in your Timeline to keep things in sync. You don't want to throw your entire Timeline out of whack. But if you do, don't panic. Remember that the Apple-Z undo shortcut keys can bring you back to an earlier sync Timeline setting.

To close up the Timeline, highlight an empty track section and press the Delete-with-Arrow key so the scenes from that point to the tail will immediately be brought forward, fitting snugly against the place where the missing portion of the scene once stood. On the other hand, if you tap the larger Delete button (no arrow), that action just vacates the tracks, leaving a gap in the Timeline.

> **NOTE:** If one Delete key doesn't work (almost like having a sticky key) when you are trying to remove tracks, just hit the other Delete key on your keyboard. A few tries will eventually make unwanted files disappear. Or temporarily cut out the highlighted tracks (Apple-X shortcut keys) and then paste them back (Apple-V).

Making Precise Cuts: Using White Edge/Black Edge as a Guide

If you are editing with two sound tracks and one picture track, you'll want to make sure that all three tracks are cut together, precisely, at exactly the same point. Look closely at the way the Playhead cursor in the Timeline interacts with the edit points of your shots. Sometimes the cursor turns white (creates a white edge to the video and soundtracks). And sometimes it looks dark, like a black line. While the final test of accuracy of cutting and rejoining the Timeline tracks will be to view them spread out to their widest lengths, after a bit of practice you will learn exactly how to position the placement of the Razor to a lined-up Playhead to make precise white-line cuts. (Black-line cuts can also represent exact-length cuts, but you need to double-check accuracy by hitting the Apple-+ keys, to inspect the cut close up, in a fully expanded Timeline view.)

Try this. Align the Razor tool to just one image/video track and, when the Playhead cursor disappears, click on the mouse, piercing the track with a cut. Now repeat that procedure for the sync soundtracks below; line up the Razor until the Timeline Playhead cursor disappears, click, and expand the Timeline to check your accuracy. That precision in positioning the Razor, before clicking the mouse to make a cut, will save you time later when cleaning up the edit. Of course, by hitting the

Apple-Z keys, you can undo any nonaligned razor cut. And don't forget to SAVE after each editing maneuver!

Using the Razor Tool with Separated Tracks

Sticking with just the Razor tool, you can accomplish basically every procedure a 16mm or 35mm filmmaker can do when editing a feature with a tape splicer. An editor would select different points at which to trim the picture or soundtrack, then remove footage from the roll and shift certain lengths of track around to achieve better clarity in a narration. Then other soundtracks would be added, as well as sound effects (birds chirping, a car driving past, a cup being placed on a table), and music. All that can now be accomplished on DV with the help of the Razor tool. The key is to click on the tiny chain-link/peanut-shaped icon found in the upper right-hand corner of the Timeline. When you click there, you'll see the sync toggle lock open. Now you can razor-cut any separate piece of picture or sound to isolate a short visual action, a single word, or even part of an utterance, whatever you need to trim. Once a section is highlighted, it can be removed or repositioned, shifted to the right, the left, up, or down with a drag of the mouse, or deleted altogether from the Timeline. When not working on particular video or audio tracks, it's worth clicking on the track-locks (padlock icons to the left of the Timeline) to give yourself absolute assurance of no odd changes occurring.

If there is a director's voice command that needs to be removed from the cut, just razor-cut on each side of the unwanted portion of soundtrack, highlight it, and, holding down on your mouse, move it to an empty track below, so that you can match it to an equal-length silent "room-tone" section of the same scene. Use the scale changing slider or Apple-+ to check on the exact positioning when precision-matching lengths. Razor-cut each side of the clean tone to match the length of the voice command (see illustration below) and highlight it. Then hit Apple-C, which copies that exact section of tone. Position the Playhead cursor past all the footage in the Timeline and hit Apple-V (repeat the "paste" enough times to create the needed length of tone for filling in). The short length of matching clean tone will magically appear. Drag it back to the gap formed by the deleted voice command and move it into place as follows: Line up the clean soundtrack length below the gap, trim it to size, click down on it, and slide the mouse upward to move the track into place. Use Apple-Z to undo and try again if any red out-of-sync numbers appear. Voila! It's really that simple to correct bad sound sections.

> **NOTE:** When you're scrolling through a feature's length of footage in the Timeline, I recommend that you temporarily highlight the picture and soundtracks you're presently working on, so that when the Timeline is expanded to its largest incremental view, you'll have a visual aid to locate your Playhead-marked cut point.
>
> And don't consider your movie fully edited until you expand the entire movie and check each cut close-up. You'll immediately see where pieces of sound and picture are not perfectly aligned in the Timeline. Make use of the magnification tool that looks like a Phillips-head screwdriver—the circle with an X in the middle, located in the same toolbox as the Razor tool. By dragging this tool onto the Timeline and clicking repeatedly, you can enlarge any por-

A voice command given to actors Christa Cesmat and Joe Gillard during the shoot of *Release the Head* is razor-cut, highlighted, pulled down, to be matched with adjacent clean tone A1/A2 track sections above for replacement.

tion of your edit (the circle with a minus sign condenses the Timeline) and examine it in full close-up detail.

Overcoming a Panic Moment with FCE/FCP When Something Goes Wrong

While cutting my movie *Bear Dance* on Final Cut Pro 3, I suddenly
found that all my footage, as seen on the canvas window, had shifted in
color, looking like a red negative readout. Where had my lovely full-
color movie gone? I must admit I freaked out a bit when I thought that
the entire hour-and-a-half movie was somehow permanently red-
saturated, and I had no idea what caused it. I had been working with
the titling generator (Window/Effects/VideoGenerators/Text/Text/
Control/Font Color) and had fiddled around with different colors for the
titles, but why would this affect the entire movie?

I tried talking to the Apple Care hot line people (I'd signed up for
just such a meltdown moment), but was told I had a 30-minute wait
ahead of me because of a high volume of calls. "The heck with that," I
thought. "I'll just go back to the computer and try again to solve it myself." Checking through the entries in the files of each heading along
the top bar (File, Edit, View, Mark, Modify, Sequence, Effects, Tools,
Windows, and Help), I came across Channels in View, clicked on the
spread arrow, and read the list. Top to bottom it included different
kinds of color frequencies: RGB, Alpha, Alpha + RGB, Red, Green,
Blue. I noticed that the little checkmark was on the Alpha + RGB setting. Remembering my Photoshop, I changed the setting to just RGB
and instantly all my images became full color again. So I guess the lesson is, when something weird happens in Final Cut Pro/Express or any
media editing or animating software system, get up, get some fresh air,
have a drink of water or a cup of tea. Relax, somehow, for a few minutes at least before returning to apply logic to solving the problem.

Importing Music from CD

While I was attending the Figueira da Foz International Film Festival
in 1998, the year our Feature Workshop DV movie *Loneliness Is Soul*
played in the Main Feature Film Competition, I met a journalist

named Américo Sarmento, who covered the festival for Portugal's largest newspaper, *Journal de Notices*. After interviewing and photographing me for an article he was doing, he handed me two CDs of a band he was producing and promoting, telling me it would be great if I could use some of their songs. Well, the years went by. Then, suddenly in the middle of editing *Bear Dance*, I awoke to the fact that I had original Portuguese music to add to the Portuguese scenes. Fortunately I had kept the CDs in a safe place and was able to locate them in a matter of minutes. Here's how I imported them into the Final Cut Timeline, an extremely easy and fast procedure.

First, insert the CD into a Mac computer. As soon as the Audio CD icon loads to the desktop, the iTunes program Player also shows up on the monitor, or you can open it with a click if it doesn't activate on your system. Before playing anything, just double-click on the icon and you'll see a window open with a file for each song, indicating the track number and that they are AIFF files. Just go to the top Finder/File and click on New Folder (in my case the new folder I created was located in the LaCie 80-gig FireWire drive on my desktop). Give the folder a suitable name (mine is called PortugueseROCK-songs), then drag the files in Audio CD over to the folder one after the other. When you let go of your mouse, each file will copy to the folder. If you have more than one CD's worth of music to copy, you should rename the first batch, since two "Track 1" files can't exist together in the same folder. At this point, you can expel your CD from the computer and put it back in its protective case.

Before you can move the music files to your Final Cut edit, you'll need to add another two blank audio tracks to the Final Cut Timeline. Go to Sequence in the top bar menu, locate Insert Tracks, click it open, and where it says Audio change the number of tracks from 0 to 2. Click OK. As soon as you see two new empty tracks appear in your Timeline, just click and grab a sound file from the new folder and drag it right into the Timeline. Just as before, when dragging picture and audio files to the Timeline, a shadowy representation will occur. Position the mouse where you'd like the sound to be located and release it. Just that quickly your new music track is part of the editorial mix.

Raising and Lowering Sound Levels: A Quick Mix

After a short period of editing you will find yourself becoming highly critical of the varying sound levels of your tracks, with scenes and music losing their punch, and you'll want to correct that deficiency. Fortunately, FCP/FCE has some good, basic audio editing capabilities built into their programs.

If you double-click on any soundtrack section in your Timeline, you'll see a new window open on the desktop that reveals the actual sound waves associated with that section. In the audio control window there is a playhead cursor (just like the one in the main editing Timeline) that can be moved right or left with your mouse. And a slider control at the bottom (again, exactly like the editing Timeline) can condense and expand your viewpoint, so that you can adjust the volume on the smallest increment of audio in a song or word of dialogue. To change the overall level of volume for a certain sequence, just hold the Apple key down and click on each track until both turn purple. For stereo tracks you'll want both tracks selected before raising or lowering volumes. Then click on the thin red line above the sound wave (you'll see the cursor morph into what looks like a tiny, two-sided clamp) and pull the track down to lower the volume, or up to raise it.

As you move the cursor, you'll see a tiny readout showing the current dB level of your audio (it changes constantly as you move the tracks). This allows you to match one volume level to another, from track to track and scene to scene, helping you determine the overall volume settings for your entire movie.

To change the sound level for a particular area of one track, you simply click on the Pen tool at the bottom of your Toolbox. (Click on Tools in the Window bar menu if the slim ¾-by-3½-inch tools window isn't available on your desktop.) Now, wherever you click along the red line that runs above your sound wave readout, you'll form a tiny red-dotted control point. Clicking again on the top pointer cursor icon at Tools, you will now be able to raise and lower a portion of the track by clicking on a red control point and mouse-dragging, while unselected points hold their place. In this manner, a sharp noise in your tracks can be quickly and efficiently lowered to a tolerable level, just by selecting the red control points on each side of the troubling volume, adding another point midway between, then grabbing that center point and dragging that part of the track to a much lower position. Click-selected control points can also be slid along horizontally, to pinpoint sound level corrections.

NOTE: Sometimes the constant double-clicking on sound files will result in an instant closing down of your Final Cut Pro/Express program; you'll be suddenly staring at your empty desktop. Before panicking, thinking that your latest round of work has been lost forever because you didn't save it in time, go to Final Cut Pro/Express Documents in the hard drive, click to open its window, and check Autosave. If you set Autosave to occur every 30 minutes at Final Cut Pro 4 (or Final Cut Express)/User Preferences/General, then at least you have your movie's cut from a half an hour ago, possibly even more recently (Check at File/Restore Project). So all is not lost. But it is worth saving your sound level changes more frequently than you're used to saving other editing changes.

Loud Volume Changes

In the soundtrack, each decibel level (dB) represents a sound change that can be barely detected by the human ear, so the changes with the control points and repositioning are fairly subtle. For more substantial changes in volume, like trying to quiet a loud bus motor, hold down the Control key and press either the minus (–) or plus (+) keys (found in the numbers keys), maybe three times for starters. You can repeat this procedure, constantly checking on results, until you reach the desired sound levels that work for your scene and overall mix.

Making sweeping changes in volume settings is vital when introducing music as an overlay. For more intricate sound mixing maneuvers, you'll want either to use the Peak DV digital Audio editing software included with FCP3 or upgrade to Final Cut Pro 4 with its new sound mixing board capabilities. Or check out the latest Pro Tools professional audio software, a version of which is now available free at their Web site (*www.digidesign.com*).

Professional Sound Mix for DV Features

No matter how well you think you've ironed out sound for your DV feature and made it consistent and effective in your 70- to 90-minute cut, you might want to consider finalizing your movie with help from a professional sound mixing technician with feature-film experience. Why? Because all you need is one screwup somewhere in the sound-track (an off sound, or a too-low/too-high volume moment, etc.) to ruin the viewing experience, especially when the movie plays in a large theater with sound running through the main speaker system. I was lucky to discover Seattle-based Scot Charles of Blue Charles Productions (206-783-6797, *info@bluecharles.com*) to help me achieve a re-fined theatrical sound mix for my DV movies. It was Scot's great sound mix for *Loneliness Is Soul* that helped that movie get selected for the Best Script award over more than thirty other million-dollar-plus features at the Main Film Competition of Figueira da Foz International Film Festival. While the resolution of the VHS video projection left much to be desired in the 500-seat theater where it screened, the super-clean and clear soundtrack running through the house speakers gave the movie its competitive edge. Good sound can make your mind see images sharper than they actually appear. Good sound controls the moviegoing experience. Our movie was the first DV feature to be included in the Main Film Competition; they now screen regularly in Betacam SP.

What does Scot do to the soundtrack that I can't accomplish with a home mix, you ask? For starters he applies more than twenty years of experience to his sound-tweaking decision making. Though it may be my natural inclination to raise the level of a phone conversation between someone seen talking in a booth and someone off camera, Scott will lower that off-camera sound a bit more than I normally would, knowing it mustn't overpower. And he'll adjust music tracks to a lower setting, because my louder levels would have pulled the viewer out of the story. These are pretty basic examples of what a sound expert does to manipulate a series of loose scenes into a cohesive motion picture experience.

But their art goes much, much deeper. When you add up, say, fifty of these subtle and not so subtle sound mix decisions, the movie that emerges is a much better one from the one you brought to the studio. So as long as Scot can tolerate my need to keep his sweetening mix down to a couple of days' duration, I'll venture over to his home studio in Seattle for each new feature. Fortunately his rates are very reasonable, making it possible to give most DV movies a professional "theatrical quality" sound mix tune-up for under $1,500.

Basic Titling with FCP

For my Figueira da Foz movie I decided to build a series of titles with no motion, just credit "cards" that would fade in and out, words in white superimposed against black and then over a final credits scene. Here's the procedure.

Open the Effects window if it isn't already on your desktop (go to window in the top bar and click on Effects, or use shortcut keys Apple-5). The Effects list will then appear in your browser. Pan down until you come to Video Generators, and open that section by clicking on the tiny triangle beside it. Then open Text (another click on the triangle control), and you'll find another Text box. Just latch onto the Text box icon located in the Text section (the Text icon sits directly under Scrolling Text), and drag it to the Timeline (a new video track V2 will suddenly load to accommodate the new title). You should then immediately see a new solid purple "text" track appear.

Double-click on the new Text track and you'll see a viewer window open with tiny graph-style checkerboard squares. At the top left bar menu you'll see several tabs. Click on Controls. That opens your text-typing window. Highlight the words "Sample Text," hit Delete, and type in your own credits. I'd recommend selecting one of the bolder type-faces for your font, since the narrow ones tend to read somewhat imperfectly in Final Cut Pro after rendering

When you've finished the first credit, just click on the Canvas window and you should see your new title appear there. What I like to do when creating a series of titles with the same height and spacing is use the Razor tool to chop the long initial title track (as it's first loaded into the V2 track) into smaller portions, after I've typed in my first title.

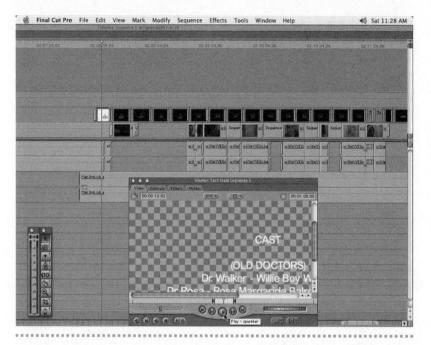

Clicking on the Video tab in the titling bar menu shows the credit as it will appear on screen, with spacing and alignment (click "Fit All" in magnification button list above checkerboard to see full title in viewer window).

That way, I have all the subsequent title boxes waiting. I then just double-click on each one, type in credits, close the window (checking titles with a click on the Canvas window), and drag the Fade-In Fade-Out box (from Windows/Effects/Video Transitions/ Dissolve/Fade-In Fade-Out Dissolves), and release it at the end of each title. You can still drag-and-drop the titles, changing their position (and length—just click-and-drag at either end) in the Video track, until you have set the screen time for each titles plate. Then add the correct fade-in/fade-out or other appropriate effect to your credit sequences.

A final titling procedure is accomplished by selecting Sequence/ Render All in the top bar menu. It shouldn't take more than a few minutes to render everything (the red and green lines in the Timeline above the titles will turn to a dull purple). That's it. Of course there are much more complicated titling procedures (I'm sure you'll learn them as need dictates!), but it's best to ease into FCP by first using the basic magic of the system, which can still get you elegant titling results.

EIGHTEEN TIPS FOR FINAL CUT PRO FINISH EDITING

Here's a basic list of editing procedures for making your cuts tighter and more effective, and some notes of caution—like *saving* often as you edit! Of course, the essence of great editing is not being satisfied with anything short of perfect transitions and seamless cuts that add up to the best pace for presenting your material. You won't want to bypass any of these procedures or final advice on mastering to safeguard all your fine work.

1. *Clean cuts (turning the playhead cursor white).* As you spend more time with Final Cut Pro/Express you'll begin to see a pattern of how the most exacting cuts are made. When a cut at the end of a section of picture and soundtrack is clean and even, the playhead cursor turns white when aligned exactly against the edge. Try it and you'll see this is true, whether the Timeline is stretched out to full, foot-long increments or not. This white morphing of the playhead is your indication that your cut is precise, perfectly aligned between all the tracks the playhead cursor touches.

To double-check the sharp and precise cutoff of several tracks, spread out the Timeline (for close-up view use either the sliding enlargement knob under Timeline or the Apple-+ keys, or click on Timeline with the Phillips-head screwdriver magnifying tool). Are the tracks even to themselves at this widest setting? If you see part of the edge of your cut, say the picture edge, looking black, while the two soundtracks are white and more invisible, then your cut is jagged and you need to correct it. Stretch out the Timeline to its widest possible setting and retrim with the Razor tool, removing the overlap with highlight and delete actions. Or, for a short end, just drag a shot up past the cut point and razor-cut it even with the other tracks.

2. *Unlocking and relocking tracks for fine cutting.* You'll soon discover the need to cut only one track at a time, and that requires unlocking the tracks so that only one section of the image or sound can be highlighted. The little piece of chain in FCP3 (peanut-shaped icon in FCP4) in the upper right part of the Timeline will have to be changed back and forth, between locked and unlocked (with a click of the mouse), so that you can work on separate, very small, selected parts of the picture and soundtrack in the Timeline. To select, or highlight, simply click on individual sections of the picture or soundtrack while holding down the Apple key.

If there is a scene made up of ten little lengths of sound and picture that you've trimmed and wish to move elsewhere as a complete unit, you'll need to hold down the Apple key and click on each element until each part of the scene has been selected and changed to the deeper highlight color. Then, by clicking on any part of the larger conglomerate and holding down the mouse, you'll see the pointed cursor change into a four-pointed star. Keeping the mouse down, you can then drag the unit to a new location.

After you've accomplished your careful work on individual tracks, completed any nonsync procedures, and repositioned work in the Timeline, make sure to click on the chain/peanut again to lock the Timeline down in its sync setting. If sync has slipped during your editing, you'll want to apply the undo (see tip 3).

3. *Using the Undo option (ninety-nine levels of returning your cut to an earlier state).* One of the most helpful keyboard shortcuts in Final Cut Pro or Final Cut Express is the Apple-Z key combination for instructing the program to revert to an earlier configuration. Each time you hit the two keys, you move the cut back one step, making the Timeline change to earlier settings. I make use of the undo keys when I need to jockey a piece of soundtrack into sync with its other stereo track if sync is lost. If I drag a track up into the Timeline and tiny red squares appear that say −1 or +1 (or other number combinations), indicating nonsync drift, I hit Apple-Z to make that portion of the track jump back to its starting position where I began the maneuver. I just keep trying and then undoing until I get it right and the soundtrack has no little out-of-sync red message. To set your level of undo to 99 in

FCP3, go to File/Preferences/General and type in "99." For FCP4, go to Final Cut Pro/User Preferences/General.

4. *Saving (and resaving) while editing.* Make sure you save your cuts often. Save after any progress you've made. Save after designing a good transition or finding the correct sound level of a scene. If you're not careful, you could be caught between autosaves, losing minutes of tedious sound crafting or fine editing that would be virtually impossible—or at least a giant pain—to duplicate. And try not to accumulate scads of copy saves that will ultimately clog the storage memory of your computer. When saving your latest cut on Final Cut, look carefully at the Save As window and remove the extra word "Copy." By deleting "Copy" you will be able to save your work without littering your entire desktop with new files that eat up memory. When the window opens asking "Replace?" click Yes.

And save your work in several locations. Save it once on the external hard drive and once on the desktop. If you have a second external hard drive, save it there as well. These backup copies are vital to adding security to the idea that the results of all your months of hard computer editing will be available for exporting to a final master tape or DVD when you start up your computer the following day. If the hard drive on my computer suddenly goes dead, I'll still have the movie at another backup location. *Save often.*

5. *Matching pieces of sound and picture for overlays and inserts.* First you need to make room for the matching of lengths of picture and soundtrack by adding new empty tracks to the Timeline. Go to Sequence/Insert Tracks in the top Final Cut bar menu and type in "2" where it indicates the number of audio tracks, type "1" in the video tracks slot, and hit OK. Then click on the chain/peanut sync control to unlock it, making the Timeline nonsync. Razor-cut and select a portion of the stereo soundtrack (click on two tracks to activate the purple highlight), while not cutting or highlighting the picture track. You can now click on the stereo tracks and move them down to the two new tracks below, adjacent to a portion of other tracks that you want to replace.

After stretching the Timeline out to full size, use your Razor tool to click cut points at each end of the replacement section (making sure that the Timeline cursor turns white through the cuts). Once you delete the bad sound (hit Delete after just those stereo track portions are highlighted purple with chain/peanut unlocked), then drag exactly the same-length replacement pieces of soundtrack (or picture) snugly into place. Click the chain/peanut to lock, and recheck your cut ends. With a few tries you'll find you can repeatedly make perfect same-sized inserts.

6. *Copying and pasting to create sound tone for replacement.*
Now that you've learned how to drag in new tracks of equal length to replace bad sound sections (see tip 5), you also need to be able to supply clean room-tone for replacement. After razor-cutting the portion of bad sound, select a nearby portion of the soundtrack where no one is talking and no distinguishable sounds are occurring. This silent stretch of room-tone between words of dialogue should be located as close to the bad sound in the track as you can find, but it doesn't have to be of equal length to the bad sound section. Slice the clean section on each side with the Razor tool, highlight it, then hit Apple-C to make a copy of that portion of the track. Then hit the Apple-V keys repeatedly until you've duplicated enough little, good sound clones to equal the full bad sound length to be replaced (listen closely to make sure the short, repeated sound-tone pieces don't produce an unsuitable reverberation).

Next, drag the good sound replacement to the bad sound area, line it up on an empty track below to match the length (using the cursor-turning-white method as already explained), and use the Razor tool to click a cut, deleting any extra length. Now delete the bad sound pieces and drag that equal-length, two-track good sound replacement into the space that bad sound used to occupy. Presto. You've patched your soundtrack! If you hear a repeating pop or other noise when you play through the replacement area, the patch needs to be redone, copied from a cleaner room-tone area than the one you selected.

7. Using FCP4 Audio Mixer/Audio Filters. When you click on Window/Arrange Audio Mixing you'll see your Final Cut Pro 4 desktop suddenly transform to a workstation with a mixing board to the right of the image screens. If you hit Play (click the spacebar) your sound levels are immediately represented in rising and lowering audio signals that are shown in three audio level monitors: the four meters representing A1–A4 soundtracks, a Master meter (both with knobs for adjusting volume), plus the ever-present desktop meter that has been appearing paired with your Tool Palette. Between these three readouts you should be able to determine the best sound levels for your movie.

As your movie plays, you want to check that no sound exceeds the 0 dB range (designated by the slightly bolder black dash about halfway up each of the four soundtracks, shown as the number "0" on the Master meter, and represented by the top of the scale on the separate desktop audio meter). Along with this "peak-level" monitoring you'll also want to control the "average loudness" of the soundtrack, which includes the level of spoken dialogue plus the music and any sound effects. The Final Cut Pro 4 manual recommends keeping the range from the soft/quiet sounds to loud volumes much more contained (shorter dB range) for Internet or computer presentations. When you mix for a movie theater/theatrical presentation, that quieter environment is more suitable to a wider range of sound subtleties. At any rate, I'd say mix your sound now for the festivals and high-quality DVD presentation, perhaps remixing for the Internet (cutting out highs and lows) at some future point.

As you adjust your sound levels for a certain cut, watch that the average dialogue levels hit around the same basic number on the meters, so there will be that constant throughout the movie. The Master meter, with its side-by-side tracks, is the quickest way to spot if levels are exceeding the necessary 0 dB limit. The 0 =+12 dB "clipping area" will help you determine how much you need to lower the levels to avoid distortion.

8. *Using professional earphones to mix sound levels and set EQ.* Wearing a professional set of earphones (my Sony MDR-7506 Professional Dynamic Stereo Headphones cost around $100, and the new for-digital version is around $150), you'll want to play your DV feature through from one end to the other, paying close attention to the sound levels and quality. If the dialogue or music is too hot or too low, make the necessary adjustment (see "Raising and Lowering Sound Levels: A Quick Mix"). In addition to listening, you'll want to watch the peak level meter (the hang-down item on your desktop, toolbox-sized, that fluctuates when sound is present in your cut), to see how the sound levels are tickling the red zone. The trick is maintaining a stringent and cohesive level for the entire movie, and you need to make decisions in a dance between what the meter says and what you hear in both ears.

Even the best mixers usually need a final step with a recording engineer or professional mixer to attain perfection in this regard—anything short of perfection will greatly disrupt the quality of your movie. If your sound is so loud that the level is buried high in the red, without any movement, that's proof that you are running sound too hot. In that case, double-click on the Final Cut soundtrack to open the control box, and then mouse-click a few times on the minus key (−) while keeping your finger on the Control key. Each click will drop the volume 1 dB. Conversely, using the plus key (+) will raise volume.

An important next step in improving sound for a movie is adjusting the EQ. If the tone seems artificial (too bass, too treble, echoey, etc.) and interferes with the content of a scene, then it must also be adjusted until it is supportive (and unnoticeable) within the filmmatic structure (go to Effects/Audio Filters/Final Cut Pro/3 Band Equalizer and adjust the sliders).

NOTE: You can drastically reduce or increase the volume levels of your scenes by clicking on the Gain −3 dB/+3 dB, etc. settings, located below the Pan commands at Modify/Audio.

9. *Splitting soundtracks for a professional mix.* If you decide to give your movie the best sound possible by spending another fifteen hundred dollars or so working with a technician who is skilled at finessing a theatrical-quality mix, you'll want to split your soundtracks into separate dialogue and music/effects while still editing in Final Cut Pro/Express. This splitting is done by double-clicking and highlighting a certain sound section, revealing the window for changing volume levels, and clicking and sliding the pan slider from the middle 0 setting completely over to one side or the other. First, repeat this clicking and sliding procedure for each and every large and small piece of dialogue soundtrack, always sliding the pan lever *completely left*, to the −1 setting, so that *Pan Left* = *dialogue.* Then repeat the procedure, only this time sliding the pan lever from the middle setting all the way right to the 1 setting, so that *Pan Right* = *music and effects.* You can also go to the top bar menu, select Modify/Audio and manually click on Pan Right or Pan Left for each separate track. (Both stereo tracks will need to be panned separately for 100 percent accuracy in this procedure. Don't rush it!)

To give your soundtrack a final test before printing to video, listen to the movie through earphones. You should hear dialogue in one ear, music and effects in the other.

10. *Creating and rechecking titles.* With Final Cut Pro/Express, to change a title or create a new credit, simply go to Window in the Final Cut Pro/Express top bar menu and click Effects/Video Generators/Text/Text (double-click), so that the checkerboarded window opens. Then click on the Control tab at the top to open your typing window. Make the change (or type in a new title's text) and click on your Canvas window to check the results.

Before printing your movie to tape or DVD, check all front and rear titles for misspellings or omissions. You will also want to check on how long each title remains on the screen. These days it doesn't seem like the front title or director's title (a DV by . . .) is on-screen very long, just a few seconds to identify the work and move on. Just one clumsy, long title can give a movie an uncool look. So be very careful with the screen time you give your opening titles.

11. *Rechecking transitional effects.* Look over each fade-in and fade-out, dissolves, and other effects, to determine if they are delivering the full measure of magic to your cut. Is that final fade-out long enough? Would a few seconds more of slow fade-out make the movie end on a more elegant note? How about the first fade-in at the beginning? Is it too long? Shouldn't the movie get started with more pep and determination? With Final Cut all you have to do to make a change is double-click on the transition icons in the Timeline (at the ends of shots where you originally installed them), which opens the Control window. Grab the end of the boxed-in rectangles (with the duration-of-fade pyramid shadow in the middle), and drag it left or right for a new duration setting. Or you can just change the numerical setting in the top left slot and click on the window. And are your soundtrack transitions working properly to bring in dialogue, ambience, and music right with the picture? Could some of them be improved?

If some sound transitions between scenes seem too abrupt, go to Window/Effects/Audio Transitions, click the control triangle, and choose Cross Fade (odB). Then click and drag the Cross Fade icon right to the break between soundtracks and release it, repeating the application to the second stereo track. You'll probably need to adjust the length of the audio fade a bit to find the best setting.

12. *Correcting the basic exposure and color with FCP.* Make use of FCP3/FCP4's superb image correction capabilities to bring a consistency to your image quality. In my *Bear Dance* DV I shot a scene in a pool room with a figure seated on a window seat, back lit by the strong Portuguese summer sun. Because the scene outside the window was overexposed, and the actress's face was underexposed on the shaded side, I decided to adjust the contrast. First I double-clicked on the image to bring it into the viewer, then went to Effects/Video Filters/Color Correction/Color Corrector. Next I clicked on the Color

By clicking on the FCP3 Auto-Balance Eye Dropper (the tiny square found below the Balance color wheel), holding down the mouse while dragging the cursor to the image, then clicking on a section of image that's believed to be white, you can perform an after-the-fact white balance and bring flesh tones back to more normal values. (Courtesy of Apple)

Corrector 3-way tab at the top bar menu of the viewer. As soon as the Balance and Hue color wheels appeared, along with the Whites, Mids (mid-range greys), Blacks, and Sat (Saturation) slider controls, I went to work.

The first step was to click the Autocontrast button, the central white-arrow-up/black-arrow-down center portion of the button to the right of the sliders. To brighten the actress's face, bringing definition back to the shaded interior side, I dragged the Mid slider to the right. Because of the autocontrast setting, the white and black values stayed mostly in place. As soon as I saw the black value diminish a bit, I increased it by moving the slider labeled "Blacks" to the left of 0. As a final check, I clicked the Before/After button near the top bar menu, and compared the corrected image with the original.

To change the color setting, just click and rotate the hue color wheel and see what changes are appealing. It doesn't take much to give your movie a distinctive color style. As with any Final Cut procedures, you can proceed along many different avenues to get similar results; so spend some time testing what's possible.

13. *Final check of the pacing throughout the movie.* Ask yourself if everything in the Timeline is absolutely necessary for the movie you've made. Is there anything you could remove that would bring extra clarity or energy to other scenes? Sometimes a last look at a movie can help the director reevaluate the state of things, see any remaining deadwood that detracts from the whole.

Here's a quick method for getting tougher on the footage before it's finished and too late to make changes. If your movie runs 77 minutes, pretend that you need to carve it back to a precise 75 minutes. Can you remove 2 minutes? Give it a try by saving the project under another name (add an A or extra number to the title when you Save As). If you have a Mini-DV camera system, then you want to limit your running time to under 80 minutes to print to tape from Final Cut on that special-length cassette. That should give you the impetus to make tougher cuts. Of course, I understand that not all movies will submit to this kind of boxing, but why not make the extra effort to get your footage pared down to its most efficient length?

If your DV feature holds up to this test (i.e., you can't extract anything), then feel confident that you've nailed the final cut.

14. *Using Joe's Filters (www.joesfilters.com) for Final Cut Pro (which includes a deinterlacer).* If you type in "Joe's Filters" in *www.google.com* search engine (or use the Web site listed above), you'll come across an array of very reasonably priced plug-ins created by Joe Maller for use with Final Cut Pro. Since his plug-ins are created with the FXScript effects language of Final Cut Pro, they are completely compatible with your editing program. Joe offers an assortment of thirty-three helpful plug-ins in his filter pack, including improved drop shadows, bevel and emboss, channel blur, diffuser (like looking through silk), noise filters, soft blurs and gradients (to keep part of your image blurred while another part is sharp), color glow (make that red coat glow as in Soderbergh's *Full Frontal* movie), and pixel controls like Maximizer to blow them up into bacteria-like balls, and Flexi-smear to create Mylar-like distortions. There is also a tool for customizing the Timeline for easier access and personalized options.

Maybe most importantly, Joe includes a deinterlacer that helps you change the look of your DV into more of a solid-frame progressive scan. That plug-in, combined with his Field Blender, will deinterlace your movie's video and combine it with a film look, so that the motion more closely resembles film. So if you are delving deeper into the intriguing mysteries of FCP, don't miss out on sampling these wonderful effects. The cost is only $95 for the whole collection of Joe's thirty-three filter plug-ins—or download a trial version at his Web site.

15. *Making a backup copy on Mini-DV cassette.* What if your computer's hard drive and external hard drive both crash at the same moment and take your precious, months-in-the-making DV feature with them (a bit of filmmaker's paranoia here)? Just to make sure you have a usable backup copy of your movie, it's worth occasionally printing your current cut to a few 60-minute Mini-DV tapes as you go along. For the best backup copies, the kind that could be immediately captured back into a Mac computer for further editing, you'd want to separate the tracks, music to pan right, dialogue to pan left (see tip 9), so that you wouldn't be stuck with "married" sound (where if you lowered music later for a final mix, it would drag down dialogue as well). To do this right, you must make sure that each and every soundtrack section, both channels, are set to the new pan settings. When I did this recently in some haste, I didn't always get the pan lever over fully to the 1 or −1 setting, so don't rush it! Be patient as you apply this process to an entire feature's worth of tracks. Keep in mind that you'll have to do this procedure later if you go the Professional mix route (discussed earlier in this chapter). Anyway, expect to give this painstaking job a full day of your life.

Once you have a few, long backup tapes, you can risk screening the recent, shorter Print-to-Video tapes on your NTSC TV, watching with an audience to check for pace and structure, being on the lookout for bad cuts, detecting too low or too high sound or music, watching for color correction needs, etc. (Make another stereo, nonpan copy for screening, in order to hear the full sound mix.) You won't see the final 16:9 letterbox on your TV unless you have an expensive monitor that resolves this format, but you will get a sense of what's succeeding or failing in the assembly.

NOTE: I recommend final remastering of your Mini-DV/DVCAM feature to Digi-Beta. Fotokem lab in Burbank, California, (818) 846-3101, can uncompress your 16:9 images into a final letterboxed "4X3 1.78 matted" master copy (probably an extra $350).

16. *Reducing the storage clog by using Media Manager.* Once you have created your movie's Mini-DV backup copy, it's worth lightening the media storage load in your hard drives by implementing Final Cut's Media Manager to extract files that aren't being used (the "long ends" of scenes you've cut down to fit the Timeline final cut). You'll be surprised how much memory you can free up using this FCP application.

The first step is just positioning your cursor on a particular length of scene (pick one that has been radically shortened during editing). If you click to highlight, then open the Media Manager (File/Media Manager), you'll immediately see two graphs displayed. It will only take a second to notice the disparity between the Original media file and the Modified one. But that readout can be deceiving if you have captured in bulk as I do, batch-capturing a 25-minute chunk at a time. You could have another part of the same shot used somewhere else in the Timeline. So although that one scene represents a small percentage of the whole scene captured, and it appears you could reclaim wasted hard drive space, it would be unwise to delete anything until a further analysis is made.

Before initiating a command to remove any files from your computer, I suggest running a small test. Copy a few scenes you don't need to a New Project window and let the Memory Manager delete the long ends. Has that disrupted your ability to edit or screen that little movie? Is this a safe procedure? If it seems OK, try it with a bigger bunch of footage. Then, after you're completely confident that you aren't deleting anything usable from your precious assembly, go for the entire housecleaning procedure. And use an excellent book like *Final Cut Pro 3 for Macintosh* by Lisa Brenneis (or her updated FCP 4 how-to) to sort out the media management issues. She devotes twenty-eight pages to using Media Manager, so it's not something to enact lightly in the middle of your final cut.

> **NOTE:** If you can afford a second 80–500-gig external hard drive, then make a full copy of your cut, media files and all—a solid backup copy—*before* using Media Manager for extraneous file removal.

17. *Saving your movie on its external drive for a year.* I know this sounds radical and extravagant, but I'm suggesting that, once you are finished editing your DV feature and completely happy with the final cut (have even mastered it to Digi-Beta, entered the dubbed VHS and DVD copies in festivals, etc.), you still maintain the option to recut. Once you've unplugged the external hard drive, where all your movie's media clips and Final Cut Pro Timeline are saved, and placed it away from the computer, up on a shelf in a good, secure, temperature-controlled environment (not in the same building where you've stored the Digi-Beta master), you can feel assured that the feature you've spent maybe a year or more making has another, good, usable backup copy (LaCie external hard drives of 80 gigs to 120 gigs like I have cost about $200).

For your next feature-length DV movie you'll of course have to purchase another external hard drive. For the cost of a new tire or two for your used car, you'll have your movie stored away on its own hard drive, which can immediately be accessed if further editing must be done. If after a few screenings (maybe six months after your movie's finished) you notice a weakness in the storytelling structure or hear a flaw in the sound mix, you can fix it. Or you might suddenly gain access to some new, cutting-edge music and want to drop it in. No problem! Possibly you have fluency in a second or third language and can translate the movie, creating your own subtitles for a European or Asian premiere. The market for your movie just suddenly expanded! But you'd be in hell trying to accomplish this task unless you saved to the hard drive and kept that working copy available.

At any rate, think of the alternative. If you delete all the information on the external hard drive, your working copy of the movie is gone, and so is your chance to improve it. Yes, you could try to reconstruct it from the Edit Decision List (EDL). (Saving your EDL to a Zip disk is a must in any case. Go to the Final Cut bar menu, click on File/Export/EDL, type in the movie's title in the top slot, click OK, and select your Zip on the desktop for destination.) But I recommend the precaution of temporarily retiring that hard drive—and who can tell what exact condition it is in after all those saves? I'd say spend the $200 and buy a brand new one for your second movie. And if after a year you're broke and desperate for the extra memory, pull that first external hard drive off the shelf, delete the files, and use it for feature 3!

18. _Most important: Learning through your FCP editing mistakes._ During the recent cutting of _Release the Head_, I decided to hold a certain scene in place—tuck it away in a holding pattern in the Timeline for later inclusion into the cut—by dragging the image track up to video track V2 and dropping the two stereo soundtracks down, to empty audio tracks A3 and A4. If you looked at the Timeline, you would have seen this swelling of the cut, an extra lump of track stacked above and below the edges of what was obviously the main Timeline edit. I had forgotten about this extra footage "in the wings" until I screened a cut for my wife one Saturday afternoon. When we entered into my place-saver footage area of the Timeline, an unexpected sound superimposition suddenly took over. We heard both audio tracks at once, while the picture still read off the V1. At any rate, I quickly appreciated this accidental effect: An interjection of the second

Sony Vaio laptop (about $2,000), preloaded with Adobe Premiere and hooked up to a Sony Hi-8 digital camera via FireWire, can get a movie cut and streaming to the Web (note the cable modem, left of screen). (Courtesy of Sony Electronics Inc., and Adobe Systems Inc.)

soundtrack was just the flair I needed at that point in the cut. I probably wouldn't have been daring enough to just lay an entire new scene atop and below my current cut, but in this case serendipity offered me a great, bold new effect. All I had to do was recognize how well the mistake worked. That's your job as well. Try to learn from everything you see and experience as you immerse yourself in the magical world of electronic editorial manipulation.

ADOBE PREMIERE PRO FOR PC

Certainly Final Cut Pro and Express aren't the only games in town for nonlinear editing. One of the first software programs on the scene was Adobe Premiere (*www.adobe.com*), a well thought-out screen and timeline editing tool that kicked off the DV revolution. And with Apple reserving FCP for the Mac-only crowd, the PC moviemaker will

Adobe Premiere monitor screen and Timeline, with clips and accompanying thumbnail reminder images stacked in the Project bin (the scene splitting Razor tool can be seen in the top right corner of the toolbox, located directly below). (Courtesy of Adobe Systems Inc.)

need Adobe Premiere, Avid Xpress DV, Discreet's Cinestream, and others as NLE alternatives. If you've browsed through the Final Cut Express and Final Cut Pro sections, you should have a good basic idea how Adobe Premiere works as well. Just like most other NLE software, Premiere begins with setting Camera (Control Device) and Capture (Capture Settings) preferences. You'll want to locate your DV camera in the extensive Control Device list (my old Sony DSR-TRV10 was listed there, though it is a discontinued model) and adjust the aspect ratio if you've shot in 16:9. You don't need to change other settings until you make a test by running the camera and seeing if the image and audio load to the screen properly (smooth video and clear audio, running at 29.97/25 fps, NTSC/PAL, quality at 100 percent).

Before actual capturing, it's necessary to set up a destination scratch disk file where the images and audio will collect in the mass of computer files on your PC (or external hard drive). Once you've named a file, it will appear in your capture bin, signaling that you can now capture by running footage (use the triangle button at the bottom of your viewing screen to Play) and clicking on the red Record button directly below. Another click on the red button stops the capture. As soon as the capture cycle has been completed for a clip, a thumbnail image with attached rectangle file will appear in the bin. Just grab hold of it and pull it directly into the Timeline, or use the keyboard commands for cut and paste to manually insert it in the video track. Now you're editing.

NOTE: If your video has taken on an unstable electronic quality in Adobe Premiere, you may want to enact the Deinterlace Desktop Playback option, which should help the image settle down.

Cutting a scene, deleting portions, and rearranging the assembly in Adobe Premiere should also feel familiar. There is a Razor tool similar to the one in Apple's Final Cut programs, located in the eight-tool toolbox found directly above the video and audio track controls at the beginning of the Timeline. Click on the Razor icon to activate the scene splitting tool, position it somewhere along the length of a shot, and click. A line will suddenly appear that bisects the track. Now you can hit the Delete key or select the Cut command in the Edit menu. Or you can drag the extra portion to some other location in the Timeline, or move it back to the bin for use later. Once you've got the rhythm of cutting and rearranging down pat, you can explore the other editing tools and finally export the results to a Windows file or QuickTime in preparation for a final tape or DVD master.

NOTE: Don't overlook the cooperative nature of Adobe products. When you purchase the Digital Video Collection with Adobe Premiere, After Effects, Photoshop, and Illustrator, you are buying software that is perfectly integrated. That means you can import an Adobe Premiere project and apply animation with After Effects (or one of the other graphic programs). When you import to AE, the Premiere movie will be received as both a new composition (containing each clip as a separate layer) and as a folder (each clip as footage). Adobe Premiere bins will also be converted to folders. Your Timeline and transitions/titles (appearing as solid layers in AE) maintain their same location and settings.

ADVANCED EFFECTS EDITING AND ANIMATION SOFTWARE AND TECHNIQUES

In the coming years, DV moviemakers will find that a little money can actually give them the potential to create a *Star Wars*–level special effects movie, right at home. Here are some incredible software programs I've had the opportunity to employ for my DV work.

Commotion 4.0 Effects Software

When the FedEx driver unexpectedly showed up at my door, I was delighted to find he was delivering a package containing Commotion Pro 4.0 software that I had requested from Pinnacle Systems (*www.pinnaclesys.com*, available for both Windows and Mac, $499). On the front of the box I read about what Commotion could accomplish: rotoscoping, motion tracking, real-time playback, matte creation with Primatte Keyer, accurate retouching with Composite Wizard, and adding photo-realistic elements with Image Lounge.

The back of the box explained more, about how you could isolate images from any color background, simulate back lighting, blur and feather edges, remove unwanted artifacts, simulate the natural elements of fire, smoke, and water with tools for adding realistic shadows and true camera blur. And with their eighty included filters a lot was certainly possible; this version contained Adobe Photoshop for easy retouching and animation—terrific news since Final Cut Pro and Express could each handle multiple-image tracks. I was eager to start testing Pinnacle System's claim that "every creative tool you need for superior image editing and visual effects is packed into this one comprehensive desktop application."

At their Web site I had learned that they offered not only a free download of Commotion 4.1 for Mac OS X, but also a new plug-in, Commotion Export XML, that allowed Commotion 4.0 and 4.1 to export a single sequence from Final Cut Pro, to create a new composite. So Final Cut Pro would have full access to the Commotion software possibilities. Commotion had also designed their composite effects software to integrate with other leading NLE software products, including Adobe Premiere and Avid Xpress DV.

With the Commotion box in my hands, I quickly did what I usually do with a completely new and complicated software application: Toss it to my teenage son Marlon and his buddy, Andrew Poling, for testing. Because they were already fluent in the use of Adobe Photoshop and very, very familiar with image manipulation—working with layers of effects, motion paths, etc.—I wanted to see if they could penetrate the program using only their intuition. They certainly weren't in the mood to read an instruction manual on their Sunday off from school. Within minutes, they had created and radically altered an island landscape (constructed with Bryce 3-D software) changing its colors, textures, and speed of play; most fabulously, they added a wall of fog to their tiny island's landscape. As the superfast dolly shot viewed the island from a 360-degree perspective and swept in for a closer examination (the island was now in B&W), a layer of fog suddenly rushed down the steep cliffs, hanging there as if suspended between us and the rocky cliff side. I had to ask the young men to replay it several times for me because the effect was so sublimely lifelike. Part of the fun of having new software is blindly experimenting, taking the program out for a test drive before you get serious and hit the books. Commotion certainly passed the test for being a user-friendly product for creating moviemaking magic.

After Effects and Magic Bullet

As you pair your Final Cut Express and Final Cut Pro editing with other software programs, you'll appreciate the fine selection of Adobe products available to help you pull off your digital moviemaking vision. Learning how Adobe Photoshop may be coupled with Final Cut Pro/Express and Commotion software as a partner in animation leads naturally to discovering Adobe After Effects, Adobe Illustrator (you can render objects by hand and include them in your images), and Red Giant's Magic Bullet, a plug-in for After Effects that can deliver amazing filmlike effects to video.

Magic Bullet from Red Giant Software (*www.redgiantsoftware.com*, 415-274-2000, $995) takes advantage of the powerful and smooth combining of Adobe software products, using After Effects 5.5 or later version as its base program. Of course, the work done with Magic Bullet can be imported back to Final Cut Pro directly. (Check out Magic Bullet Editors for FCP, only $299.)

Here's what Magic Bullet can do for your movie. First and foremost it can convert your 29.97-fps DV into a 24-fps filmlike movie. It actually recreates missing pixels and eliminates unwanted color artifacts and interlacing (with a one click operation). If your movie needs to be reformatted into letterbox, the software can deliver the new aspect ratio, up to superwide-screen *Lawrence of Arabia*–style settings. And if you miss the way a film lab–style dissolve feels, along with fades to white, those subtle effects will now be available in your After Effects menu.

In the Look Suite you can select the right look for your story's subject matter (from a vast list), just as cinematographers would do when designing visuals for a feature film they were preparing to shoot. While Academy Award–winning DP Vilmos Zsigmond would need to arrange for a lab to "bleach" the negative for a certain mood he and his director were after, you can just click on "bleach" and your movie footage will immediately shift into that pictorial mode. Broadcast Spec helps you attain the NTSC broadcast standards your movie may be lacking by first identifying areas of the frame that are blown out (too bright) or dark and repairing them while leaving the rest of your movie's image alone. Finally, there's Deepcolor Technology, which Magic Bullet claims will supply a higher color depth than any other plug-in.

Magic Bullet was created by Stu Maschwitz, programmed by Douglas Applewhite, with design by Dav Rauch. I'll definitely be looking forward to their next breakthrough! (Courtesy of Red Giant Software)

The Magic Bullet manual includes an insightful account of Stuart Maschwitz inventing this software based on his needs as a filmmaker, the history of their product, and "The Science and Philosophy of the Bullet," which encapsulates the history of DV—an informative primer on where DV came from and where it's headed. If you don't quite get all the digital jargon surrounding DV activity, the Bullet manual will be a big help.

This is real new-millennium magic and should be on everyone's wish list. Maybe you and three other DV buddies can pop in $250 each to share the full-product cost (much less for Magic Bullet Editors), invent a company name, and rock the film festival circuit!

PERSONAL EDITING NEEDS

When you shoot a feature in any medium (DV or film), you have to expect that it will take months to satisfactorily edit the results. Editing is a very demanding job, and one you probably cannot afford to hire someone else to do. And the stakes are very high. A bad cut can destroy a good movie. What you're after is creating a clarity of concept, maintaining good and believable performances, and engineering a pace for that audible and pictorial information so that the audience can absorb and digest what you are communicating. Certain genres demand special talents. And if you have a comedy, then you need to create opportunities for the audience to laugh as well. So you'll need to test the cut occasionally, checking to see whether you and a small preview audience are on the same page.

With the radical speed and demands of computer editing, there is the likelihood that deeper concepts within your footage may get overlooked because you don't have time to absorb the subtext created by all the juxtapositions resulting from footage stuck end to end. Computers seem to demand that *we* speed up to match their technical efficiency. They somehow make us impatient for results. We spend too long staring into their screens, often getting physically exhausted from working too many hours at a stretch and failing to breathe deeply enough while we work. To buck these tendencies I suggest the following:

1. Before getting too far into editing, make a small printed sign that reads BREATHE! and place it somewhere below the computer screen. Most of the time it will sit there unnoticed, but occasionally you will be reminded to take a breath, snap out of your computer trance, and come up for air!

2. Also, you may want to add another sign (DRINK!) to remind yourself to take a gulp from your nearby water bottle every so often.

3. Count four, maybe five hours from the time you sit down in front of your DV editing workstation and write that number in bold script on a letter-sized sheet of paper. Pin the sign somewhere within your view (a kitchen timer or alarm clock would also work of course). When the later time rolls around (sometimes it feels just like the blink of an eye when editing is progressing well), get up and follow your own instructions. TAKE A BREAK!

4. Of course, while editing (thinking hard under pressure), you'll still need to EAT AT MEAL TIMES (7–8 A.M., noon–1 P.M., 6:30–7:30 P.M.), just like everybody else, because you'll need energy for all the hard mental and physical work ahead.

5. And you must GET SOME PROPER SLEEP, hitting the sack somewhere around 10–11 P.M. each night—no later—since you don't want to overtax yourself any one day at the cost of the next. Forget the 18-hour editing sessions.

A final word: If you never quit, you *will* edit your DV feature to completion before you die. Good luck on finding the breakthrough cut!

8

GUERILLA PROMOTION: A QUICKTIME MOVIE PLAYER AT EVERY WEB SITE

Congratulations! You've survived the moviemaking wars and emerged with a solid product in your hands: a DV feature. Looking back for a minute at the process you went through, can you believe all the twists and turns that fate dealt you so that you could reach this spot? It was probably quite a roller coaster ride. Yet somehow you pulled people together, got equipment, and shot for days on end. Then, with a good deal of discipline, you carefully captured, assembled, and honed down the shots into scenes, sequences, and a final cut. And after applying a good sound mix (with ProTools or Final Cut's built-in audio mixer) and color correction (Final Cut Pro/ Express color wheels), and maybe fancy titles (LiveTitles, again from Final Cut) and effects (Lightwave, Commotion, Adobe's After Effects, Magic Bullet, Final Cut), you got it completed.

What was it like screening it for an audience for the first time? It was probably a thrilling mix of fear and expectation, as it always is for me. We wonder, "Will it work?" Moviemakers just want their effort to operate on all cylinders, to deliver the goods inherent in the material. When the cuts are right, the drama, comedy, or adventure has a life of its own, and the audience rides it from the beginning title to the last frame. Little can they imagine the countless little puzzle pieces we are presenting at a screening. Hundreds of images and sounds that we recorded on tape or DVD have merged into one cohesive experience— or at least that's the hoped-for result!

How did the first screening go? Was it successful, better than you expected, or a little on the iffy side? Sometimes a hometown screening or in-house cast and crew "premiere" can be somewhat disappointing. After all, everyone has a vested interest in what they see on the screen or TV set. If they're actors, they wonder if they look good enough. They will certainly be super-critical of their performances, and that can make it difficult for them to just fall into the movie as they'd normally do at the local cineplex. And crew members may be watching for their favorite shots or remembering funny on-location incidents that no one else will be privy to. So they may be reliving the job more than watching the movie. And your investors—if they can catch a breath—are analyzing your work from their viewpoint as well. (Is it good enough to *sell*?)

And, of course, you have your own mix of heavy emotions surrounding these first few screenings. As leader of the production, you want it to be a rip-roaring success, and anything short of total adulation is going to give you pause. As the movie runs, your sensitivity picks up on all these people's vibes, tuning into their reactions. Are they laughing in all the right places? Are they involved in the story, relating to the characters, properly moved when the drama hits? It's as if you can sense the mood of all your friends and new compatriots who have worked on and nurtured your project, as they sit there in the dark of the theater. With all that static in your head, how can you really see your movie at the same time?

First screenings can be rough, especially if you've never experienced the completion of a feature. If you had the level of sensitivity required to envision, shoot, and complete a DV feature, then that sensitivity will certainly persist through your screenings. And, in a large sense, you're still editing. Even a big festival screening will feel like you're testing the cut. Does it work? That's what you want to find out. Does it work in New York City? Does it work in Berlin? Does it work in Park City, Utah (home of the Sundance Film Festival)? It may work at one of those highfalutin world-class international festivals, but not in your living room. So after testing the waters in your hometown, you'll want to start actively entering the movie you made in film festivals. And the Internet provides one-stop shopping for doing that. It's called "Without a Box."

WWW.WITHOUTABOX.COM
FESTIVAL-ENTERING WEB SITE

Joining *www.withoutabox.com* is the best choice you can make toward coordinating your promotional campaign. After the many months of scripting or creating improvisational outlines, the weeks of shooting, the untold hours sitting at a computer editing—after all the work of acquiring music and keeping all those people in the loop who have been so eagerly awaiting your movie's world premiere—you owe it to yourself to have this able, online assistance. Now that the yearly membership is free (!) you can enjoy the feeling of having an actual staff helping your feature get the recognition you believe it deserves. So, before you go through the old filmmaking routine of putting together a pressbook by hand, getting multiple photos printed, and filling out a separate application for each festival (a terribly draining procedure if you apply to twenty different festivals), go directly to *www.withoutabox. com* and sign up.

The Web site *www.withoutabox.com* has revolutionized the festival application process. Join thousands of other enlightened moviemakers by sending your applications via the Internet after filling out just *one* submission form, and save on entry fees with WAB's special discounts!

After you've registered, the first step toward applying to festivals will be to enter all the pertinent data about your movie in the supplied information slots. Withoutabox will require you to type in the contact information for your feature, including the names, addresses, phone numbers, and e-mail addresses of the producer, director, and scriptwriter, along with a few different-length synopses, the names of lead actors, main crew members, composer of musical score, etc. You'll list any festivals where your movie has previously shown and supply a statement by the director—in other words, all the usual data that festivals need before they will select a movie and eventually publicize it at its world premiere.

Withoutabox has made the painstaking process of entering and promoting your DV feature a thousand times easier, not only by having a one-time fill-in slot for all this festival information, but also by offering the option of posting a full press kit online, complete with stills, a one-sheet artwork (your movie's poster), reviews, résumés of cast and crew, biography, filmography, and even a photo gallery from the shoot. All this will get sent out to the festivals with a click of a button. Now you can enter as many festivals as you can afford. (Many festival submission fees are discounted through Withoutabox.)

> **NOTE:** Be careful not to give your World Premiere away to a small, relatively unknown film festival before you've tested the waters and entered the top festivals in the United States, Asia, and Europe. Patiently start by applying to these important festivals (see the next section for listings, deadlines, and contact information) before settling for the other showcases.

SELECTING FESTIVALS FOR A WORLD PREMIERE

While there will be many festivals to enter that seem tempting because of their exotic locations (Bermuda, Hawaii), you need to have a method to your madness of trying to break through with your DV feature. Put the most important festivals *first*—enter them before less prominent venues, even if you must sit on your movie for a few months while waiting to hear the verdict. Here's a short list of top festivals with maximum press coverage. Not all accept DV features yet (unless they're blown up to 35mm film), but it's worth assuming that they will at some point in the near future. Check at their Web sites for prequalifications or use the *www.withoutabox.com* one-click, prequalifying button. Since these important festivals are "life-changing" ones, the kind that can put you on the map, it is well worth entering them first before moving on.

> **NOTE:** Make sure to carefully read each festival's submission requirements, since some will not accept features with prior screenings (Cannes refuses entries with even Internet exposure!).

U.S. Film Festivals/Web Sites and Deadlines

Sundance Film Festival (January)
http://www.sundance.org
DEADLINE: LATE SEPT.
Surprisingly, the odds aren't as bad as trying to get into Slamdance (see below) which received more than three thousand submissions for just seventeen feature slots. Still, this festival has to be considered a longshot.

New Directors/New Films (March)
www.filmlinc.com
DEADLINE: OCTOBER–NOVEMBER
They select only twenty or so features from around the world, but maybe you'll be fortunate to be screened and heavily reviewed in the New York papers.

New York Film Festival (October)
www.filmlinc.com/nyff/Nyff.htm
DEADLINE: JULY 9
Look into their new section "Views from the Avant Garde," which shows experimental, nonnarrative abstract works.

Telluride Film Festival (May)
www.telluridefilmfestival.com
ACCEPTS SUBMISSIONS FROM MAY 1 TO JULY 15.
Telluride recommends applying early so that movies can be properly considered. From all accounts, this is a great festival experience.

Denver International Film Festival
(October)
www.denverfilm.org
DEADLINE: JULY 15
It gives a John Cassavetes
Award each year (so you know it's
indie-friendly). My *Morgan's
Cake* feature premiered here
before making it to Sundance,
Berlin, and New Directors/New
Films.

Slamdance Film Festival (January)
www.slamdance.com

DEADLINE: AUGUST 30–OCTOBER 1
Check out their Anarchy online
festival for under ten-minute movies,
and give some support to this great
indie filmmaker–created festival.

Seattle International Film Festival
(May)
http://www.seattlefilm.com
DEADLINE: JANUARY
Seattle International has been
called one of the top five in the
U.S., and you can't argue with the
strong audience support.

European Film Festivals and Deadlines

Berlin International Film Festival
(February)
www.berlinale.de
DEADLINE: NOVEMBER 5
This is a huge, but precisely run
affair. An important premiere for
your work, either in the Forum of
Young Cinema or Panorama, where
many American indies have shown.

Biennale di Venezia (September)
www.labiennale.org
DEADLINE: JULY 21
A great festival in Venice, Italy.
Check out their new section, "New
Territories," that welcomes
submissions of experimental movies
on Betacam PAL and DVD.

Toronto International (August)
www.e.bell.ca/filmfest/asp
DEADLINE: JUNE 6
For many, this is the kickoff event
on the festival circuit, for discovering
the next big trend.

**Cannes International Film
Festival** (May)
www.festival-cannes.fr
DEADLINE: APRIL 1
Large, important, and expensive.
But if you get accepted in the *Un
Certain Regard* section, you can
make some big news.

Karlovy Vary International Film Festival (July)

www.iffkv.cz

DEADLINE: APRIL 14

An important Eastern European festival near Prague, Czech Republic, that can launch your cutting-edge work.

London Film Festival

(October–November)

www.lff.org.uk

DEADLINE: EARLY SUMMER

A classy festival with appreciative audiences and a chance to sell a movie to Channel Four (as I did with my feature *1988—The Remake*).

Rotterdam International

(February)

www.iffrotterdam.nl

DEADLINE: NOVEMBER 1

The audiences pack into every theater to see the international offerings. Lots of interesting indie fare to see. This is a great place to show a first feature (where my first feature, *A Man, a Woman, and a Killer* was premiered).

Locarno International

(August)

www.pardo.ch

DEADLINE: JUNE 13

If you have the goods, enter their "Filmmakers in the Present" section, which presents "first person" works, "treading the confines between fiction and documentary."

Since I've experienced the high of being selected by some of these festivals (though many remain on my promotion wish list), I can testify to the pleasurable rush of adrenalin in store for you when any of them contact you with an affirmative reply. If they believe your work is worthy of their festival's exposure, the tables suddenly turn and they'll want your assurance (in writing) that you will allow your work to premiere at their venue, adding glory to their stature as a world-class organization. So what you are actually doing by applying to festivals of stature is giving festival directors the opportunity to make their mark on world cinema. I hope your work will be considered good enough to have that kind of impact.

Other Viable Film Festivals

Of course, what often comes along with making a cutting-edge work is a series of early rejections. So be prepared to face some adversity. Keep in mind that none of the festivals listed below should be considered a "consolation prize," but as a real opportunity for making a splash with your world premiere. Check out the Web sites for:

Mill Valley Film Festival *http://cafilm.org* (June)
AFI Fest *www.afi.com/onscreen/afifest* (November)
Hamptons Film Festival *www.hamptonsfest.org* (October)
Palm Springs International Film Festival *www.psfilmfest.org* (September), with three hundred films shown!)
Boston International Film Festival *www.bifilmfestival.com* (July 3–5)
Edinburgh International Film Festival *www.edfilmfest.org.uk* (August 13–24)
Cinequest *www.cinequest.org* (February)
Tribeca Film Festival *www.tribecafilmfestival.org* (April/May)
Rome International *www.riff.tv* (September)
Southern Triad—*www.magfilmfest.com* (February)
　　　　　www.ozarkfoothillsfilmfest.org (April)
　　　　　www.indiememphis.com (October)
Los Angeles Film Festival *www.lafilmfest.com* (June)

You'll want to check the Web sites for exact deadlines, which usually occur three to four months before the actual festival date.

Aside from the recognizable names, there are numerous small-town festivals sprouting up everywhere, including in my own Port Townsend (*www.ptfilmfest.com*, a "film-lover's block party," in September). Even if you are only selected for screening in an out-of-the-way place, your movie will still have the chance to win fans and perhaps send a few chills down your spine as you become the in-person speaker and honored guest of the proceedings. That rare experience alone is worth all the promotion effort.

If you still want to examine a full list of festivals, go to *www.film festivals.com*, and browse their selections. Some of these sites offer a nice Web site link that will take you directly to numerous film festival home pages (just as you will be able to do at *www.withoutabox.com*). At *www.marklitwak.com/filmfes.asp* attorney Mark Litwak offers a well-organized selection of festivals, as part of his entertainment law resources for film, TV, and multimedia design producers. And at *www.filmfestivalsource.com* there are two hundred twenty-five links to festivals in just the American section alone.

YOUR OWN INTERNET SIX-PLEX MOVIE THEATER

After the major film festival options have been exhausted (you're still entering smaller underground fests . . .), it's time to use the Internet for PR and screenings.

I was very pleased when I learned from my Arcadiaweb Services webmaster, Jeff Sherman (also a mainstay of the band Glass *www.rpursuit.com/glass/index.asp*), that his design associate, Erik Poulsen, was going to create a movie theater online at my site (see *www.vangoghsDV.com*, Chapter 11) to show my movies as QuickTime files. This offers the promise of showing not just footage but entire features, especially now with the faster speed of cable modem lines for the home consumer. At every step, though, you must watch for deals, since fast lines can easily add $50 to your monthly Internet fees. But with a fast cable connection you will find a world of movies to watch online, and many previews of the latest theatrical releases.

QUICKTIME MOVIES

Start by dropping in at *http://www.apple.com/quicktime/* and trying to download some of their movie trailers. If they run smoothly on your computer and the sound is clean and clear, then your system of computer (memory and speed) and modem (rate of download) are adequate. How does it feel watching movies this way? Suddenly your computer has turned into a small TV set. Can you imagine your own movie screening in this format? (Go to an Internet "cafe" if you don't have a fast enough Internet connection.) If you have the ability to enlarge the QuickTime screen, then do so, making the image of the streaming video as large as you can. While sites like Miramax, Dreamworks, and USA Films have been designed to present trailers to persuade moviegoers to buy tickets for their movies, your site could be designed to screen full movies, or at least preview clips as a way of selling VHS tapes or DVDs. The point of browsing other streaming videos and getting a taste of what QuickTime has to offer is to learn just what your potential audience might expect from your Web site. Having a sense of the status of current Internet streaming will help you make decisions regarding your personal bankrolling of an online movie theater. Once you commit to a certain Internet server, Internet connection, and computer hardware and software, you are kind of stuck for a while, even as video streaming breakthroughs are made by other companies and applications. So make informed decisions.

PLAYING MOVIES ON A FREE SERVER

In this information age, it pays to stay informed about things large and small, from computer software and hardware inventions and new Web sites (sign up for *www.yahoo.com*'s Best Site of the Week announcements), to cutting-edge health bulletins. So take advantage of what's being developed in the new millennium. You might start by asking Web-savvy teenagers what they know about file sharing. My teenage son Marlon helped me (a) register as the administrator at a low-cost file sharing server, KDX, (b) set up my log-in name and password, and (c) create a directory for my feature-length DV movies in QuickTime format for file sharing over the Internet. Essentially, what Marlon did was help me create an Internet screening room, providing free access to people anywhere in the world who are interested in seeing my work.

To join a low-cost server, all you need is a computer with an Internet hookup and your movie in QuickTime, or some other Internet-friendly media format. As long as your KDX server is online, people with your IP can access the server as a KDX client at *www.haxial.com/products/kdx/index2.html* (you'll go here to download the Client and Server, as described below). As soon as your Internet audience learns the address to plug in (mine is 66.235. 26.243:10700), they can download your movie. Here are the steps to becoming administrator of your own PR machine, sailing your DV product out into cyberspace, with under $50 spent in the pursuit of an Internet audience:

Step 1: Go to *www.haxial.com/products/kdx*, click on the logo, and at the full information page scroll down to KDX server and client downloads for your particular platform (Mac or PC) and load them onto your desktop.

Step 2: Open the KDX server with a click. A window will appear with three field slots, asking for Name, Administration Password, and Confirm Password. Fill them in and unclick the Guest Access box. You'll want to wait until your movie is ready for file sharing to grant access to the public. Click Save (the window will disappear).

Step 3: Now double-click on the KDX Server (in Finder, if you have a Mac), and you'll get a window with a line of type that includes the current date, time, and an IP address. Keep that window open as you proceed to Step 4.

Step 4: Open the KDX Client folder, copy the IP number (see above) onto your clipboard (Apple-C), and click Connect in the KDX toolbox. Paste the IP address into the address slot (Apple-V), type your login name and password, then click Files in the toolbox.

Step 5: Click on the striped rectangular icon in the top bar; that gives you the full screen for creating your movie file. After you name the folder, click Normal Folder, then click Create.

Step 6: Go to the KDX folder, open the original folder for the application, and go to KDX/server/Folder/Bases/Default/*your folder's*

After you type in the tracking number/IP address, log-in, and password at the KDX file sharing site (*www.haxial.com/products/kdx*) and click Files at the left-side bar menu, you can add your movie folders (Feature Length Movies, Shorts, whatever you call yours), in QuickTime drag-and-drop movie files for others on the Internet to access and enjoy.

name. Drag and drop your QuickTime movie into the folder. That's it. Congratulations! You've just expanded your horizons, gone from being a local moviemaker to one of the world! (For further assistance with this procedure, access the KDX help menu at Web site above.)

The next PR challenge now becomes: How can you get your file sharing information out beyond your immediate circle of DV moviemaking friends? An inexpensive method of promoting your Web site address and tracking number is to use 8½-by 11-inch fliers (or even full-sized posters) posted throughout your neighborhood, as music groups do. Later, if you have a small advertising budget, take out an ad in an affordable moviemaking magazine, like *Film-*

Click to enter...

Playing off the no-frills Dogme 95 ethics, I designed our *Chetzemoka's Curse* (Dogme No. 10) poster with just one image (the Hill building in Port Townsend, photographed by collaborator Lawrence E. Pado) and a copy of our official certificate from the Dogme 95 Secretariat in Denmark.

maker, MovieMaker (*MM* publisher and editor Tim Rhys has produced his own indie feature and may offer you an indie discount), *Film Comment, Res, Videographer*, or *DV magazine*.

As streaming formats change, and the demand for high-resolution, "clean" streaming images and sound increases, you'll want to consider the purchase of the industry standard video encoder software, like Discreet's Cleaner 6 (*www.discreet.com/products/cleaner/*, about $500), which produces razor-sharp video in all major formats: MPEG 2–pass variable bit rate for DVD, MPEG 4 and AAC compression for Quick-Time 6, and Kinoma for hand-held PDAs.

PROMOTION FINALE (TV SALES AND SO ON)

It has been said that, of the entire moviemaking process, promotion for a movie takes the longest period of time, and I've found that to be true. If you shot a movie in ten to twenty days and edited it for a year or so, you'll most likely be promoting it diligently for at least a few years following its release. And after that, if no major distributor has signed your movie to a distribution deal, you'll probably still keep trying to get it into DVD markets and video stores in the United States and elsewhere, the places that accept films released in the last five years.

Beyond that, you could always visit one video store at a time and try to get your tapes and DVD placed where they can be seen by an appreciative at-home audience. At the same time, you might want to approach TV outlets like the Independent Film Channel (*www.ifctv.com*), Sundance Channel (*www.sundancechannel.com*), WNET/Thirteen (*www.thirteen.org*), HBO (*www.hbo.com*), or National Asian American TV (*www.naatanet.org*) for a sale. And why not contact Independent Television Service (ITVS) (*www.itvs.org*) and find out what grants are available for new projects?

Your promotion period will probably extend into the realm of traveling filmmaker tours, where you and your movie will be on display at museums and independent showcases, for an in-person premiere. In other words, you'll exhaust all the possibilities, trying to get your flick as far as it can possibly go during the small window of time you have during which it is considered current.

NOTE: If you can target a final cut and mastering to occur sometime in late spring (April or May), you can start promoting your feature in the last week of May. This gives you a window for meeting deadlines for the most indie-friendly and important festivals and markets, such as September's IFP Market in New York City (*www.ifp.org*), where you can screen your finished movie (or work-in-progress) for the industry-only audience, conduct targeted networking, and perhaps even win a chunk of the $100,000 in awards given out each year to emerging moviemakers. You'll also be able to enter Toronto (August, if you hit the June 6 deadline for submission), Venice (June 15), Denver (July 15), Sundance (Oct. 15), Rotterdam or Berlin (Nov. 1), New Directors/New Films (Jan. 17), and others, while entering smaller, less exclusive festivals as a backup. Check the Internet for up-to-date submission deadlines.

You can see how the promotion period easily takes longer than the production itself, especially if you don't ever feel like giving up on getting new exposure for your work. And while PR can be exciting and challenging, it can also be very demoralizing when you're repeatedly rejected and finally drained of financial and spiritual resources, perhaps to the point of being discouraged from ever putting on the indie moviemaking hat again. Your mettle will be tested over and over during promotion. If you can't get any show at all, make your own. Project your DV movie on a flat wall at night, right in Greenwich Village or in your town's mall (using a borrowed DLP projector would be nice). Of course, this is probably illegal, so be prepared to fend off the authorities with a plea of "moviemaking insanity." You never know—you might get your brave new movie seen by a *New York Times* critic heading home. Give the world a chance to discover you and your good work.

9
REALITY CHECK:
MORE FROM RAY CARNEY'S
"THE PATH OF THE ARTIST"

After rereading Ray Carney's introduction to his second install-ment of "The Path of the Artist," as it appeared in *MovieMaker* magazine (*www.moviemaker.com*), I realized that it was saying everything I wanted to say about the commercialization of art and the disorientation true artists feel when their work doesn't even come close to earning them a living. As you work toward becoming an indepen-dent artist, it doesn't help to have a sugarcoated idea about what you're up against. Here's what Ray has to say:

■ ■ ■

I have a recurring dream about a world where the museums have been bought up by the superstores and are run the way they are. Decisions on acquiring paintings are no longer made by art curators and specialists, but are governed by the marketplace. Artists buy their way in by purchasing "wall space" for ten thousand dollars a square foot, just like Coca-Cola or Dockers does to get into your local Wal-Mart. But since there is always more demand than space avail-able, simply getting a painting into the store is not sufficient; a work has to bring people in to justify its existence, to keep the shelf space from being re-assigned to something else.

The museum of the future keeps track of how many people look at each painting each day. The figures are published and studied by the heads of other museums to see which paintings attract the most viewers. Bidding wars en-sue to get the hottest paintings. Paintings whose drawing power falls off after a few days or weeks are removed and replaced by others. Work that doesn't seem certain to attract viewers is not put up in the first place, even if it can pay the wall fee. Corporate entities grow up to evaluate the potential popularity of each painting and to invest in it (or withhold investment) according to the predictions. In order to attract viewers and boost attendance figures, the artists of the future work in concert with vast armies of publicists and press flacks, whose job is to attract an audience to their work.

The artists themselves do everything they can to stoke up interest, giving magazine and newspaper interviews, making the rounds of television talk shows, making outrageous claims for the importance of their work. Of course, there are no more landscapes and still lifes. And no more portraits. In the museum of the future, paintings that require time and experience to understand were long ago shoved aside by works with flashy, dazzling effects. Individual works vie for attention with every gimmick imaginable—free baseball caps, t-shirts, light shows, neon-lighted frames, holographic posters, multimillion-dollar television, radio, and newspaper ad campaigns. The hushed subtlety of classic art gives way to coarse obviousness; the quiet beckoning of the old-fashioned museum is replaced by blatant hucksterism. The paintings of the future are full of violence and nudity and sensational allusions to contemporary issues. It is the end of art as we know it.

The reason the dream scares me is that when I wake up I realize that it is not a vision of some hellish nightmare future, but the world we actually live in. It's only that what the dream symbolically represents as museums and paintings is our present movie theaters and the films that play in them.

—From Ray Carney's "The Path of the Artist"
(*www.cassavetes.com*).

■   ■   ■

Some readers will, no doubt, still wish commercial success upon themselves, imagine their movies being heralded from the rooftops, and great wads of money raining down from the heavens (condos in Aspen, tabloid fame). As the old saying goes, "Be careful what you wish for." Those success-oriented fantasies can work to undercut the real activity of being an artist, that is, positioning yourself for a lifetime of seeking out and speaking the truth through your work.

Ray Carney's dream of the full commercialization of art is frightening to me because, as Ray says, this reality already exists. Just insert the keywords "cottage paintings" in any search engine, and your computer screen will load up with the "artwork" of Thomas Kinkade. This "artist" has made millions of dollars merchandising paintings of cozy little English-style cottages sitting perched on a hill somewhere. He's become fabulously successful by selling that idyllic image of happy home at the peaceful golden-hour. Obviously there must be a huge yearning in people for such a perfectly tranquil state of being, because his suppliers can't produce the duplicate editions fast enough. There are numerous print runs, of varying complexity, materials, and price; his hand-signed prints cost thousands and original Kinkade oils sell in the five to six figures. Kinkade's merchandising has branched out to include not only selling actual cottages (based on images right out of his paintings) but also a line of furniture, wristwatches, books, bible covers, candles, lamps, screen savers, neckties, and more. There aren't any Kinkade Crunchy cereals or Kinkade cars yet, but just wait! Anyway, this capitalist alone warrants Ray's nightmare.

So look out, you classic artists, you subtle painters of edgy portraits and provocative landscapes, you moviemakers of the obscure. Banality is epidemic. The point for us media artists—and for DV moviemakers in particular—is that you can be supremely commercial, if that's your desire. (Just go out and shoot movies of cozy cottages.) If that isn't your dream, then please prepare yourself to pay some artistic dues.

10
DV VAGABONDS:
SHOOTING BY VAN

I n our cockeyed world, where rents can be as much as $1,500 per month or more, it seems like a big waste of time (a lifetime) to try to stay ahead of the economic curve, letting all our moviemaking dreams take a back seat to thirty-day billing cycles. For some who have experienced the difficulty of trying to have a life (paying rent, gas and electric, phone, etc.) *and* make movies, there is an alternative.

Please allow me to beat around the bush for a second. There was a scene with actor Yahn Soon that didn't make it into my 2001 DV feature *The 5th Wall,* but was especially poignant for me. In the scene, Yahn spoke with his then girlfriend about their monthly struggle just to make ends meet and brought up the point (at my voice command) that they could live maybe as long as four months if they were careful with one month of his income (from his TV cameraman's job) and got rid of the apartment. Why couldn't they just hit the road, he asked, traveling around by van, checking out different parts of America? They could visit places that he'd only seen in movies, like the coast of Maine or the hills of Vermont—all those autumn leaves in a blaze of colors. The open road beckoned.

In the next scene, I had Yahn, in character, make a list on-camera of what he "never wanted to do again." Here is his list:

> I never want to shoot news again. I never want to shoot news again [he repeated this mantra]. I never want a boss. I don't want to pay rent. I never want to hear the phone ring again. I never want to pay

credit card bills. I never want responsibility again. I never want to work sixteen hours a day. I never want to smile when I don't feel like it. I never want to pretend I like people that I don't like. I never want to wear shoes again. [This line was fed to him to connect with an upcoming scene I had in mind.] I want to bring seeds to people. I want a van . . .

Of course, in the scene his girlfriend shot him down. Living in a van wasn't her cup of tea. But something has to give if you see your life being wasted, ground up by the high costs of maintenance. Maybe buying a van will set you free.

In December 2001, I saw an ad in my local paper. It read "High-Top camper van, 1972; ¾ ton, starts right up. Stove, refrigerator, sink, and fold-out bed. Perfect for the mobile Shedboy/girl. $600." Perhaps you caught the National Public Radio piece about our city of Port Townsend having a large population of "shedboys"—men (and women) who survive without jobs or any visible means of support, by living with friends, renting small and inexpensive rooms, or dwelling in cars or boat sheds, quite happily thriving off the grid. Well, even though I was still trying, along with my wife, to wage the battle of keeping up with a mortgage and raising a teenage son, I thought the van, as affordable as it sounded, might pump an idea of freedom into my thirty-day cycle of financial grind. Hell, it could even pay for itself, I explained to Julie. I could (a) use it as a portable office; (b) take off for a few days when I needed a solitary break from family life and re-sponsibilities, sparing the high cost of motel rooms; (c) even travel to gigs at film festivals where I conduct seminars and film showings; and at the same time (d) perhaps shoot a DV feature on the road while I'm gone.

I had written a road movie script several years prior to this time, enti-tled *Secret Time*, about a man who disengages from his daily life to spend solitary time out on the road, contemplating what happened to the spiri-tual quest he'd begun in the 1960s. Now I could conceivably shoot it and save hundreds of dollars by eating and sleeping in a van, and it would also hold a few helpers and all the moviemaking equipment. So the idea

My 1972 Ford Econoline van parked at Chuck's Auto for mechanical evaluation. How much will it cost to make a used vehicle roadworthy?

of owning a van opened up creative possibilities. I bought it, realizing that even if I had to double the cost to get it running perfectly (tune up the engine, replace the radiator, clean up and recarpet the interior, etc.), it would still be a bargain.

Acquiring the van suddenly made my daily life seem freer. Just seeing it sitting out there on the grass overlooking the Port Townsend Bay helped me concentrate better. "Yes" it said to me, "you *are* going to get to see new things, take in new vistas and experiences in the coming year." Just the thought that I might be on the road making movies gave me an increased sense of inner peace. Suddenly it felt like there would be adequate time to *do everything*.

Mad Monks

In the first few days of the shock of being a van owner, I searched Google.com on the Web to see how I'd done with the purchase price. But as often happens with the Internet, I was brought into contact with various forms of information way beyond what I thought I was looking for. When I clicked on one entry about a "1972 Ford van" I found myself at a site that celebrated a couple of guys from San Francisco who had bought a van (same year as mine!) in the mid-1980s and just took off for Oregon. From their new Northwest digs they decided to send a long letter back home to friends. The letter soon grew into a twenty-four-page diary of daily life. Like explorers before them, they had a lot to impart, and donning an alias, The Monks, they raised enough money to print the article in newspaper form. By the second issue they had inadvertently founded *Monk: The Mobile Magazine*.

The Monks gave the magazine out for free and sold advertising to keep up with the costs of production and gas. The theme was always the same: two guys (usually pictured on the cover) and what they were doing with their lives away from the big city. Without dependence on critical reviews (or even copy editing—many readers say they enjoyed

Jim Crotty (left) and Michael Lane were happy campers as they occupied a 1972 Ford Econoline and produced *Monk* magazine from the road (*www.monk.com*). (Photo by John Deming)

the grammatical errors), their magazine and van lifestyle have survived and flourished for over fifteen years and more than nineteen issues (see *Mad Monks' Guides* to U.S. cities at their Web site).

Getting the Right Van

Now imagine this in DV terms. You and your partner buy an old, low-priced van, cheap enough that you can afford to get it roadworthy. By sharing costs, perhaps living out of it for two or three months, saving maybe $4,500 or more in rent and utilities, you are able to purchase your 3-chip/FireWire-ready DV camera ($1,600), laptop computer ($2,000), NLE software (Final Cut Express at $299, or win an eBay Final Cut Pro 4 for $500), and hit the road ($400+ for gas).

But before we get to on-the-road filmmaking, here's a little car talk. If you decide to purchase an older van for your temporary living quarters and moviemaking vehicle, you need to be very careful to know exactly what you are buying before you trade cash for a bill of sale. The wrong van can cost you plenty of maintenance money, every extra dollar out of your pocket, just when you've finally started making your (DV) dreams a reality. I know this book isn't an auto repair manual, but with "used-car" in the title I'll risk putting in a few pages on automotive information.

> **NOTE:** Before you buy your moviemaking van, do the following: Take the vehicle to a good mechanic and let him or her give it a $100 once-over examination. For a hundred bucks a mechanic will usually follow a standard list of checkpoints (engine compression, transmission, U-joint, rear end, suspension, steering, brake pads, etc). Yes, you'll lose your hundred dollars if you don't buy the van, but you'll save the thousands—not to mention the aggravation it might have cost if you'd bought a lemon.

I was in a friend's van once, merrily speeding down a desert highway in Death Valley, when suddenly the front tie rod gave out and snapped apart, making both the tires flare out independently. The van slid to a screeching halt, ending up on the wrong side of the road's shoulder. We were lucky we weren't hitting eighty on the Hollywood Freeway. So make sure the engine and running gear are OK, with a special emphasis on the front rack and pinion that keep your steering tight.

The 1972 Ford Van Restoration Estimate

When I bought my '72 Econoline van for $600 I figured that I'd have some repairs to make before I could call the vehicle roadworthy. After all, the van was basically thirty years old; in fact, it qualified for zero payments on yearly registration as soon as I could purchase a vintage license plate and place on a '72 generic sticker. So I had a local mechanic (Chuck) write me up a full estimate on parts and labor, giving me the full cost for restoring the mechanical end of the vehicle, in an attempt to bring it completely up to present-day reliability. Here's the damage: steering repair, $1,070; engine tune-up, $251; radiator repair, $441; transmission servicing, $200; grand total, $1,962.

OK. So to get the front end shaped up as new, stop the leak of transmission fluid, replace the radiator, and tune it up was a couple grand. Was this a reasonable expenditure? Whatever van I bought that was in the old-age bracket (that cost under $1,000) would probably need similar repairs. And wasn't it worth it to know that the undercarriage, steering arms, and bushings all would be in order, much like new? And the radiator would be sound as well, so I wouldn't have to fear blowing out my cooling system on the road in some highly inconvenient spot in the desert somewhere. And the engine would run well for a period of time that I could depend on. By supplying new points and plugs occasionally, which are easy for even a novice to replace in an older car as opposed to a newer, computer-controlled one, I might actually be, once again, master of my own transportation system. The leak from the transmission could have caused some damage if not caught periodically on a long trip, so it was good to catch that. Yes, it would feel good bringing an old car up to safety standards, restore it, be the guardian of this veteran of the roads.

I looked hard again at the numbers. Even though the van would, in the end, cost me a grand total of $2,700, was it a good expenditure? I went to the Internet and entered the keywords "Blue Book" and clicked on *http://www.autoweb.com/content/research/index.cfm?id=10869*, which said it offered the current worth of new and used automotive vehicles. I clicked on Pre-Owned Vehicles, a slot for data, and entered the vital statistics of my van. I was searching for the cutoff point where buying a newer van for more money would make more sense than restoring an older one. What could I buy for $2,700? Well, I could find some mid-1970s vans for around that price, get myself almost up to 1980, but all those vehicles were subject to the same amount of natural deterioration and need of work.

When you finally plop down your G4 (G5 or G-6) Mac or current high-powered PC laptop on the little table in your camper van (lots of campgrounds have electrical hookups . . .), and start editing with Final Cut Pro or Express, Avid DV Xpress, or Adobe Premiere while enjoying the ocean breezes and views (Malibu or Big Sur), it might be a bit disorienting at first. But sometimes a shake-up in your life is necessary to get things back on track. Isn't it worth shedding the "normal" lifestyle comfort to become a full-time artist? And with the Internet/ e-mail, friends and a support system are at your fingertips.

The main thing is to jump-start yourself out of your rut and get back on track with the things that are most vital to your life, like making movies (and not suffering needlessly at a dead-end job). Make the strong American economy (robust even in a recession) work for you. Use creative concepts to get yourself disentangled from the nine-to-five, forty-hour workweek. Then apply that same kind of original, out-of-the-box thinking to your future moviemaking projects.

Laws and Admonitions of the Road

For those who still have doubts about this so-called great adventure of vanning around the United States, here's a final bit of sage paranoia-busting advice from Jim "Mad Monk" Crotty. Jim's admonition may not be a one-size-fits-all kind of reality check, but at least it may give you a few laughs and spare you, when we meet at a film festival somewhere, from having to say, "Rick, you didn't warn me!"

LAWS AND ADMONITIONS OF A MADCAP RV NOMAD

By James Marshall Crotty ©2002

I lived on the road for over thirteen years, publishing *Monk*, the Mobile Magazine, from the confines of a 26-foot RV. Along with my illustrious partner, Michael Lane, I invented dashboard publishing, and helped launch the zine revolution. I know about trying to lay out story boards on the back bed of a camper. I know about plugging the power cord into lampposts, so I can copy edit an article. I know about Federal Express showing up at obscure campgrounds in the middle of the Arizona desert. I know about selling advertisements from pay phones in freezing cold rain. I know about finding a bank of pay phones, so you can make calls on one and get return calls on the other (I once tied up five different pay phones at the Sanbusco mall in Santa Fe using this method). I know about the hazards of having your overpriced mobile publishing house suddenly go kaput. And I intimately know about calling up the Good Sam Emergency Road Service, waiting two hours, and then being towed to the nearest garage, which doesn't open till Monday. I know about waiting in the RV in the parking lot of said garage until it does open Monday morning. I know about being stuck there for a few more days selling ads from the nearby pay phones trying to raise the money to replace the transmission or the carburetor or the alternator or the ignition or whatever decided to go wrong this time. I know about making my home right where I am. And finding a way to pray, play, run, cook and write anywhere, any time, under any and all conditions.

You can talk all you want about Charles Kuralt and Jack Kerouac and some other fair-weather nomad trying to write or publish from the road, but no one in the history of this country has deliberately lived entirely on the go for over a decade, without a direct phone line, without a home to return to, without a second car, and managed to publish, sell ads for and write a 40,000 circulation magazine. No one in today's America is that dedicated or mad.

I am.

Therefore, I am eminently qualified to tell you the twelve unforgiving and unforgettable laws of the road. Especially the laws of the road in a 1986 Fleetwood Bounder motorhome bought from Leach Camper Sales in Lincoln, Nebraska in the middle of the coldest winter in recent memory when my previous '72 Ford Econoline van had just died leaving me completely homeless and desperate. Here they are:

1. Never buy anything from a guy named Leach.

2. Never buy any model of vehicle in its first year off the line. I bought my Bounder in 1986, but it was a 1985 model. The ignition kept shorting out and forty-three different mechanics over a decade could never figure it out. Which brings up . . .

3. Stick with the same mechanic.

4. Don't buy a used motorhome. Nothing depreciates faster than a motorhome. For good reason—they're a cheap house on wheels. When the Germans start making American-sized motorhomes, buy one of those.

5. Be absolutely vigilant about staying on top of every single squeak, burp, or other strange sound coming out of your vehicle. When a car breaks down, no big deal. You just cab it over to Motel 6 for the night. When a motorhome breaks down, there goes your house. Plus, you usually have to wait a lot longer for the part.

6. When things are going smoothly, and you're just tooling down the highway, observing the scenery through the big windows of your big beast on wheels . . . at just the moment when you are experiencing some minor satori, some subtle oneness with all living things, when you are feeling at peace with your self, your life, and the world, a tire will blow. Guaranteed.

7. Things will never ever go like you read in the books. I have spent ten years deconstructing the road myth. I am the anti-road myth. People read "On the Road" or "Travels with Charley" or "Blue Highways" and concoct some fantasy of peripatetic bliss. In a motorhome, especially a 1986 Fleetwood Bounder motorhome bought from Leach Camper Sales in Lincoln, Nebraska during the coldest winter on record, you are destined to break down. In fact, a corollary is: YOU MUST BREAK DOWN. If you don't break down, you will not have enough crises to turn into compelling stories in your mobile magazine.

8. When you absolutely must leave the campground, your cat will suddenly disappear into the woods. And you will have to wait two, sometimes three days for it to come out of the neighboring drainage pipe.

9. When you feel hopelessly lost, and stop for directions, you are invariably ⅛th of a mile from your destination. Which is sad because . . .

10. When you are closest to your destination, people will inevitably give you the wrong directions. Corollary: you must ask three (not four and not two) different people to get back on track.

11. No one will believe you. No one will care. They simply will not comprehend the sheer terror you feel every time you enter the motorhome, knowing at some point in the next three hundred miles, this thing is going to stop running. You will begin to lose a fundamental trust in the universe. You will start to feel this planet is a very shaky place to be. You will develop strange sicknesses from sleeping above a gas tank for thirteen years, and from living so close to the smells of a cat's litter box. You will develop allergies from the mold growing in the decaying particle board walls, which got wet from leakage in the roof, which one day just suddenly started leaking for no other reason than it is a Fleetwood Bounder in the first year off the line bought from a guy named Leach in Lincoln, Nebraska in the middle of the coldest damn winter in the history of this solar system!

12. You will forget all of this, crank up the engine and hit the road again!

James M. Crotty is the cofounder of *Monk: The Mobile Magazine*, the travel/culture Web site Monk.com, and the Web development firm Monk E-Biz (*http://www.monk.com/web/*). To read other writings by Crotty, please go to *http://www.JamesCrotty.com.*

Shopping for Vans Online (in England!)

Still with me? You aren't deterred? Really? Maybe you are crazy enough to become a traveling DV moviemaker after all. Perhaps you'd like to combine your love of digital video on the open road with that European vacation you always promised yourself you'd take after college, and head to . . . England!

The other day, while I was entering the keywords "camper van" in my *www.google.com* search engine, I found an amazing Web site located in England that lists hundreds of vans for sale at varying prices, most for under £3K (see *www.ukmotorhomes.net/*). Remember, in England prices are in pounds and euros, not dollars! Maybe you could buy a van from this site, catch a cheap ticket to London, and shoot DV in the English countryside. Then, when you're done with your European shoot, just resubmit the van for sale, back at the UK Motorhomes Web site, listing it as a "moviemaking" van, maybe even adding the name of your DV feature to its roadworthy attributes.

That will be your first PR! Suddenly your movie's title will be in bold type, added into the text of your web-ad. Once the ad is successfully submitted, you can test your favorite search engine (Safari or Google), for its investigatory powers, by entering your movie's title and seeing if your ad loads in the browser window. Or you can print the ad in the classified section of a local English newspaper and read the name of your upcoming movie in bold type on newsprint. In either case, your PR media blitz has begun.

Webcasting from the Road

If you have a Web site already in place, you could certainly record and transmit images of your road trip as you go, sharing tasty previews of your adventures as you compile your first DV used-car feature. Suddenly you'll have fans on the Internet, wondering what city you'll roll into next. If they notice it's their city, you can bet on receiving some e-mail hellos, a few complimentary meals, good companionship, and helping hands for shooting in their locality. You'll be able to (1) build the initial DV-Moviemaking-by-Van Web site, (2) load still images and text (maybe offering an Internet fill-in slot for people joining your mailing list), and (3) set up a streaming video movie theater at your Web site, where people can see the movie-in-progress.

With the Web we can make new (DV) friends, celebrate our progress as moviemakers (is your site up yet with that map of your DV moviemaking stops across America?), and give ourselves the respect we deserve for doing the difficult work of being artists in a culture that's considerably less supportive of that activity than our European counterparts. Going upstream isn't easy. Making movies that are likely not commercial (it takes money to hire name actors, and without that clout you will have difficulty making your indie feature commercial) means that you have to be aware of the difficult road ahead, both literally and figuratively. Your parents, even your friends, will wonder what you're doing, leaving that good, high-paying job and expensive apartment behind—for what? And perhaps they'll even be thrown by your new positive energy, not to mention the weird movies you are sending back from America's heartland. Don't be surprised. Try not to let your feelings be hurt. When you think in original ways you will have to ride out the criticism and somehow remain strong-willed. At the end of the day, when you've made your artistic statement, I can assure you that people of importance will finally take notice. Your

Mad Monks celebrate their liberation from mundane eight-to-five lifestyles.
(Photo by Ingrid Lundahl)

control over your career depends on your ability to persevere against the odds. So keep the pedal to the metal!

Cell Phone Instead of Shortwave

In this modern age, we've been supplied with all the interconnective tools we could ever need, often at affordable prices if you search out the perfect deals long enough. Have you seen the e-mail pocket pal Hip Hop? Do you have a cell phone yet? Just a few years ago it would have been almost mandatory for a traveling truck or van to carry a shortwave hookup for road emergencies. Now, of course, cell phones supply that same convenience. At any rate, for a minimal cost you can acquire a cell phone for road emergencies, and perhaps spend a few of those introductory hours trying to talk friends into flying into Boise or somewhere and joining the fun. (They've seen the .jpegs you e-mailed from the road!) Tell them to look for a van that's flying the banner "I got DV!" off its antenna.

If you've been a filmmaker for a while, but only lately joined the DV revolution, you'll laugh at the irony that this time I recommend purchasing a used car (van) to make a movie instead of selling your automobile to make a (16mm) movie—what I advocated in *Feature Filmmaking at Used-Car Prices*. The point is that we all need to overcome economic and emotional obstacles to keep our moviemaking dreams alive. Whatever it takes. Buying *or* selling a used car can make a movie happen, as soon as you let your subconscious help determine your true path. Suddenly you can live for your art, put it first, make it a top priority.

Endnote: My Van Saga

When I discovered that the costs of repairing my impulsively purchased van would top the Blue Book value of the vehicle, I moved it on to a local junkyard, where it had a chance of becoming a find for another soul with romance for the road in his or her heart. Fortunately, I could reconcile the relatively small financial loss through my corporate recordkeeping, while looking forward to the day when having a usable van could mobilize my DV moviemaking venture. In a way, the van I bought so hastily was a sacrifice to the contents of this chapter. Without owning a van of the exact year, make, and model I acquired (a 1972 Ford Econoline), I would never have discovered the Mad Monks online and thus would not have had the opportunity of presenting these open road DV-moviemaking visions for your consideration.

I think it's time we stop second-guessing our every move in life. If the price tag for such an adventure is less than $1,000 and leads to other positive things, then I'd say pat yourself on the back. You're doing well! Let that left side of your brain kick the tires and check the compression on a van-for-purchase, while allowing the right side to absorb information about roads yet untaken, imagining exciting destinations. Some new-millennium history is waiting to be recorded. The story that encompasses it is up to you.

11

WWW.VANGOGHSDV.COM:
MAKING ART WITH DV

Awhile back, I decided to purchase the domain name *www.van goghsDV.com*. At the time, I had a vague notion that somewhere in the media universe there existed the Vincent van Gogh of DV, a super-creative but undiscovered and unappreciated media artist—genius-level—who was putting together a portfolio of the most amazing and provocative artistic movies the world has ever seen. Of course, no one would know about the work until this supremely gifted individual died. I imagined this scenario could actually be taking place somewhere in the world during my own lifetime, and hoped I'd be around to witness the momentous occasion, the announcements on TV, the books, documentaries, and other spin-off flicks about this person. I could see a Hollywood docudrama as well, like the life story of Jean-Michel Basquiat (Andy Warhol's protégé), only this time it would be about this new, dynamic, and heretofore unknown DV moviemaker.

So spending the $95 to register the domain name for three years got the wheels turning in my head. Have you ever done something like that—leaping before you looked? I simply felt that I must get that domain name: vangoghsDV. But if anyone had asked me why, I would have had no suitable response to explain such reckless spending. If pressed, all I could have offered in my defense was that I allowed myself to buy a Web site name for some reason as yet unknown to me. I just acted on impulse, allowed my ideas to flow, and indulged my intuition.

But nothing happened for a while. I didn't seem to have any time to focus on the site, and I just let it sit idle for more than a year. All you got when you plugged in the Web address was a loaded page trying to sell you all the other combinations with "vangoghsDV" in the title—you know the ones: .net, .org, .tv, .biz, .cc, .ws., etc.—or variations of the word itself, like van-goghs-DV.com, or vangoghDV.com. They also offered several lists of movie-related links. OK. Enough time being sucked into the Web.

I decided it was time to get the site up and running, have it do something. I sent a quick e-mail to a local Web artist, Jef (*jef@snarg.net*), and arranged to buy him lunch. Then, before the luncheon date, I clicked onto the Snarg Web site, *www.snarg.net*, to get an idea of what Jef had been doing lately. As happened the last time I went there, I had to click at random for a while before activating a screen alive with shifting colors, shapes, and sounds. Was it a Web site or a painting? (Check it out for yourself!) Was it something like van Gogh would have done if he had the Internet medium and a simple build-your-own-Web site kit? Anyway, once you're in the site you need to give it time to ramp up, since there is a lot to see and enjoy if you are patient enough, as with any good work of art. So pour some coffee, tea, or hot chocolate, or set up a cold beverage and just sit back, letting the seemingly random images and music and sound effects tickle your brain. Just the very existence of such a site helps move ideas ahead, expanding our consciousness regarding what's possible in this computer-based medium.

TRAVELING ARTIST AND DOCUMENTARIAN

Another artist friend, Galen Garwood, had introduced me to the Snargs, having hired them to create PR for his own DV project *Panom, Cousin to the Clouds*, a documentary about an elephant hospital in Thailand. Galen is a painter whose work had for many years been well received at top Seattle galleries. One day, he happened to read an article in *Smithsonian Magazine* describing the plight of the Asian elephant. Right then, tears streaming down his face, Galen experienced a kind of epiphany. Soon after that, he sold just about everything he

Jef of *www.snarg.net* on the street in Port Townsend, collecting DV images for his ongoing random Web collages.

owned, auctioned off all his own paintings and other works in his private collection, and emptied his bank accounts to buy DV gear. He purchased a new DV camera (Cannon SL-1), sound equipment, a computer, and camping gear, left for Thailand and disappeared into the jungle to shoot a DV feature. (If you attended the IFP Market in New York in 2000, you might have caught Galen's work-in-progress, edited partially in the field on his Mac laptop loaded with Final Cut Pro.)

In 2002, Galen arranged with Jef of Snarg.net to set up a method by which he could add images and reportage directly to his Web site from the road. Jef designed a program that enabled Galen to supply images to a worldwide Internet audience, no matter where he was located on the planet. This seemed like a good advancement for the art of indie moviemaking. The world could watch DV footage as it was shot on location, however remote, without the expensive satellite feed that the networks use when covering something overseas. The DV camera would be put on a footing with the ham radio. Now if someone

Galen Garwood hefts his Canon XL-1 DV camera amid the Karen tribe, in the remote Umgoi region of Thailand. E-mail him at *ggarwood2001@yahoo.com* to see where his DV-making adventure has taken him next! (Photo by Chakkree ©2002)

can just figure out a way to get those images inserted into the nightly news we might learn some unfiltered truths about what's really happening around the world.

LIGHTWAVE 3D ANIMATIONS

For some, like Port Townsend's Andrew Poling, the DV revolution means having access to fantastic computer animation systems for the price of a used car. If a college-bound high school senior like Andrew is resourceful, he can save from a summer job, perhaps get parents to match dollars, and end up with a cutting-edge program like LightWave 3D (NewTek Inc., 1-800-TOASTER, *www.newtek.com/products/lightwave*). For $1,595 ($395 with educational discount) it offers an amazing array of professional 3D graphics surface-modeling options (airbrushing between morphs, combination move-and-rotate tools, interactive scale), animation for DV (spreadsheet-style scene editor, squash and stretch tools, simple crowd simulation, motion mixer, and nonlinear animation, all of which is fully compatible with Final Cut Pro), and speedy photo-real or stylized rendering on a Mac G5.

As soon as Andrew helped me upgrade my OS X to the Jaguar 10.2 I'd recently purchased, we installed LightWave 3 into the Applications folder of my hard drive. Then, after inserting the dongle key into the keyboard's second USB port (the other port is used for the mouse), Andrew opened the Modeler program and I watched as the four-section work grid filled the screen. To demonstrate how to design a three-dimensional spaceship, he began by clicking on the Box button, located under the left-side Objects menu heading, which made four box-shaped objects appear, one in each quadrant.

He next scrolled his mouse up to the upper right corner quadrant and selected the center Rotation Key tool button (the symbol with two planets in an orbit path). After clicking this rotational button, he moved the mouse around to reveal the box as a 3D cube shape. It would be from this basic cubic volume that Andrew said he would

NewTek's LightWave work screen, with the upper-right quadrant supplying a 360-degree wraparound three-dimensional view.

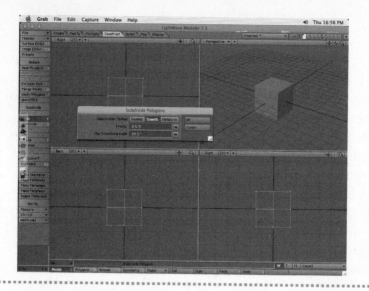

Clicking the Rotation key in the top-right bar menu (a tiny symbol with orbiting planets) shows off the square as a cube.

stretch points out, add angles, and reunite volumes until he achieved a spacecraft shape in the grid.

He next clicked on Construct in the top menu bar and then on Sub-divide (the D shortcut key, side menu). In the Subdivide Polygons control box that appeared at the middle of the computer screen, he selected Smooth and adjusted the Fractal amount to read 15 percent, which he said made the grid size smaller. Then he selected Points in the bottom menu, and clicked on the top corners of the box/cube to form control points (the Apple key must be held down for each click-created control point). With a click on the Top (view) perspective button at the upper left corner, Andrew then clicked Move (in the left-side menu) and pushed the mouse up the mouse pad to magically stretch the cube's corners high above its surface, forming what he called a "king's crown" (see illustration next page).

With a click on Polygons (bottom menu) and holding down the Apple key, he circled the pointed cube, drawing a line that encircled the object to select it in total, then clicked on Stretch (in the side

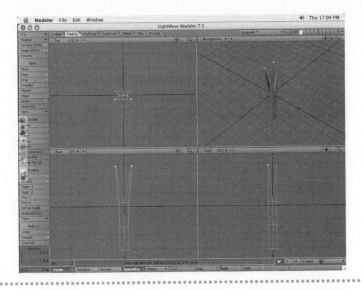

The elongated form, stretched thin by its control points, starts to look aerodynamic.

menu), selected the magnifying glass (near center of grid), and stretched again.

After that, his routine for making changes was to (a) click on empty Clearing Box at the lower left (the word Grid below), (b) click on Move, (c) click Points and select, (d) click on Move and hold down the points to stretch them out, (e) disable Move by clicking anywhere on the surface, and (f) click on the empty box to repeat the procedure [clicking on the Rotational tool (upper right corner) to check on progress]. It was exciting to see the first glimpse of the spacecraft-to-be, when the two control points atop of the king's crown were moved down to a midpoint.

As with any new software program, the user must enjoy the process, have fun playing around, and be enthralled by the potential. The learning curve is a necessary part of the process, so try not to get too frustrated as you proceed. Plan on spending a few weeks just experimenting, learning from your mistakes, and building up a design vocabulary like Andrew has done.

If animation is your DV field of choice, then also check out Universe (*www.electricimage.com*), Maya (*www.alias.com/eng/index.shtml*),

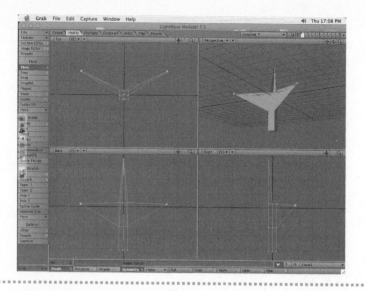

Stretching selected control points at a 90-degree angle produces winglike protrusions.

With Artmatic's easy, space-age software console loaded to the screen, strange shapes like a slotted spiral can be built and altered (a click on the dice), then saved in a sequence (left-side image column) for export as a QuickTime movie (U & I Software, *www.artmatic.com*, $299).

Apple's new Shake (*www.apple.com/shake*), and various other programs you can find on the Internet using Google or Safari with the keyword "animation." What's exciting is looking forward to new DV features that use these space-age programs in conjunction with live action shooting. Out of this mix will surely come some amazing indie creations.

12
SPACE-AGE DV

HOLOGRAPHIC TECHNOLOGY AND MORE

This chapter could just as easily be called "Holographic Disk Technology" because that development alone promises to revolutionize the computer and DV industry. One thing that all computer-based activities have in common is the need for data storage. And with corporate data storage needs doubling each year, several companies have been working to develop new methods beyond the known CD and DVD route, holographic digital storage (HDS) in particular.

DV FILMMAKING AND DATA

To understand the impact holographic disks will have on DV (cameras to digital editing), it may help to review the methods of data storage developed in recent years. Remember CDs? Their technology offered around 680 mb of storage. Then came DVD, which offered 4.7 gigs of memory, a huge leap forward for those of us who wished to copy a feature-length movie (DV) on a single disk. And in 2001, Apple Computers gave us the possibility of actually burning to a DVD disk after editing our movies on a Mac. At that point it was clear that our media artworks were intrinsically tied to the problem of data storage. If we had the storage, we could shoot more video and juggle it around in our editing, using software that didn't freeze up for lack of storage or slow data rates.

Those of us who demanded storage space in our computers for longer film and DV projects learned the pertinent numbers: for each second of full-motion video (thirty video "frames" per second) played full-screen on our computer, we needed a data rate of approximately 30 megabytes (MB) per second, or 1.8 gigs for each minute on screen. So when the Mac came out with 30 gigs of storage built in, we suddenly had access to editing and viewing longer projects. Still, data storage and data rate remained an issue. What if we shot 7 hours of DV? We'd have to look at it in careful data bundles. We could always feel the pressure of needing storage as we worked.

HOLOGRAPHIC STORAGE

Now, it was impressive that a CD could hold three hundred thousand pages of text, approximately three hundred times more than a floppy disk. But image data was much more demanding. That's where holographic data storage (HDS) comes in. Instead of riding the line of 1.8 gigs per minute for playing video, HDS offers the possibility of incorporating rates of 10 gigs *per second*, far beyond the minimal requirements of image presentation. This laser technology seems to be turning science fiction into fact.

What is holographic technology? How does it work? In basic terms, holographic storage is the 3D recording of information, using a laser to record wave-front data in photo-reflective crystals (initially a strontium-barium-niobate compound), as 3D holograms. These grids of light and shadow dots of binary code sit in layers called multiplexes, allowing a vast amount of data accessed from numerous pages to be stored in a very small area. This technology has been around since the early 1990s when Nippon Telephone & Telegraph company announced that they had developed holographic technology that could record approximately 30 hours of moving image in a piece of crystal the size of a fingernail.

I'll let that sink in a bit. I'm fighting to edit *one hour* of DV on my computer. But that's *30 hours* of video footage—on a fingernail. Yes, that would solve my problem. While companies like Lucent Technology (In Phase Technologies) couldn't afford to research and build the holographic technology for a few (at that point) struggling video artists, the fact that storage needs double every six months for corporations (more than a $100 billion data-storage industry by 2005) means that HDS laser technology will soon have solid product demand. That's why I've registered the domain name *www.holographicdv.com* until 2006 (and beyond?). That's what we'll all be doing: *Making Holographic Features at Used-Spaceship Prices!*

Watch for the use of holographic technology invading other parts of daily life, in applications such as identity cards, on which vast amounts of personal information (voice recognition, eye scans, fingerprints, image, etc.) can be incorporated. And the video games you play on your computer screen will not be limited to the flat screen of your monitor. Click on *www.dti3d.com* and other companies that offer true 3D interaction, thanks to laser technology.

Holographic storage will undoubtedly have a huge impact on the mobile wireless revolution, certainly on how we stream and receive images and audio. No longer is Dick Tracy's TV wristwatch a sci-fi fantasy. Soon we'll all be talking to each other via postage stamp–sized TV screens, viewing movies while riding to work, shooting and editing DV features without any cords to connect. And if investors or other interested parties want to watch our shoot (the minute-by-minute on-location progress), we can stream documentary footage or the actual rushes to our Web sites. Presto! We'll offer our own indie miniseries.

So these are exciting times, certainly the best for making DV movies at used-car prices. I'll be looking forward to seeing your new works at festivals and on the Internet, while trying to serve up a few surprises myself. Until then, happy DV-ing!

APPENDIX A

MULTIPERSON COLLABORATIVE CONTRACT

RICK SCHMIDT ("Schmidt") doing business as FEATURE WORKSHOPS, intends to produce and exploit a DV (digital video) feature-length movie tentatively entitled _____[Movie Title]_____ ("The Picture").

The following people named below will participate in the creation of The Picture, and upon completion of their collaborative services therein **will each receive an equal share of the gross profits** derived by Schmidt from the picture and ancillary rights. In exchange for the additional $50,000 or so needed to transfer the DV feature from videotape to 35mm film for theatrical exhibition, 10% of the gross will be reserved for an investor. Also, FEATURE WORKSHOPS will receive 5% of the gross profits to cover overhead during distribution/sales.

On my own behalf, and on behalf of my heirs, next of kin, executors, administrators, successors and assigns, I hereby release FEATURE WORKSHOPS, and RICK SCHMIDT, his agents, licensees, successors and assigns, from any and all claims, liabilities and damages arising out of my participation with the production of this motion picture. This agreement may be executed in several counterparts, each of which shall be deemed an original and such counterparts shall together constitute one and the same agreement, binding all the parties hereto notwithstanding all of the parties are not signatory to the original on the same counterpart. Unclaimed profit points from Actor's ½% assigns, page 4, or unused "10% gross to Investor," will be divided equally among the writer/director collaborators listed below:

Signatures

Date and Place of Execution

INVESTOR (10%)

_____

FEATURE WORKSHOPS (5%)

_____

RICK SCHMIDT

_____

_____   _____

_____   _____

_____   _____

_____   _____

_____   _____

_____   _____

_____   _____

_____   _____

_____   _____

_____   _____

On my own behalf, and on behalf of my heirs, next of kin, executors, administrators and assigns, I hearby release FEATURE WORKSHOPS and RICK SCHMIDT, his agents, licensees, successors and assigns, from any and all claims, liabilities and damages arising out of my participation with the production of this digital video Pro-DVCAM feature, tentatively entitled _____[Movie Title]_____. Upon completion of my services as defined below, I will receive one half percent (½%) of the gross profits as derived by Schmidt from the picture and its ancillary rights.

Signatures (actors)   Date and Place of Execution

_____   _____

_____   _____

_____   _____

_____   _____

_____   _____

_____   _____

_____   _____

_____   _____

AUTHORIZED BY RICK SCHMIDT_____

APPENDIX B

FEATURE WORKSHOPS AGREEMENT

RICK SCHMIDT ("Schmidt") doing business as FEATURE WORKSHOPS, intends to produce and exploit a DV (digital video) feature-length movie tentatively entitled _____ [Movie Title] _____ ("The Picture").

The following people named below will participate in the creation of The Picture, and upon completion of their collaborative services therein **will each receive an equal share of the gross profits** derived by Schmidt from the picture and ancillary rights. These gross payments will be paid to collaborators after the following debts to the production are paid in full: (a) out-of-pocket fees paid by Schmidt to actors and technicians, plus related food, lodging, and travel costs incurred during the shoot, (b) salaries paid by Schmidt to editor(s) during postproduction, sound mixer, and lab video dubbing/duplication costs, and (c) money spent by Schmidt for advertisement, distribution, and exhibition of The Picture ("four-walling," etc.), along with any food, lodging, and travel costs incurred. In addition, if it is necessary to legally enforce this contract, then the prevailing party (or parties) are entitled to reimbursement of attorney's fees and cost of suit. Venue and jurisdiction for any legal proceedings will be in Jefferson County, Washington, USA.

In exchange for the additional $50,000 or so needed to transfer the DV feature from videotape to 35mm film for theatrical exhibition, 10% of the gross will be reserved for an investor. Also, FEATURE WORKSHOPS will receive 5% for operating costs.

On my own behalf, and on behalf of my heirs, next of kin, executors, administrators, successors and assigns, I hereby release FEATURE WORKSHOPS, and RICK SCHMIDT, his agents, licensees, successors and assigns, from any and all claims, liabilities and damages arising out of my participation with the production of this motion picture. This agreement may be executed in several counterparts, each of which shall be deemed an original and such counterparts shall together constitute one and the same agreement, binding all the parties hereto notwithstanding all of the parties are not signatory to the original on the same counterpart. Unclaimed profit points assigned actors on page 3, or unused "10% gross to Investor," will be divided equally among the writer/director collaborators listed below:

Signatures   Date and Place of Execution

_____   _____
INVESTOR (10%)

_____   _____
FEATURE WORKSHOPS (5%)

_____   _____
RICK SCHMIDT

_____   _____

_____   _____

_____   _____

_____   _____

_____   _____

_____   _____

_____   _____

On my own behalf, and on behalf of my heirs, next of kin, executors, administrators and assigns, I hearby release FEATURE WORKSHOPS and RICK SCHMIDT, his agents, licensees, successors and assigns, from any and all claims, liabilities and damages arising out of my participation with the production of this digital video feature, tentatively entitled _____ [Movie Title] _____

_____. Upon completion of my services as defined below, I will receive one half percent (½%) unless otherwise noted, of the gross profits as derived by Schmidt from the picture and its ancillary rights.

Signatures (actors)   Date and Place of Execution

_____   _____

_____   _____

_____   _____

_____   _____

_____   _____

_____   _____

_____   _____

_____   _____

_____   _____

AUTHORIZED BY RICK SCHMIDT_____

APPENDIX C

LITERARY PURCHASE OPTION AGREEMENT

THIS AGREEMENT, effective as of _____, 200__, made by and between _____, _____, and- _____, or their nominee, located at _____[address]_____ (hereinafter collectively referred to as "Producer") and _____ located at _____ [address]_____ (the "Writer"), concerning the rights to an unpublished stage play entitled _____ and the materials upon which it is based, the following terms and conditions shall apply:

1. DEFINITION OF "WORK": For purposes of this Agreement, "Work" means the unpublished stage play entitled _____[Movie Title]_____, written by Author and any and all other literary materials, titles, themes, formats, formula, incidents, action, story, dialogue, ideas, plots, phrases, slogans, catchwords, art, designs, compositions, sketches, drawings, characters, characterizations, names and trademarks now contained therein, as well as such elements as may at any time hereafter be added or incorporated therein, and all versions thereof in any form.

2. GRANT OF OPTION: In consideration of the mutual promises contained herein, and the payment to Writer of $1,000.00 (the "Option Price"), Writer hereby grants to Producer the exclusive, irrevocable right and option (the "Option") for eighteen (18) months (the "Option Period") to acquire the exclusive motion picture, television, videocassette, and all subsidiary, allied and ancillary rights in and to the Work pursuant to the terms set forth below.

3. EXTENSION OF OPTION:

a. Producer shall have the right to extend the Option Period for one (1) period of eighteen (18) months. For the right to the extension of the first Option Period there must be one of the following:

    i. the project is set up at a company, major studio or mini-major studio able to fund the project,

    ii. substantial negotiations in progress for complete financing of the film,

    iii. letter of commitment to act in the film from one star, or

    iv. a full-length feature-film script has been completed, or

    v. Producer pays Author the sum of $1,000.00.

4. EXERCISE OF OPTION: Producer may exercise this Option at any time during the Option Period, as it may be extended, by giving written notice of such exercise to Writer and delivery to Writer of the minimum Purchase Price as set forth below. In the event Producer does not exercise said Option during the period as it may be extended, this Agreement shall be of no further force or effect whatsoever. All rights granted hereunder become property of Writer. Upon exercise of the Option, Producer shall have the right to file the Assignment, Exhibit A, with the Copyright Office.

5. PENDING EXERCISE OF OPTION: Producer shall have the right to engage in all customary development and preproduction activities during the Option Period as it may be extended.

6. GRANT OF RIGHTS: Effective upon Producer's exercise of the Option. Writer does hereby exclusively sell, grant, and assign to Producer, all rights in and to the Work not explicitly reserved by Writer (below), throughout the universe, in perpetuity, in any and all media, whether now existing or hereafter invented, including but not limited to, the following: all motion picture rights, all rights to make motion picture versions or adaptations of the Work, to make remakes and sequels to and new versions or adaptations of the Work or any part thereof, to make series and serials of the Work or any part thereof; the right, for advertising and publicity purposes only, to prepare, broadcast, exhibit, and publish in any form or media, any synopses, excerpts, novelizations, serializations, dramatizations, summaries and stories of the Work, or any part thereof; and all rights of every kind and character whatsoever in and to the Work and all the characters and elements contained therein except as explicitly reserved as follows:

a. Rights reserved by the Writer:

i. The right to publish the Work in its original adapted stage play form; the stage rights, radio play rights, and the right to use characters included in the Property in a new story, novel, stage or radio play, or screenplay.

ii. In any case where the Writer exercises her/his right as herein described, the Writer agrees that the excluded property may not be based on any screenplay adaptation owned by the Producer for the terms of this agreement—regardless of screenwriter—in the course of developing the Work for the screen, without the permission of the Producer.

iii. In any case where the Writer exercises her/his right as herein described, the Producer requests that the Writer include a mention of the motion picture based upon the Work, as a courtesy, whether in production or completed, when/if within the Writer's control.

7. PURCHASE PRICE: As consideration for all rights and property herein granted, and all warranties, and covenants herein made by Writer, Producer agrees to pay Writer such sum, not later than the commencement of principal photography of a production, a sum greater than or equal to applicable Writer's Guild Minimum fees. Writer shall deliver a first draft of a screenplay within sixty (60) days of the execution of this Agreement. Producer shall pay Writer the sum of FIVE THOUSAND DOLLARS ($5,000.00) as an advance on the full payment defined above, for said first draft. Payment will be in advance of commencing the draft's writing. Subsequent drafts of said screenplay shall be paid at rates commensurate with industry norms, (e.g., Writer's Guild in U.S.A.); or industry standard for the country in which the film is produced; or rates mutually acceptable to "writer" and "producer."

8. CREDITS:

a. In the event a motion picture based substantially on the Work is produced hereunder, Writer shall receive credit in the following form:

Based on the stage play by Author

or if the film has a different title from the Work, then:

Based on the stage play _____[Title]_____ by Author.

b. Such credit shall be accorded on a single card in the main titles on all positive prints of the picture and in all paid advertising in which the director has received credit, except for advertising of eight (8) column inches or less; group and list advertisements, teasers, publicity; special advertising; billboards, television trailers; film clips ("excluded ads"). Nothing contained in this Paragraph shall be construed to prevent the use of so-called "teaser," trailer, or other special advertising, publicity or congratulatory advertising. All other matters regarding prominence, placement, size, style, and color of said credits shall be in Producer's sole discretion.

c. No casual or inadvertent failure to comply with credit requirements hereunder shall be deemed a breach of this Agreement.

9. RESERVED RIGHTS: All publication rights are reserved to Writer for Writer's use and disposition, including but not limited to the right to publish and distribute printed versions of the Work and Writer-written sequels thereof (owned or controlled by Writer) in book form, whether hardcover or softcover, and in magazines or other periodicals, comics or coloring books, whether in installments or otherwise subject to Producer's limited rights to promote and advertise. Producer shall have the right of first negotiation and last refusal to enter an agreement such as this one with regard to any works created by Writer pursuant to this paragraph.

10. RIGHT OF FIRST NEGOTIATION: If Writer desires to dispose of or exercise a particular right reserved to Writer herein ("Reserved Right"), then Writer shall notify Producer in writing and immediately negotiate with Producer regarding such Reserved Right. If, after the expiration of thirty (30) days following the receipt of such notice, no agreement has been reached, then Writer may negotiate with third parties regarding such Reserved Right subject to the next paragraph.

11. RIGHT OF LAST REFUSAL: If Producer and Writer fail to reach an agreement pursuant to Producer's right of first negotiation, and:

a. Writer makes and/or receives any bona fide offer to license and/or purchase the particular Reserved Right or any interest therein in a context other than an auction ("Third Party Offer"), Writer shall notify Producer, if Writer proposes to accept such Third Party Offer, of the name of the offeror, the proposed purchase price, and other such terms of Third Party Offer. During the period of ten (10) days after Producer's receipt of such notice, Producer shall have the exclusive option to license and/or purchase said Reserved Right upon the same terms and conditions of said Third Party Offer. If Producer elects to exercise the right to purchase such Reserved Right, Producer shall notify Writer of the exercise thereof within said ten (10) day period, failing which Writer shall be free to accept such Third Party Offer. If any such proposed license and/or sale is not consummated with a third party within thirty (30) days following the expiration of the aforesaid ten (10) day period, Producer's Right of Last Refusal shall revive and shall apply to each and every further offer or offers at any time received by Writer relating to the particular Reserved Right or any interest therein; provided, further, that Producer's option shall continue in full force and effect, upon all of the terms and conditions of this Clause, so long as Writer retains any rights, title or interests in or to the particular Reserved Right, or

b. Writer seeks to obtain bona fide offers to license and/or purchase the particular Reserved Right or any interest therein by means of auction ("Auction"). Writer shall notify Producer of the time, date, location and rules of such Auction within (30) days thereof. Writer shall be entitled to license and/or sell the Reserved Right to the highest bidder at such Auction, provided that the terms and conditions of the license and/or sale to any party other than Producer shall be at least as favorable to Writer as those terms and conditions last offered by Producer to Writer under Clause 3 above. If any such license and/or sale is not consummated with any party in the course of said Auction, Producer's Right of Last Refusal shall revive and shall apply to each and every further Auction relating to the particular Reserved Right or any interest therein; provided, further, that Producer's option shall continue in full force and effect upon all of the terms and conditions of this Clause, so long as Writer retains any rights, title or interests in or to the particular Reserved Right.

Provisions

1. NAME AND LIKENESS: Producer shall have the right to publish, advertise, announce and use in any manner or medium the name, biography and photographs or other likeness of Writer in connection with the exhibition, distribution, advertising and promotion or other exploitation of any film created as a result of the exercise by Producer of its rights hereunder, including merchandising, if merchandising rights are granted herein.

2. PUBLICITY RESTRICTIONS: Writer agrees that, except as merely incidental to Writer's personal publicity endeavors, Writer shall not issue, authorize or permit the issuance of any advertising or publicity of any kind or nature relating to this Agreement, Producer, the material, any exercise of any rights in the Work or any versions or productions based in whole or in part thereon, without the prior written consent of Producer.

3. NO OBLIGATION TO PRODUCE: Nothing herein shall be construed to obligate Producer to produce, distribute, release, perform or exhibit any production based upon or suggested by the results of Writer's services hereunder.

4. REVERSION: If Producer exercises the option and fails to commence principal photography within four (4) years thereafter, Writer may send Producer written notice that the rights will revert to Writer unless principal photography commences within ninety (90) days of such notice. If Producer fails to so commence principal photography, the rights shall revert to Writer. Writer shall reimburse Producer all out-of-pocket costs paid by Producer out of first moneys received by Writer in connection with the Picture but no later than the commencement of principal photography.

5. REMEDIES: Writer acknowledges and agrees that Writer's sole remedy for any breach or alleged breach of this Agreement by Producer shall be an action at law to recover monetary damages. In no event shall any of the rights granted or to be granted and/or the releases made herein revert to Writer except as provided herein, nor shall Writer have a right of rescission or right to injunctive or other equitable relief.

6. FORCE MAJEURE: If the development or production of the Picture is materially interrupted or delayed by reason of epidemic, fire, action of the elements, walk-out, labor dispute, strike, governmental order, court order or order of any other legally constituted Authority, act of God or public enemy, war, riot, civil commotion or any other cause beyond Producer's control, whether of the same or of any other nature, or if because of the illness or incapacity of any principal member of the cast, any unexpired portion of the term hereof shall be postponed for the period of such interruption or interference.

7. ASSIGNMENT: Producer has the right to assign this contract to any person or entity in Producer's sole discretion.

8. REPRESENTATIONS AND WARRANTIES: Writer represents, warrants and agrees that:

a. The Work itself is original with Writer and no part of the Work is in the public domain,

b. Writer has not and will not enter into any agreements or activities which will hinder, compete, conflict, or interfere with the exercise of any of the rights granted to Producer. Writer has no knowledge of any claim or potential claim by any party which might in any way affect Producer's rights herein,

c. The Work does not, and no use thereof will, infringe upon or violate any personal, proprietary or other right of any third party, including, without limitation, defamation, libel, slander, false light or violation of any right of privacy or publicity or any copyright law.

d. The exercise of the rights herein granted to Producer will not in any way, directly or indirectly, infringe upon any rights of any person, or entity whatsoever.

9. INDEMNIFICATION: Writer agrees to defend, indemnify and hold Producer, and Producer's employees, agents, successors licensees and assigns harmless from and against any and all claims, damages, liabilities, losses or expenses (including reasonable attorney's fees and costs) suffered or incurred by Producer on account of or in connection with the breach of any of Writer's representations, warranties or covenants set forth herein.

10. PUBLIC INFORMATION: Producer, and Producer's successors, licensees or assigns, shall have no less rights by reason of this Agreement to material in the public domain than any member of the public may now or hereafter have.

11. ARBITRATION: Any claim, controversy or dispute arising hereunder shall be settled pursuant to California law by arbitration before a single arbitrator in accordance with the rules of the American Film Marketing Association (AFMA) held in Los Angeles, California. The award of the arbitrator shall be binding upon the parties and judgment there may be entered in any court The prevailing party shall be entitled to all arbitration costs, and reasonable attorney's fees.

12. ADDITIONAL ASSURANCES AND DOCUMENTS: This Agreement is irrevocable, and applies equally to any and all motion pictures produced hereunder and is not only for Producer's benefit, but also for the benefit of any other party to

whom Producer may sell, assign, and/or license any or all of the rights, privileges, powers and/or immunities granted herein. Writer, to the best of Writer's ability, will prevent the use by others of the rights granted hereunder in a manner inconsistent with the grant of rights to Producer. Producer may prosecute, and Writer irrevocably grants to Producer full power and Authority to do so, in Writer's name, and to take any and all steps as Producer, in Producer's sole discretion may elect, to restrain and prevent others from so using such rights. Writer further agrees to execute, acknowledge and deliver to Producer any and all further assignments and other instruments, in form approved by counsel for Producer, necessary or expedient to carry out and effectuate the purposes and intent of the parties as herein expressed. If Writer shall fail to so execute and deliver or cause to be so executed and delivered any such assignment or other instruments within ten (10) days of being presented, Producer shall be deemed to be, and Writer irrevocably appoints Producer, the true and lawful attorney-in-fact of Writer to execute and deliver any and all such assignments and other instruments in the name of Writer, which right is coupled with an interest.

13. OTHER DOCUMENTS: Writer agrees to execute such assignments or other instruments as Producer may from time to time deem necessary or desirable to establish, or defend its title to any material created hereunder or rights granted hereunder. Writer hereby irrevocably appoints Producer the true and lawful attorney-in-fact of Writer (which right is coupled with an interest) to execute, verify, acknowledge and deliver any and all such instruments or documents which Writer shall fail or refuse to execute, verify, acknowledge or deliver within ten (10) days of receipt thereof. Producer shall provide Writer with copies of any such instruments or documents executed, verified, acknowledged and delivered by Producer on Writer's behalf hereunder.

PRODUCER _____

_____

_____

WRITER: _____

WRITER'S SOCIAL SECURITY # _____

EXHIBIT A

ASSIGNMENT (Short Form)

FOR good and valuable consideration, receipt of which is hereby acknowledged, the undersigned Writer does hereby sell, grant, assign and set over unto the Producer's heirs, successors, licensees and assigns, forever, the sole and exclusive motion picture rights, television motion picture and other television rights, videocassette rights, and certain subsidiary allied and ancillary rights, including merchandising rights and limited publication rights, for advertising and exploitation purposes only, throughout the universe in perpetuity, in and to that certain original short story Work described as follows

TITLE: _____

By: Author

including all contents thereof, all present and future adaptations and versions thereof, and the theme, title and characters thereof. The undersigned and Producer have entered into a formal purchase agreement dated _____, 200__, to the transfer and assignment of the foregoing rights in and to said work, which rights are more fully described in said Purchase Agreement, and this Assignment is expressly made subject to all of the terms and conditions of said Agreement.

IN WITNESS WHEREOF, the undersigned has executed this assignment on

_____[DATE] _____

WRITER: _____

APPENDIX D

ACTOR'S RELEASE

FOR VALUABLE CONSIDERATION, including the agreement to produce the motion picture tentatively entitled _____[Movie Title]_____ , I hereby irrevocably grant to RICK SCHMIDT ("Producer") and FEATURE WORKSHOPS, its licensees, agents, successors and assigns, the right (but not the obligation), in perpetuity throughout the world, in all media, now and hereafter known, to use (in any manner it deems appropriate, and without limitation) in and in connection with the motion picture, by whatever means exhibited, advertised or exploited: my appearance in the motion picture, still photographs of me, recordings of my voice taken or made of me by it, any music sung or played by me, and my actual or fictitious name.

On my own behalf, and on behalf of my heirs, next of kin, executors, administrators, successors and assigns, I hereby release FEATURE WORKSHOPS, its agents, licensees, successors and assigns, from any and all claims, liabilities and damages arising out of the rights granted hereunder, or the exercise thereof.

I understand that I am an independent contractor, solely responsible for all medical and other related insurance coverage. I shall hold FEATURE WORKSHOPS and RICK SCHMIDT harmless and not liable for any and all accidental occurrences relating to the production of the movie, which may result in personal injury to me. Additionally, I understand that as an independent contractor, I am responsible for reporting, paying and deducting my own federal and appropriate local income taxes. The salary and profit points, if any, will be paid to me in gross, without any withholding or funds for taxes and/or insurance.

DATE

SIGNATURE

STREET ADDRESS

CITY, STATE, ZIP CODE, COUNTRY

TELEPHONE NUMBER

SOCIAL SECURITY NUMBER

I am the parent or legal guardian of _____. I hereby irrevocably consent to the foregoing grant and agreement. I agree to indemnify RICK SCHMIDT and FEATURE WORKSHOPS, its licensees, agents, successors and assigns, and hold each of the foregoing harmless from any and all damages, losses and expenses resulting from any actual or purported disaffirmance or rescission of the above agreement by the signatory thereto.

DATE

SIGNATURE OF PARENT OR GUARDIAN

(PRINT NAME.)

APPENDIX E

LOCATION RELEASE

I (we) hearby grant to you, your successors, assigns and licensees, the right to photograph, videotape, reproduce and use (either accurately or with such liberties as they may deem necessary) the exteriors and interiors of the premises located at _____, and to bring personnel and equipment onto the premises and remove same.

You may have possession of the premises on or about _____, 200__, and may continue in possession thereof until the completion of your proposed scenes and work, estimated to require about _____ days of occupancy over a period of _____ days.

However, in the event of illness or actors, director, or other essential artists and crew, or weather conditions, or any other occurrence beyond your control, preventing you from starting work on the date designated above, or in the event of damaged or imperfect video/film or equipment, you shall have the right to use the premises at a later date to be mutually agreed upon.

This is in connection with the motion picture DV (digital video)/photoplay tentatively entitled _____ [Movie Title] _____, and includes the right to reuse the DV/photography in connection with other motion picture DV/photoplays as you, your successors, assigns, and licensees shall elect, and, in connection with the exhibition, advertising and exploitation thereof, in any manner whatsoever and at any time in any part of the world.

You agree to hold me (us) free from any claims for damage or injury arising during your occupancy of the premises and arising out of your negligence thereon, and to leave the premises in as good order and condition as when received by you, reasonable wear, tear, force majeure, and use herein permitted excepted.

I (we) acknowledge that, in videotaping/photographing the premises, you are not in any way depicting or portraying me (us) in the motion picture DV/photoplay, either directly or indirectly. I (we) will not assert or maintain against you any claim of any kind or nature whatsoever, including, without limitation, those based upon invasion of privacy or other civil rights, defamation, libel or slander, in connection with the exercise of the permission herein granted.

I (we) represent that I (we) are the owner(s) and/or authorized representative of the premises, and that I (we) have the authority to grant you the permission and rights herein granted, and that no one else's permission is required.

_____

DATE

_____

SIGNATURE OF OWNER OR AUTHORIZED AGENT

_____

SIGNATURE OF OWNER OR AUTHORIZED AGENT

_____

(PRINT NAME[S].)

APPENDIX F

MUSIC RIGHTS AGREEMENT

LICENSOR:_____

This Synchronization License Agreement ("License") is made and entered into this _____ day of _____, 200__, by and between _____ ("Licensor") and Rick Schmidt/ FW Productions.

1. Licensor grants to Rick Schmidt/FW Productions the nonexclusive, irrevocable right, license, privilege, and authority to record on film or videotape and use the musical composition and recording entitled _____ in synchronization or timed relation with the film/DV (digital video) production currently entitled _____.

2. Licensor authorizes Rick Schmidt/FW Productions to use or cause to be used the aforesaid musical compositions and recordings in conjunction with the aforesaid film/DV production in any manner he deems fit including, but not limited to, the purpose of advertising and exploiting said film/DV production and the right to license and distribute the aforesaid musical compositions in conjunction with said film/DV production throughout the world on any medium or forum, whether now known or hereinafter created.

3. The musical compositions and recordings licensed pursuant to this agreement shall not be distributed or exploited separately or independently of said film/DV production.

4. Liscensor hereby represents and warrants that he has the full legal right, power and authority to grant this license and that the performance rights to the aforesaid musical compositions and recordings are available through ASCAP, BMI, or SESAC.

5. Licensor warrants, represents and agrees that Licensor will obtain in writing all requisite consents and permissions of labor organizations, the copyright owners, and the Artist (if applicable) whose performances are embodied in the compositions and recordings and that Licensor will pay all reuse payments, fees, royalties, and other sums required to be paid for such consents and permission, in connection with _Schmidt's_ use of the compositions and recordings. If _Schmidt_ so requires, Licensor will obtain such person's to deliver to him any documents that he requires to confirm that they will not look to _Schmidt_ for any payments in connection with the compositions and recordings in the film/DV production. Licensor will indemnify and hold _Rick Schmidt/FW Productions_ and its officers and directors harmless from any and all limitation, attorney's fees and legal expenses arising from any breach of Licensor's warranties, representations or covenants under this license, or in any way resulting from or connected with _Schmidt's_ use of the compositions and recordings.

6. The term of this license is for the worldwide period of all copyrights in and to the musical compositions and recordings and any and all renewals or extensions thereof that Licensor may now and hereafter own or control.

7. The rights granted herein shall inure to the benefit of _Rick Schmidt/FW Productions_, its licensees, successors and assigns.

DATE

BY

WITNESS

(PRINT WITNESS NAME.)

INDEX

Page numbers in italics refer to figures.